Nancy E. Sullivan
Ellen Sue Mesbur
Norma C. Lang
Deborah Goodman
Lynne Mitchell
Editors

D0061258

Social Work with Groups
Social Justice Through Personal, Community, and Societal Change

Pre-publication
REVIEWS,
COMMENTARIES,
EVALUATIONS . . .

"This outstanding book fills a gap in our existing group work literature. Focusing upon a single theme of 'group work and social justice,' this volume provides breadth and depth, and has important material for educators, practitioners, and students. The organization of the book is excellent and provides direction for readers interested in a particular theme, e.g., social justice in theory for social work with groups. Particularly impressive is the ways in which the articles in different sections complement each other. For example, having read the earlier chapters on 'social justice in theory for social work with groups' the reader can then proceed to the practice chapters with an increased depth of understanding. Reading this volume makes one proud to be a social worker practicing with groups."

Toby Berman-Rossi, DSW
*President, Association
for the Advancement
of Social Work with Groups;
Professor, Barry University
School of Social Work*

The Haworth Press®
New York • London • Oxford

Social Work with Groups
Social Justice Through Personal, Community, and Societal Change

THE HAWORTH PRESS
Titles of Related Interest

Social Work with Groups
Social Justice Through Personal, Community, and Societal Change

Nancy E. Sullivan
Ellen Sue Mesbur
Norma C. Lang
Deborah Goodman
Lynne Mitchell
Editors

The Haworth Press®
New York • London • Oxford

The Haworth Press, Inc., 10 Alice Street, Binghamton, NY 13904-1580.

PUBLISHER'S NOTE
Identities and circumstances of individuals discussed in this book have been changed to protect confidentiality.

Cover design by Marylouise E. Doyle.

Library of Congress Cataloging-in-Publication Data

Association for the Advancement of Social Work with Groups.
International Symposium (22nd : 2000 : Toronto, Ont.)
    Social work with groups : social justice through personal, community, and societal change / Nancy Sullivan . . . [et al.] editors.
       p. cm.
Selected proceedings of the 22nd International Symposium of the Association for the Advancement of Social Work with Groups, held in Toronto, Canada, Oct. 2000.
Includes bibliographical references and index.
    ISBN 0-7890-1815-2 (alk. paper)—ISBN 0-7890-1816-0 (soft)
    1. Social work with groups—Congresses. 2. Social justice—Congresses. I. Sullivan, Nancy Elizabeth, 1949- II. Title.
    HV45 .A79 2002
    361.4—dc21

                                                  2002068753

CONTENTS

ABOUT THE EDITORS

Nancy E. Sullivan, MSW, PhD, RSW, is Associate Professor in the School of Social Work, Memorial University of Newfoundland, St. John's, Newfoundland. She is vice president of the AASWG, and has served as acting president. She was co-chair of the 22nd Annual International Symposium of AASWG, Toronto, 2000. She can be reached by e-mail at <nancys@mun.ca>.

Ellen Sue Mesbur, MSW, EdD, has been a professor at Ryerson University, School of Social Work, Toronto, Ontario, where she has also served as director. Currently, she is director of the BSW program at Renison College, University of Waterloo, in Waterloo, Ontario. She was co-chair of the 22nd Annual International Symposium of AASWG, Toronto, 2000. She can be reached by e-mail at <esmesbur@sympatico. ca>.

Norma C. Lang, MSW, PhD, is Professor Emerita, Faculty of Social Work, University of Toronto, Toronto, Ontario. She was co-chair of the Program Committee for the 22nd Annual International Symposium of the AASWG, Toronto, 2000. She has a major interest in developing theory for social work with groups, and has written extensively. She was chairperson for the Fourth Symposium, held in Toronto, 1982. She can be reached by e-mail at <norma.lang@utoronto. ca>.

Deborah Goodman, MSW, PhD, is the Supervisor of Research and Quality Improvement at the Toronto Children's Aid Society who has worked, taught, and conducted research in the Ontario child and family welfare system. She was co-chair of the Finance Committee for the 22nd Annual International Symposium of the AASWG, Toronto, 2000. She can be reached by e-mail at <D.goodman@sympatico.ca>.

Lynne Mitchell, MES, MEd, is a clinical supervisor at Youth Clinical Services, Toronto, Ontario. She was co-chair of the Program Committee for the 22nd Annual International Symposium of the AASWG, Toronto, 2000. She can be reached by e-mail at <michael. mitchell@sympatico.ca>.

CONTRIBUTORS

Susan Ciardiello, CSW, is a doctoral student at Yeshiva University, School of Social Work, New York City, and works at the Community Counseling Center of Larchmont and Mamaroneck in Westchester County, New York. She has a special interest in the use of activities with children and adolescents in groups. She can be reached by e-mail at <Sue23@optonline.net>.

Carol S. Cohen, DSW, CSW, is Associate Professor at the Adelphi University School of Social Work, and Chair of the Social Work Board of New York State. Her present work centers on community-based practice with groups, field education, program evaluation, and group methods in research. She can be reached by e-mail at <carol_cohen@hotmail.com>.

Sue Devor, BSW, is a graduate of the University of Toronto. She has worked for the Province of Ontario Department of Welfare, Rehabilitation Branch. Currently, she volunteers at Stop 103 (a food bank) and is a cooking instructor there. She coordinates volunteer drivers weekly for Kosher Meals on Wheels, and supervises dinner preparation for over 100 guests each Thursday night for one of the Out of the Cold programs serving the homeless. She can be reached by e-mail at <devorsue@home.ca>.

Arielle Dylan, MSW, graduated from the University of Toronto Faculty of Social Work where she is now a doctoral student. She has a special interest in clinical social work and First Nations issues. Dylan resides near and works part time in a First Nations community agency. She also works as a consultant for Homes First Society, a supportive housing provider for hard-to-house people, where she is conducting research and developing an internal crisis response team. She can be reached by e-mail at <aubriedylan@hotmail. com>.

George S. Getzel, DSW, is Professor Emeritus, Hunter College School of Social Work of the City University of New York. He has written extensively on aging, crime victimization, HIV/AIDS, group work theory and practice, and value concerns to the profession. Getzel is currently a consultant to agencies in New York City serving the homeless, addicts, and people with AIDS. He can be reached by e-mail at <ggetzel@hotmail.com>.

Alex Gitterman, EdD, is Professor, University of Connecticut School of Social Work, Hartford. He is past president of the Association for the Advancement of Social Work with Groups and has written extensively about life-modeled practice, vulnerable and resilient populations, and mutual aid groups. He can be reached by e-mail at <Alex.Gitterman@uconn.edu>.

Mari Ann Graham, PhD, LISW, is Associate Professor and Interim MSW Program Director at the College of St. Catherine, University of St. Thomas, School of Social Work, St. Paul, Minnesota. She teaches a variety of courses and directs the Spirituality Institute. She can be reached by e-mail at <MAGRAHAM@Stthomas.edu>.

Sue Henry, MSc, DSW, is Professor Emerita at the University of Denver. Her MSc (Soc. Admin.) is from Case Western Reserve University, and her DSW is from the University of Denver. Author and practitioner, she has taught at the University of Pennsylvania and the University of Denver. She can be reached by e-mail at <shenry@du.edu>.

Estelle Hopmeyer, MSW, is a member of the faculty and Associate Director (academic) at the School of Social Work, McGill University, Montreal, Quebec. She teaches group work courses at the undergraduate and graduate levels. She also teaches a graduate course on loss and bereavement, and directs the McGill University Center for Loss and Bereavement, which offers free support group services for the Montreal community. She can be reached by e-mail at <Hopmeyer@leacock.lan.McGill.ca>.

Linda Hutton, MALS, MSW, CSW, graduated from Fordham University School of Social Work in 2000. She is a candidate in the four-year program at the National Institute for the Psychotherapies in New York City. She has a private psychotherapy and psychoanalytic practice in Manhattan and is founder of the Irish Women's Consultation Association, an experiential group that focuses on the effect of Irish culture, mythology, and family on Irish women's sense of power, guilt, and accomplishment, including identity issues particularly relevant to all Irish women. She can be reached by e-mail at <stella6290@aol.com>.

Claudia Lawrence-Webb, DSW, is Assistant Professor at the University of Maryland, Baltimore. Her recent research and publications address kinship care, the Flemming Rule, child placements, spirituality, and black feminist thought. She possesses extensive knowledge and practice experience in public child welfare services and training. She is certified in marital and family therapy. Currently, she is principal investigator on a five-year project examining managed care in child welfare. She can be reached by e-mail at <clawrenc@umbc.edu>.

Stephen Lewis is currently UN Special Envoy for HIV/AIDS in Africa. He is the former deputy executive director of UNICEF, former Canadian ambassador to the United Nations, and served on the International Panel of Emminent Personalities to Investigate the 1994 Genocide in Rwanda. Prior to his international appointments, he was the leader of the New Democratic Party for Ontario, Canada.

Merike Mannik, BA, BSA, is employed at Helping Hand Aged Care in Adelaide, South Australia, as Program Director of Healthy Lifestyles, an innovative rehabilitation and therapy program for older people. Mannik also guest lectures on group work at the Flinders University of South Australia, teaches adult education, and runs Wild Women's Weekends for older women wishing to get more out of life. She has a BA from the University of Adelaide, and a BSA from the Flinders University of South Australia. She can be reached by e-mail at <mmannik@helpinghand.org.au>.

Flavio Francisco Marsiglia, PhD, is Associate Professor with the Arizona State University School of Social Work at Tempe, where he is the lead instructor of the cultural diversity sequence. He is Principal Investigator of the Drug Resistance Strategies—Next Generation Project, an NIDA/NIMH-funded drug-prevention research grant involving more than 5,000 students and their teachers at forty-two middle schools in Phoenix, Arizona. He can be reached by e-mail at <marsiglia@asu.edu>.

Paule McNicoll, PhD, is Associate Professor in the School of Social Work and Family Studies at the University of British Columbia, in

Vancouver, Canada. She has a special interest in community development and social action group work. Her recent publications address health and mental health issues of the Innuit people, group work education, and participatory action research. She can be reached by e-mail at <mcnicoll@ubc.ca>.

Zelda Moldofsky, MSW, CSW, is a graduate of the University of Toronto Faculty of Social Work. She has been in private social work practice, and has worked as a volunteer at Stop 103, a food bank in Toronto, Canada, where she established a social group work program. Her concerns for the nutritional and social problems of the food bank users led to the development of groups that focused on low-cost recipes made by the group members in her Meals Made Easy cooking groups. She can be reached by e-mail at <z.moldofsky@utoronto.ca>.

Dominique Moyse-Steinberg, DSW, after teaching for over ten years in New York City, joined the adjunct faculty of Smith College, Northampton, Massachusetts, in 1997, to teach group work, research, and professional writing, and to serve as thesis advisor. She is the author of *The Mutual-Aid Approach to Working with Groups* (Aronson, 1997). She can be reached by e-mail at <IrwinSteinberg@RCN.com>.

David B. Nicholas, PhD, is Academic and Clinical Specialist in the Department of Social Work at the Hospital for Sick Children, Toronto, Canada. A focus of his work is the psychosocial impact of childhood chronic health conditions on families and caregivers. He can be reached by e-mail at <david.nicholas@sickkids.ca>.

Michael Phillips, DSW, is Associate Dean at Fordham University Graduate School of Social Service, New York City. He has conducted many practice evaluations with a particular emphasis on the use of group work interventions with children who have a substance-abusing family member and/or a family history of domestic violence. He can be reached by e-mail at <mphillips@Fordham.edu>.

Ben Zion Shapiro, PhD, is Professor Emeritus in the Faculty of Social Work, University of Toronto. He has done extensive research on the meanings of help in various cultures, and has made major contributions to theory for social work with groups. He can be reached by e-mail at <benzion.shapiro@utoronto.ca>.

Betty L. Welsh, MSW, is Professor Emerita, Wayne State University, Detroit, Michigan. She is co-author with Paula Allen-Mears and Robert O. Washington, of three editions of *Social Work in Schools* (Prentice-Hall, 1986; Allyn & Bacon, 1996, 2000). She is a recent volunteer in the field of gerontology, both locally and statewide, and employs her group work skills broadly within the retirement community where she is a resident. She can be reached by e-mail at <bwbluebird@aol.com>.

Foreword

Social Work with Groups: Social Justice Through Personal, Community, and Societal Change! was the theme and title of the 22nd Annual International Symposium of the Association for the Advancement of Social Work with Groups (AASWG), held in Toronto, Canada, in October 2000. This collection of papers, selected from the more than 150 prepared and presented by social group work practitioners, educators, and theorists at the symposium, retains the title.

In opening a book thus titled, one may ask oneself, "What is the meaning of the concept of social justice? What does this collection of papers purport to say that will explain and illuminate the concept, which is surely value-based? What do social workers who work with groups know about such a value concept?" Surely social justice means very simply that it is desirable for a society to make its resources available to all people equally and fully, and, yes, that includes social work services, which certainly are, or ought to be, available to all people.

In viewing the contents of this book, one is immediately struck by the breadth and complexity in the application of the concept. Herein, it seems to refer to a range of people, for example, adolescent youth confined to a residential setting, First Nations people and their cultural activities, sexually abused African-American children, older women and their reclaimed lives, parents who use a food bank for their children, fathers of children with spina bifida. The implication is that persons such as these, and many others addressed in these pages, are deprived of societal resources and affected by societal injustice.

This could bring the reader to question further, "What do these social workers who offer their services in groups know about this subject?" There must be more to it. As one begins to read further, one discovers the depth of philosophical, societal, social, and psychological knowledge and insight that guides the professional skill of these authors whose work is assembled here. They seem to be presenting, in many different ways, some very important understandings about the human condition:

1. Social justice is a process, not an absolute. Achieving it is hard and ever-continuing work.
2. Human needs are not finite. Human situations create new needs to be addressed by society equally and fully.
3. A society requires structures that are continually vigilant to all human needs, past, present, and future.
4. Social work is such a structure, always seeking a just society and always alert to new needs and new injustices.
5. Social group work, working from a democratic value base with mutual aid goals, is intrinsically concerned with equality and inequality.
6. Social group workers, always cognizant of human situations that produce new societal needs, reach out to help people, and to help people help each other.
7. The group is a unit in human societies that embodies the potential for social justice encounters and, in achieving its groupness, represents relationship in vivo.
8. In the group, humanness is rooted and humanity can be realized.

This is a remarkable collection, informing the reader about the values, knowledge, and skills of social work with groups through the presentations of practice, the education of social workers for practice, and the application of theory in skillful practice. It is a contribution to the dreams and goals of humanity, demonstrating that social justice can be enhanced.

The profession of social work, and particularly those social workers who believe deeply and work skillfully in offering human services in groups, can be proud—as am I in accepting the invitation to write this foreword.

Catherine P. Papell
Professor Emerita
Adelphi University School of Social Work

Acknowledgments

The Symposium Planning Committee gratefully acknowledges the support of the Social Sciences and Humanities Research Council of Canada (SSHRC), and The Hospital for Sick Children Foundation, Toronto, Ontario. Their generous support contributed to the success of the symposium and the production of these juried review proceedings.

Introduction

From its origins in the Settlement House Movement of the late nineteenth century, social group work has served as a means to assist people to integrate into or rejoin society, and to enable people who are marginalized and devalued, due to economic, emotional, or other social circumstances, to gain a sense of inclusion as participants in community with others. Our group work heritage prepares us to work with people based on values that accept difference among them, acknowledge and respect their personal realities, and shape our professional role as a collaborative resource working with them. Groups in social work can and should redress social injustices as part of our profession's mission toward the goal of a more equitable life for everyone.

The theme of this symposium, Social Work with Groups: Social Justice through Personal, Community, and Societal Change, was chosen by the aptly named Genesis Committee, a task group launched by the Toronto Region Groupworkers' Network, the Toronto Region Chapter of AASWG, and composed of a cross section of practitioners and academics in the Toronto area. At a time when social work's focus, settings, and modalities of practice are so diverse, the symposium planners wished to profile the centrality of social action and social justice as unifying foundation elements of our work, whether it be in direct practice with groups, research, theory-building, or teaching. The Program Committee, in its early formulating meetings, undertook the exercise of looking at the practices of those around the table for evidence of social action and social justice elements. Amazingly and reassuringly, in even the most "clinical" practices represented, we could reframe or discover these elements present in each example. The hope and goal of the symposium planners was then confirmed: that participants would leave the symposium with a renewed realization that social justice can and should be present as an objective in social work with groups.

This symposium was the product of a corps of dedicated, hardworking volunteers, who contributed their competencies, energy, and good humour in generous measure. As individual committees and the overall planning group, we welcomed the opportunity to host the 22nd Annual International Symposium of AASWG, and now to present these selected proceedings as a representation of the rich program of the symposium.

The book is divided into four parts. Section I contains four chapters addressed to social justice and its connections to social work with groups. Section II presents four chapters concerned with elements of social justice in the theory of social work with groups. Section III offers seven practice chapters, all of which address issues of social justice in some way, whether implicitly or explicitly. Section IV contains three chapters concerned with social justice in social work education and research.

In Section I, Stephen Lewis sets the context for the symposium and the proceedings, with his extraordinary global perspective on social justice from his extensive work with the UN and UNICEF. He presents a portrait of social inequities so vast as to render normal social intervention helpless. "We need voices . . . we need your voices," he states, calling for the response of the profession of social work to the tragedies of international civil conflict and atrocity, HIV/AIDS pandemics, poverty, and globalization. Ben Zion Shapiro explores the fragility both of social justice and of social work with groups, and presents an astonishing new conceptualization of the several forms of small groups that together constitute groups in society and in practice and serve as the varied entities with which we work. Alex Gitterman examines several types of social justice that impinge on the practice of social work with groups in various ways, providing rich practice illustrations. Paule McNicoll reviews some innovations in practice, both within the profession of social work and beyond it, which address social justice through social actions undertaken by groups in particular ways.

Section II begins with the writing of George S. Getzel, whose thinking about social justice is defined in the term *justice-centered group work,* and who identifies some tools for implementing social justice elements in practice. Sue Henry defines small-group experiences in and through social work with groups as the prototype of social justice encounters. She explores the concept of social justice in our literature and presents illustrative materials from practice. Flavio Francisco Marsiglia examines elements in contemporary society that work against the achievement of social justice through social work practice with groups and presents materials on practice, which is culturally grounded. Dominique Moyse-Steinberg explores the relationship between mutual aid and social justice.

Section III begins with Susan Ciardiello's chapter describing her work with adolescent girls in residential care, using hip-hop therapy as the medium for helping the group members to deal with their important issues. Arielle Dylan presents an analysis of a First Nations form of group work known as Talking Circles, and compares it to social work with groups. Claudia Lawrence-Webb contributes new perspectives on social work with groups with sexually abused African-American children, highlighting culturally sensitive elements in the practice. Estelle Hopmeyer explores the nature of worker self-disclosure in social work with groups, developing guidelines for its use. Zelda Moldofsky and Sue Devor describe an innovative practice developed as a cooking group for parents of young children at a food bank, the group quickly moving beyond the need for low-cost nutritious meals to generate an entity with important social benefits for its members. Betty L. Welsh displays her continuing professional skills as a practitioner/educator in social work with groups, as she develops needed social group components in a retirement community in which she is a resident. Merike Mannik presents a practice with senior women in Australia, designed to enable them to regain independence, with small groups serving as the means of reclaiming their sense of themselves and their future lives.

Section IV begins with the chapter by Michael Phillips, Carol S. Cohen, and Linda Hutton on the field seminar in social work education as a significant group work experience bridging the passage from student to professional practitioner. Mari Ann Graham presents an innovative approach to teaching, which addresses issues of social justice in the classroom, and alters the role of the instructor. David B. Nicholas reports a research study of an online support group for fathers of children with spina bifida.

It is the hope of the editors that this book of selected proceedings will serve as a substantive sampling of the program of the 22nd Annual International AASWG Symposium, and will provide models and inspiration for the continuing efforts of professional social workers with groups to keep social justice prominent in our practice objectives.

The reader will note that there are a number of terms in use in this book to describe practice with groups. These include *social group work, group work,* and *social work with groups.* This range of descriptors reflects a change in the terminology of practice over time, from the earliest designation of *social group work* to the more current *social work with groups.* The term *group work* is sometimes a shorthand term, and sometimes a reflection of a practice with groups that is not informed by the practice theory of the profession of social work. For purposes of this text, these variations in terminology are taken to be equivalent to one another with regard to the group work practices that they describe.

SECTION I:
SOCIAL JUSTICE
AND SOCIAL WORK WITH GROUPS

Chapter 1

Social Justice: A Global Perspective

Stephen Lewis

There is, in my mind, very little social justice globally. If we are to achieve even a semblance of it, whether in developed or developing societies, there will have to be a renewed, passionate, and indefatigable advocacy on behalf of the uprooted and disinherited in this world. I want to approach the subject by speaking about international civil conflict, pandemics, poverty, and globalization.

Let me begin with a discussion of conflict. Instead of moving into the new century with a kind of elixir of prospect, we entered it with a devastating sense of fratricide and human desolation in many areas of the planet, including Sierra Leone, East Timor, Srebrenica, Angola, and Sudan. I believe there is a considerable touch of madness in the international community. It makes the prospect of social justice ever more difficult.

There are moments when one senses a certain positive breakthrough. Never has that been more real than in the apparent diminution of the culture of impunity. Now we have an international criminal court statute that will become an instrument of binding international law over the next year or two. We have individual tribunals in countries as far afield as Cambodia, Sierra Leone, Rwanda, and the former Yugoslavia. There is a tiny fragment of hope that individuals who are responsible for the savaging of human beings will be held accountable one day for their acts. Sadly, we have not come very far at all.

Let me say, painfully, that had it not been for the position of the United States of America and France in preventing the UN Security Council from intervening in Rwanda, we might have saved several

---

This chapter is a synopsis of Stephen Lewis's keynote address given for the Beulah G. Rothman Memorial Lecture.

hundred thousand human lives. I remind you that 800,000 people were mercilessly slaughtered between April and mid-July 1994, while the entire world looked on and did nothing! What is the void in moral and ethical response to such a happening—when the entire world knows it is occurring and no one intervenes? By sheer coincidence, the United Nations' forces were headed by a Canadian general, a magnificent fellow named Romeo Dallaire. To this day, he suffers terribly from post-traumatic stress syndrome because he begged for help and did not receive it.

I cannot begin to convey adequately the testimony that those of us who were on the panel—a panel of seventy-four Africans and three from outside Africa—heard from many individuals in Rwanda. None of us could answer the question, "What do we do now?" How do you pretend a reconciliation in a population that has been engaged in a fratricide so monumental as to depreciate the meaning of the human person, while the world looks on? It may be that there are people here who would intuitively understand how to bring these individuals back into a rational, full, and productive life. I am not sure it is in any way possible.

It will interest you to know that in UNICEF and in many international agencies, there is always a bizarre debate about these human predicaments, which consists of, "Do you engage in individual psychotherapy, or do you do group work?" How do you conduct individual therapy under circumstances like that? However, the trauma on an individual basis is so intense, I wonder if it can even be broken by the most sophisticated group dynamics.

The women of Rwanda suffered the greatest toll, because what was done to them defies imagination. The use of rape as an instrument of war was never more palpable than in that genocide. None of us on the panel could emotionally cope. We all thought as we were listening to the women who spoke with us, "How do you summon a human response sufficient to be of some help and assistance?" If it happens, it will be in the context within which all of you labor.

I want to discuss the pandemic of HIV/AIDS briefly. In sub-Saharan Africa, it has absolutely devastated the infrastructure in every respect imaginable, as fifteen to sixteen million people have been lost, nearly half of those infected. Africa is a continent of funerals. Because in many of these countries, the oppression of women is so intense, HIV/AIDS is a gender-based disease. Until the world wakes up and understands that if one does not move on prevention and protection for women and girls, we will never defeat HIV/AIDS.

One of the things which is so sudden about HIV/AIDS is that there are now thirteen million orphans. By the year 2010, it is estimated that in eastern-southern Africa, there will be fourteen million *more*. There is no way that the so-called "extended family" can thrive, because there are few adults left. Young girls are looking after their siblings or large merging families. There is no food or shelter to speak of, and absolutely no schooling. There is a subsequent pattern of child labour and child prostitution.

Dealing with and responding to these children is the absolute ultimate test of group intervention. It is an intervention in which many of the international agencies are not terribly adept, because it is all so foreign. We all know that by introducing AZT (and even other less expensive drugs) into the process of mother-to-child transmission, transmission can be reduced by 46 to 50 percent. Sadly, this is not happening. Voluntary testing and counselling will allow women to know their HIV status and give them a choice about how they want to live their lives and handle their infants. Women want to be tested, but it is almost an impossible problem with which to cope, because there are so many cases and the societies are so fractured. It is one thing to deal with the stigma, political denial, and insensitivity, yet it is another thing to deal with a lack of resources.

Three-hundred million dollars have been spent in sub-Saharan Africa on prevention, care, and treatment, while everyone knows that a minimum of three to four *billion* dollars a year are required in that area. If something is not done soon in India, Pakistan, China, Kazakhstan, Kyrgyzstan, and Uzbekistan, then we have a human calamity of almost indescribable proportions in the making.

The third point I want to make is about poverty. More than one billion people on this planet live on less than one dollar a day. I want to know the meaning of the phrase *social justice* in the face of that reality. The disparity between poverty and wealth becomes more obscene with every passing day, as poverty seems to be entrenched, not only in the developing world, but also increasingly in the developed world as well. To handle poverty, one has to employ official development assistance programs that speak to health, education, nutrition, water, and sanitation, and this assistance must come from Western governments.

When the latest Canadian federal budget was tabled by the minister of finance, all he talked about was deficit, tax, and debt reduction. How do we establish a sense of social justice in our communities when all of the emphasis is on economic variables rather than the human condition? Everyone is feeling the excruciating dilemma of plagues, of the tragedy of HIV/AIDS, of the impossibly impenetrable phenomenon of poverty persisting so determinedly, and of globalization that seems to complicate everything while pretending to emancipate the world. There have to be forces that keep struggling and hammering home the human values that appear expendable in this crazy world.

I would like to appeal to you as social workers—we need your voices. I know that the social work profession likes to do what it does best, working with clients, labouring in vineyards of change in human behaviour. You have a passion for working in the dynamics of groups and seeing the changes that one person can derive. But in the midst of it all (and you never signed up for this when you got your degrees), it is vital for people who understand what is at stake—the vulnerability of the human condition—to be a voice. I am not asking you to "storm the barricades"; I will do that for you. What I am saying is that there is a need to pronounce on the issues, to take stands, to make voices heard, and to let the community know that thinking, sensitive, decent human beings engage in dealing with people who are vulnerable, isolated, and marginalized. Most of us have social justice; it would be nice to share that in more ways with the rest of the world which do not.

Chapter 2

Social Justice
and Social Work with Groups:
Fragile—Handle with Care

Ben Zion Shapiro

INTRODUCTION: AN IMAGE OF FRAGILITY

In Jewish tradition, there is a festival called Sukkot—the Festival of Booths. Each household is supposed to construct a frail hut—a *sukkah*—open to the elements. It may have temporary, but sturdy, walls. Although the roof must provide shade, it must also be open enough to be able to see the stars. The very observant will actually establish residence in the *sukkah,* and eat and sleep there, unless the weather gets really bad. The *sukkah* symbolizes the existential fragility of life, especially as fall and winter approach.

But this is more than a ritual enactment. The experience is very real. It is a kind of postmodern challenge to all the truth and sense of security that we may take for granted. And it is a great leveler. In the last analysis, the structures of safety and security and quality and aesthetics that some of us are privileged to acquire mask a more fragile reality that all humans share. The image of the fragile *sukkah* is a metaphor for the fragility of justice in the world.

But we also need to remind ourselves that the *sukkah* first appeared in the story of a people who had been liberated from slavery and who needed protection from the elements throughout their forty-year journey in the wilderness on the way to a better future. The image, therefore, is also one of shelter and hope. Guests are invited to participate in meals. Fragility is combined with festival joy and inclusiveness, a sense of liberation, and hope for the future.

7

The laws of *sukkah* construction are very specific about the frailty of what goes overhead—usually some branches and greenery—and how it must not be too high or too low—just enough for a person to stand. But the walls! There is no limit to the area covered by the *sukkah*. It may include anyone and everyone. Those who seek shelter from the wilderness may sit down in the *sukkah* with those who leave behind their comfortable homes even for a week, and together they can experience what a just society might look like.

Social structure is my organizing concept. I see social justice as a value that has to do with the way society and human relationships organize themselves in order to ensure fairness and equity. I also see social injustice in structural terms—arising from the marginalization and exclusion of people from resources that are important to them. It is the fragility of society's structure that makes injustice possible.

As social workers we are concerned with responding to social injustice, and helping those who are most affected by injustice. But, for a number of reasons, our responses are also fragile. If social justice and social injustice can be understood in social structural terms, it might be useful to consider responses that have a social structural dimension. I argue that our groups can play a pivotal and strategic role in addressing injustice because groups are part of what makes up the structure of societies, and because issues of exclusion and inclusion are at the very core of every group, both internally and externally. How can a group-centered approach to social injustice respond to fragility?

FRAGILITY AND INJUSTICE

Experiencing and Understanding Injustice

Fragility of the Victims

At the micro level, the sheer weight of injustice upon those who are most directly affected can be unimaginably difficult to bear. People may in fact be at further risk precisely because of the injustice they are subjected to. The traumatized may be retraumatized, the marginalized may be stigmatized, and the oppressed may internalize their oppression and identify with the oppressor. And those who associate with the oppressed, marginalized, and stigmatized may also be tarred with the same brush, as may our agencies, programs, and projects.

But we must also acknowledge the deeply rooted intractability of social injustice that makes every effort appear difficult and beyond reach. Deeply entrenched interests frequently support the maintenance of the status quo that includes some and excludes others from resources that are important to them.

The world we live in may give lip service to social justice and related values, and at times even provide unprecedented opportunities for human welfare and quality of life that, paradoxically, have the opposite effect as well. The forces of globalization, the advances of information technology, the allures of popular culture, the rhetoric of privatization, and the ideologies of postmodernism, all proclaim the dawning of a new age—yet they may contain within themselves the renewed seeds of injustice and fragility.

Theory Building and Its Limits

Perhaps some of the difficulty lies in our inability to come to a common definition and understanding of the nature of social justice and injustice. Conflicting definitions may in fact reflect power differentials; social power also includes the power to define values, rights, roles, and rules. The social justice of the philosophers (Rawls, 1971; Sen, 1999), the politicians and policymakers, the academics, and the professionals, is not necessarily the social justice of affected groups. People define their values, including values associated with social justice, in terms of their personal and collective experience and perceived interests. These are not necessarily values that are shared among affected groups. The differences among them may be inherent, pervasive, and consequential. The defining process may itself bring about a state of social injustice.

Social workers have contributed conceptual and theoretical perspectives that have a particular bearing on social justice issues. They have learned to think of their work as playing a role in the transformation of society as well as contributing to the well-being of particular individuals, families, groups, and communities (Swenson, 1998).

We know how much we owe to those who planted the roots of our practice with groups—Addams (1910), Coyle (1930), Klein (1953), Konopka (1963, 1983), Schwartz (1985), and many others. We have learned from the social gospel movement and from the Inquiry (Siporin, 1986), from liberation movements and liberation theology (Breton, 1989).

Among the more particular contributions in the group work literature that have helped us do our analysis, I would include the Social Goals Model (Papell and Rothman, 1966), which saw groups as possessing a potential for effecting change through a combination of collective group action and individual social competence. I would include writings on social action (Vinik and Levin, 1991; Shapiro, 1991; Breton, 1995); on empowerment of individuals, groups, and communities (Breton, 1994, 1999b; Lee, 1994; Shera and Wells, 1999; Rondeau, 2000); on the strength perspective (Saleeby, 1992); on competence (Breton, 1994); on consciousness-raising in groups (Home, 1999); on mutual aid, building on related concepts such as the reciprocal model, the mediating model, and interactional social work (Schwartz, 1985; Gitterman and Shulman, 1994; Shulman, 1999); on the self-directed group (Mullender and Ward, 1991; Cohen and Mullender, 1999), which incorporates Lang's earlier conceptualization of the autonomous group (Lang, 1972; Sullivan, 1995); and on structural practice (Wood and Middleman, 1989; Breton, 1999a).

More recently, we have learned and contributed to thinking in social work that has been characterized as radical, feminist, critical, constructivist, postmodern, and participatory action research. A growing body of our literature has paid attention to a range of oppressed and marginalized groups; socio-economic, racial, ethnic, and cultural issues; women's issues; issues concerning gays, lesbians, and bisexuals; poverty, homelessness, disease, and violence in different societies and cultures; and issues that cut across political, social, and cultural borders.

Our practice has grown and developed by leaps and bounds in recent years in a more systematic consideration of the implications of difference, in the development of skills for working with populations who are oppressed because of their difference, and in the development of sensitivities and skills for working with people who may be different from us. We have learned how people have suffered discrimination, humiliation, deprivation, and death because of their differences. We have learned how many social justice issues revolve around the distortion and abuse of difference that leads to marginalization and exclusion practices.

However, we must recognize that the realities of theorizing and conceptualizing are such that they do influence how we see and understand things and, as a consequence, they influence our action and our interaction with others. As Foucault has taught us (Chambon, Irving, and Epstein, 1999), our theorizing is dead serious and has the power to divide and harm.

Has our thinking about social justice and injustice changed over time in order to capture the realities of how they are experienced, and to correspond to the current realities of people's needs and problems and of how societies function in the twenty-first century? Are all social injustice issues alike? Can they all be addressed within the same theoretical framework? Can we avoid the very tempting slide toward reductionism as we attempt to make the necessary links between theory and reality, and, for our urgent purposes, the links between theory and practice?

Response Fragility

Yes, we must analyze. But we do not have the luxury to wait until we fully understand. We must respond without being overwhelmed by the complexity of the issues. But we must also be careful to maintain the delicate balance between the response that is too little and too late and the response that is too much and too soon.

But our responses are also fragile. When we think of responding to social injustice, we can posit a ladder of response, with a series of rungs leading from commitment to social justice as a value, to awareness of social injustice when and where it occurs, to analysis and understanding, to mobilization, and to response to injustice through action. The process is not necessarily a linear process. The ladder of response is not a ladder that works best when it stands up straight. It may have loops and spirals and it may have ups and downs. In fact, it involves all of the rungs at every stage.

Despite the very impressive accumulation of theory, perspective, and practice, we are exposed to external constraints as we engage in our responses to social injustice. Breton (1999b) has pointed out that, in recent years, much of our empowerment work has had to be done in a "postempowerment" era—a time when we have more often than not found ourselves paddling upstream against prevailing currents of policy and theory in order to develop and bring these ideas into practice. Social workers are constantly called upon to justify programs that are considered to be politically risky because they might offend major funders and supporters of their agencies. Social workers must constantly battle to ensure adequate budgets to carry out what is often considered "a frill" or a low-priority program in contrast with "core" programs. Programs that deal with social justice issues are the very ones that may go the route of the budgetary guillotine. The international counterpart of these pressures may be far more dangerous to workers and their clients than loss of budget and employment.

Garvin (1991) has addressed and summarized the issue of barriers to effective social action by groups. He includes factors in the education and training of group workers, expectations of clients, the focus of various models of theory and group practice, and contextual issues within and beyond the agency, and suggests solutions for overcoming each of these barriers. Repeated failure to achieve discernable change can lead to frustration and response fatigue. The struggle is all too often slow, lonely, and unrewarding. Those who engage in the struggle risk the pain of backtracking and burnout. This, too, can be a barrier to response.

Ultimately, social action is not for the sake of action alone. We need to be concerned with effective action, and with the social justice outcomes of the action. The responses we engage in do not necessarily work as we intend or expect them to, if at all. From experience we know that solutions and resolutions are themselves fragile. Sometimes we would be better advised to think in less ambitious terms, particularly when even the best-intentioned responses to social injustice may generate unintended new and different forms of injustice.

Reframing Fragility

We have seen that the fragility of social justice itself can contribute to the considerable social injustice that we see all around us, close at hand and far away, flagrant and subtle. We have also seen that, in many ways, responses to injustice are themselves fragile.

But we have a tendency to think about fragility as weakness, vulnerability, brittleness, and breakability. How can we understand fragility in a way that will help us to do our social justice work more effectively? There is another sense of the word. Objects that are precious and delicate are also described as fragile. They require extremely careful handling, because they are so delicate. Justice has been described as always in a state of dynamic equilibrium—a state of precarious balance—similar to a scale perched on its fulcrum. The slightest change on either side will tip the scale. Justice is so precious precisely because of its extreme sensitivity to even the most subtle of threats. This delicacy is inherent in the nature of social justice. It is part of its very essence. Indeed, it is part of its power. In this sense I suggest that we look at the *power of fragility*—the *strength of weakness,* and that we examine the implications for building on this essential fragility in responding to injustice. Delicacy and its powerful potentials requires "handling with care." Can we as group workers apply our theory and knowledge about social structure in society and in the group as well as the potentially pivotal structural location of our groups in society to make fragility work for them? Can we build on the potential power of fragility? Can we address both the built-in fragility of social justice and the built-in fragility of our responses? What does "handling with care" mean in practice terms?

GROUP PRACTICE AS SOCIAL JUSTICE PRACTICE

A Framework for Social Justice Practice

Group: A Strategic Modality for Social Justice Practice

The contention underlying this chapter is that social justice, social injustice, and responses to social injustice can be conceptualized in social structural terms, at both the macro and micro levels. This has implications for how we think about the groups we work with.

We have always made the link between our practice and achieving justice and combating injustice when and where it occurs, but there have been changes over the years in terms of how social work groups have been conceptualized. Groups have been seen as vehicles to educate for democracy through democratic procedures within the group and the agency, as vehicles for social action within and beyond the agency, as opportunities for members to learn to accept and respect differences, and as microcosms of society.

However, the social work group is not merely an instrument for accomplishing objectives, even objectives that have to do with social justice and fragility. The social work group is a social invention purposefully designed as a helping form. The involvement of a helping professional within a human service environment defines the purpose and scope of the experience for everyone who participates in the experience.

But this social invention we speak of goes further. The social work group has to be seen also as a part of the structure of society—part of the structure of the particular society in which it has been assembled. It belongs to that extremely important realm of association and activity that lies between the interpersonal on one hand and the vast impersonal institutional maze of formal governance on the other. Referred to variously as the third sector, the third force, civil society, and the voluntary sector, it also includes the self-help movement, grassroots organizations, political action groups, the union movement, religious movements, intentional communities, women's collectives, not-for-profit organizations, community organizations, cooperatives, settlements and community centers, and many human service organizations. They all provide opportunities for citizens to come together with common purpose to meet mutual needs and the needs of their communities. The strengthening of the third sector in all its various forms at the interface between the micro/interpersonal and the macro/governance/corporate has the potential as an arena for people to construct bridges and links across boundaries and barriers. A stronger third sector can have an impact on both the micro and the macro, perhaps stronger than direct impacts on each of them considered separately.

Within this large sector there is also a particular kind of phenomenon that involves the construction of social forms which emulate natural forms. They include "befriending" programs that bring together people for helping purposes, who would not ordinarily form friendship relationships. Many of the groups we work with are in many respects friendship-like, family-like, and community-like. Members frequently begin as strangers and work their way through to a structure of relationships that best suits their purposes and needs. Emulations of these primary human forms are capable of entering into the social arena as influential social entities in their own right, at times beyond our expectations and original mandate.

The social work group, therefore, is not only a social invention; it is also a self-inventing form. It has the capacity for giving group members, in and through their group, a role in mediating and articulating the strands of relationships between and among themselves, and between themselves and their society.

We also know from our practice that no interpersonal set of relationships within the group can be understood solely on the basis of what occurs within the group—it must be understood in the group members' wider networks of relationships, and how these are influenced by and in turn influence the social world. The personal is political in the widest sense—just as the political is personal. We are able to articulate a position that places the social work group at the interface *between* the micro and the macro, in which human interaction has both a micro and a macro dimension. Any fragility at the interface may have an impact at other levels.

This reality involves us in another kind of fragility: the social structural fragility that comes from being "in between"—neither wholly here nor wholly there, neither part of the highly personalized, privatized, and isolated world of the individual nor part of the highly impersonalized, bureaucratized, and globalized world of governance and corporate society. In creating the group, we are creating a *marginal* entity that could create a perception of exclusion, isolation, and powerlessness.

But this marginality and potential for fragility can also contain the potential for freedom of self-invention action. It is this very potential that provides a foundation and a framework for a social justice practice with groups. This potential stems precisely from the strategic location of our social work groups in society.

Group Membership and Group Types:
A Proposed Matrix

A framework is proposed to show how several forms of social justice practice with groups can be derived from this strategic positioning of our practice. This is a two-dimensional framework based on combinations of different group membership structures (insiders, outsiders, or a coming together of both), and three group types (classic group, proto-group, or intergroup/intragroup). Three specific types of social justice practice with groups are then selected for discussion (classic group practice with insiders, proto-group practice with outsiders, and intergroup/intragroup practice with insiders and outsiders together). Our task becomes clear: to explicate the implications for member competencies and worker skill that will equip us to function in each of these contexts.

Group membership: insiders and outsiders, inclusion and exclusion. Inclusion and exclusion are major social issues. The experience of injustice divides society into insiders and outsiders, the included and the excluded. The boundaries are sometimes distinct and sometimes blurred. They may be simple or complex. They are invariably painful and could literally spell life or death for those outside and beyond the divide.

The group-level counterpart is the issue of group membership, which also differentiates insiders from outsiders. We know that one of the core tasks for any group and for each of its members as the group develops over time is to define membership: who is part of the group and who is not, and what does it mean to be or not be part of the group. How do these issues change at various stages of the group's life? How do these issues interact with issues of relationship, group structure, and the substance of the group's agenda? These issues of inclusion and exclusion absorb much of every group's energy. As part of our everyday practice we are constantly helping members to accept and gain acceptance, to include, and to overcome exclusion.

Insiders differentiate themselves from outsiders not only in terms of membership and not-membership, but also in terms of the norms that govern their internal relationships as well as their relationships with the "others." Insiders may tend to treat one another as family, extended family, friends, neighbours, or colleagues. Outsiders are "others" who are not privy to the same benefits and values. Formal rules of justice are not usually required for governing relationships among insiders, nor indeed, from their point of view, for governing their relationships with outsiders. Insiders have a different obligation toward one another: "compassion"—a license to bend the rules. For those beyond the pale there are no formal rules or obligations.

The only recourse for outsiders, beyond the voluntary beneficence of insiders, is to invoke formal rules of justice—rules that lay claim to superordinate status and value. But, paradoxically, for many outsiders the category of justice is only a second-best substitute for the category of compassion. From their standpoint, why shouldn't they be treated as insiders? Why should there be boundaries? The real alternative to exclusion is inclusion—not the neutral social justice of the philosopher. We know these things because it is natural for most of us to prefer inclusion over so-called objective neutrality. It is only when we are denied inclusion that we demand justice.

As social workers, we sometimes have difficulty acknowledging our own professional ethnocentricity—our core traditions, commitments and ideas, evolving theoretical frameworks, accumulated practice wisdom, norms of research and knowledge-building curricula, approaches to education for practice, and our approaches to practice itself. In effect, we, too, are outsiders because we are frequently different in this sense from either or both insider and outsider. We find ourselves invoking the "rules" of professional-client relationships in order to make our entry possible. It is in the encounter of the insider with the outsider that the delicacy of this process of rule construction is most complex, difficult, and fateful.

Group types: group, protogroup, and intergroup/intragroup. I have suggested that social structural issues, further defined as insider/outsider issues, provide a possible link between the problem and the response structure. I suggest that we extend our perspective to a broad range of grouplike vehicles for response, including, but not limited to, "the classic group" as we usually think about it. This would include "protogroups" that do not, and perhaps never will, develop in the same way as "classic groups," and "intergroups" and "intragroups" that are composites of identifiable groups or subgroups. These are structural variations that could expand our arsenal of social justice practice.

Social Justice Practice

Classic Group Practice with Insiders

Our "classic" idea of a social work group is one that reflects expectations about group processes characteristic of the society in which social work practice with groups developed, expectations that are both normative and empirical. We tend to think in terms of group development that moves along predictable lines, allowing each group to develop its own culture and distinctive qualities. A broad range of group purposes and characteristics is encompassed. These groups are more characteristic of insiders who are comfortable with themselves, their peers, their surroundings, and their acceptance.

The development of group relationships among insiders who are about to embark on a social justice project needs to begin with a perception of how they are viewed by others. This in turn can provide a powerful motivation for personal change, for group mobilization, and for exploring the grounds for the development of a group solidarity that is not exclusionary or paternalistic.

Social justice practice in and with such a group involves movement outward in a conscious and deliberate process of reaching for a broader set of interactions and encounters. These interactions will not necessarily guarantee social solidarity and harmony. They may engender tension and conflict as groups and their members negotiate what they consider to be more just structures of relationships. Part of the skills and competencies that members will need to learn is how to develop and maintain their own group's integrity and efficacy while respecting the integrity and efficacy of other groups with whom it seeks to interact. This is learning to function as a group in a pluralistic society.

Protogroup Practice with Outsiders

A social justice perspective requires us to appreciate that the classic idea of a group is not always achievable, desirable, or appropriate in every situation. Why is this relevant to group workers? Because here we see the potential for developing "collectivities" that are not exactly groups (Lang and Sulman, 1987).

We know that even in classic groups there is an internal structure that is made up of dyads, triads, and other subgroup formations. We also know that, in early phases of pregroup and group formation, and sometimes in later phases as well, these interpersonal structures are more salient for their members than the group itself. In some cases, these structures are the closest thing to a group experience that their members will ever have. These are protogroups.

Sometimes protogroups are the potential building blocks of groups. The extent to which the potential will be realized may depend on the capacities and relationship skills of the individuals, and also on the culture of interpersonal relationships that these individuals have experienced. There may be a host of other physical, intellectual, emotional, economic, cultural, or experiential factors that may make it difficult to fully engage as group members. Norma Lang (2000, 2001) has written about groups with socially noncompetent members. Some casualties of social injustice and exclusion have lost, or never had the chance to acquire, the necessary trust to become fully engaged group members.

In a more general sense, social networks are not exactly groups (Shapiro, 1987), but they constitute the structural underworld of society. They provide people with access to resources. Their members are social actors who do the networking, weaving webs of support, communication, and action. They are not dependent on physical proximity, and can span the globe. They use the telephone and the Internet. The apparent anarchy of the Internet is a promising possibility provided by information technology for overriding the constraints of boundary-maintaining social structures. In a broader sense, a social network constitutes a protogroup, potentially on a global scale.

Granovetter (1973) demonstrates that the structure of weak networks can be significant. Ties with members of networks who are somewhat marginal to their networks may actually provide better links to needed resources than the ties of "dense networks."

Participants in protogroups may experience interpersonal processes with others who share their predicament of exclusion that can provide a most powerful potential for personal, interpersonal, and social change. We have to help them penetrate social boundaries, link-by-link and tie-by-tie, if necessary, in order to help them gain access to needed resources. Our roles as advocates, brokers, and mediators become particularly important. The perception that they are marginal, stigmatized, and weak can form part of their initial identity as a collectivity. But we need to develop our sensitivity to the exclusionary implications of developing the group's boundaries, even when the group is made up of members who are themselves excluded from the mainstream of society.

Will the objectives of social justice practice be better served if we bring those who are affected by an injustice together with those who are identified with the perpetrators of the injustice? This may not always be feasible or desirable; separate development may be a precondition to an effective engagement at another stage.

Intragroup/Intergroup Practice with Outsiders and Insiders

Newstetter (1948), in using the term intergroup, was thinking primarily of groups of representatives at various levels of mandate, of the implications for managing the "from and to" between the members of an intergroup and their constituencies, and the implications for the practitioner role. His contribution was seen as moving beyond group work and into community organization. This introduces another stratum of group process that is concerned with how the group and its members relate to groups and constituencies beyond the group's boundaries.

We can broaden Newstetter's perspectives for our purposes. We may indeed be talking about coalitions and partnerships of groups and organizations for a particular social justice objective. This is what some community organizers refer to as the creation of an "action system." But in our working with such an action system we will be particularly sensitive to the individual, interpersonal, group, and intergroup processes, and the "from and to" that Newstetter discussed. Solidarity and boundaries may be issues, not givens.

Again, we may be involved in creating an intergroup structure that acknowledges and values the separate existence of groups in society and provides opportunities for them to engage in common action to combat injustice. This is a particularly challenging form of social justice practice. It highlights boundaries, operates at the margins, implicates itself directly in issues of inclusion and exclusion, exposes the fragility of social relations, and is obligated to confront that fragility. Its power is precisely derived from its willingness to become involved at the most fragile junctures of society, helping the individual and group constituents of an intergroup explore their differences and use them to achieve a greater measure of social justice.

Our purpose may be to bring persons together who belong to groups that are in direct conflict with one another, in order to work on the conflict at an interpersonal level, and not necessarily to resolve it. David Bargal (1994) reports on a model of workshops for this purpose that has been developed with Arab and Jewish youth in Israel over a number of years.

An extension of this model may be to enlarge an existing group by increasing the diversity of its members. The focus is on bringing the diversity of society—and its issues—into the group in order to explore its implications for the relationships among the group members themselves. Here we have the group as the microcosm of a pluralistic society. It must struggle to work out its own internal structure in order to achieve social justice for its own members in a conscious and deliberate way.

These latter examples may involve creating a group, which, in essence, is an intragroup. That is, there are clearly demarcated subgroups, each with its own integrity, working out a modus vivendi that will enable and enhance their ability to achieve individual, interpersonal, group, and/or communal goals. We already have some important experience in designing the composition of groups with a diversity of membership characteristics (Brown and Mistry, 1994).

An Agenda for Practice Development

"Handle with care" means helping group members acknowledge, understand, and grapple with cross-boundary issues. It means studying and acquiring the practice competencies that have to do with protogroup, intragroup, and intergroup development, and in particular the competencies for engaging in cross-boundary encounters that may be fragile, tense, and conflictual. It means learning to enhance the power potential of working at the margins of society.

CONCLUSION: AN IMAGE OF PRACTICE

Recently, I was privileged to participate in a project that involved a partnership of several university-based social workers together with staff and volunteers of the Canadian Centre for the Victims of Torture (Chambon et al., 2001). Its "befriending" program matches clients with volunteers from the community with a view to helping survivors reconstruct their lives, establish new relationships, and integrate into their new communities. The agency staff works hard to create a safe place for the client and for the befriending relationship to begin and to develop and to flourish and to provide a resource for the development of a web of relationships that expands beyond the agency and into the community. The program helps volunteer befrienders from the host community to reach out to newcomers, and become involved in working on oppression and injustice at home and throughout the world.

The struggle is to ensure that the voice of the survivor of torture is at the core of the work, to ensure that volunteers begin to understand how clients' past lives have been destroyed, how the structure of their personal relationships has come apart, how trust has been betrayed, how the memory of trauma casts a shadow over their present lives, and how the fragility of justice haunts every new relationship.

The formation of the befriending relationship had to be seen as a basic, primary social structure, a building block on which other new structures could be built by befriender and befriended together. The fragility in the lives and relationships of these refugees, a consequence of the fragility of social justice in their former lives, has brought them to a place where this fragility could be respected and cared for, and where they could rediscover their own strength and power. As the befriender and befriended, members of the agency staff and, ultimately, members of the wider community learn to cross difficult and unaccustomed boundaries and to include one another in their lives, they also learn to work together to create communities where membership is open and accessible to individuals and to their preferred groups.

REFERENCES

Addams, J. (1910). *Twenty years at Hull House.* New York: MacMillan.

Bargal, D. and Bar, H. (1994). The encounter of social selves: Intergroup workshops for Arab and Jewish youth. *Social Work with Groups,* 17(3): 39-59.

Breton, M. (1989). Liberation theology, group work, and the right of the poor and oppressed to participate in the life of the community. *Social Work with Groups,* 12(3): 5-18.

Breton, M. (1994). On the meaning of empowerment and empowerment-oriented social work practice. *Social Work with Groups,* 17(3): 23-37.

Breton, M. (1995). The potential for social action in groups. *Social Work with Groups,* 18(2/3): 5-13.

Breton, M. (1999a). The relevance of the structural approach to group work with immigrant and refugee women. *Social Work with Groups,* 22(2/3): 11-29.

Breton, M. (1999b). Empowerment practice in a post-empowerment era. In Shera, W. and Wells, L. M., *Empowerment practice in social work: Developing richer conceptual foundations.* Toronto: Canadian Scholars' Press: 223-233.

Brown, A. and Mistry, T. (1994). Group work with "mixed membership" groups: Issues of race and gender. *Social Work with Groups,* 17(3): 5-21.

Chambon, A., Irving, A., and Epstein, L. (Eds.) (1999). *Reading Foucault for social work.* New York: Columbia.

Chambon, A., McGrath, S., Abai, M., Dudziak, S., Shapiro, B. Z., and Dremetsikas, T. (2001). From interpersonal links to webs of relations: Creating befriending relationships with survivors of torture and war. *Journal of Social Work Research and Evaluation*, 2(2): 157-171.

Cohen, M. B. and Mullender, A. (1999). The personal in the political: Exploring the group work continuum from individual to social change goals. *Social Work with Groups*, 22(1): 13-31.

Coyle, G. (1930). *Social process in organized groups*. New York: Harper and Row.

Garvin, C. (1991). Barriers to effective social action by groups. In Vinik, A. and Levin, M. (Eds.), *Social action and group work*. Binghamton, NY: The Haworth Press: 65-76.

Gitterman, A. and Shulman, L. (Eds.) (1994). *Mutual aid groups, vulnerable populations, and the life cycle* (Second edition). Itasca, IL: Peacock.

Granovetter, M. (1973). The strength of weak ties. *American Journal of Sociology*, 78: 1360-1380.

Home, A. (1999). Group empowerment: An elusive goal. In Shera, W. and Wells, L. M., *Empowerment practice in social work: Developing richer conceptual foundations*. Toronto: Canadian Scholars' Press: 235-245.

Klein, A. (1953). *Society, democracy, and the group*. New York: Association Press.

Konopka, G. (1963, 1983). *Social group work: A helping process*. Englewood Cliffs, NJ: Prentice-Hall.

Lang, N. (1972). A broad-range model of practice in the social work group. *Social Service Review*, 46(1): 76-89.

Lang, N. (2000). An emergent model of social work practice with groups with socially disabled populations. Paper presented at 22nd International Symposium of the Association for the Advancement of Social Work with Groups, Toronto, Canada.

Lang, N. (2001). A typology of forms of non-competent social interaction requiring special adaptations to social work practice with groups: The means of growth and development for persons who cannot form groups unaided. Paper presented at 23rd International Symposium of the Association for the Advancement of Social Work with Groups, Akron, OH.

Lang, N. and Sulman, J. (Eds.) (1987). *Collectivity in social group work: Concept and practice*. Binghamton, NY: The Haworth Press.

Lee, J.A.B. (1994). *The empowerment approach to social work practice*. New York: Columbia.

Mullender, A. and Ward, D. (1991). *Self-directed groupwork: Users take action for empowerment*. London: Whiting and Birch.

Newstetter, W.I. (1948). The social intergroup work process—How does it differ from the social group work process? *Proceedings—National Conference of Social Work, 1947*. New York: Columbia University.

Papell, C. and Rothman, B. (1966). Social group work models: Possession and heritage. *Journal of Education for Social Work*, 2: 66-77.

Rawls, J. (1971). *A theory of justice*. Cambridge, MA: Harvard University.

Rondeau, G. (2000). Empowerment and social practice, or the issue of power in social work. In Rowe, B. (Ed.), *Social work and globalization*. Special Issue. Ottawa: CASW: 216-222.

Saleeby, D. (Ed.) (1992). *The strengths perspective in social work practice*. New York: Longman.

Schwartz, W. (1985). The group work tradition and social work practice. In Gitterman, A. and Shulman, L. (Eds.), *The legacy of William Schwartz: Group practice as shared interaction. Social Work with Groups*, 8(4): 7–27.

Sen, A. (1999). *Development as freedom*. New York: Alfred A. Knopf.

Shapiro, B.Z. (1987). The weak-tie collectivity: A network perspective. In Lang, N.C. and Sulman, J., *Collectivity in social group work: Concept and practice*. Binghamton, NY: The Haworth Press: 113-125.

Shapiro, B.Z. (1991). Social action, the group and society. In Vinik, A. and Levin, M. (Eds.), *Social action and group work*. Binghamton, NY: The Haworth Press: 7-34.

Shera, W. and Wells, L.M. (Eds.) (1999). *Empowerment practice in social work: Developing richer conceptual foundations*. Toronto: Canadian Scholars' Press.

Shulman, L. (1999). *The skills of helping individuals, families, groups and communities* (Fourth edition). Itasca, IL: Peacock.

Siporin, M. (1986). Group work method and the inquiry. In Glasser, P.H. and Mayadas, N.S. (Eds.), *Group workers at work: Theory and practice of the '80s*. Totowa, NJ: Rowman and Littlefield: 34-49.

Sullivan, N. (1995). Who owns the group? The role of worker control in the development of a group: A qualitative research study of practice. *Social Work with Groups*, 18(2/3): 15-32.

Swenson, C.R. (1998). Clinical social work's contribution to a social justice perspective. *Social Work*, 43(6): 527-537.

Vinik, A. and Levin, M. (Eds.) (1991). *Social action in group work*. Binghamton, NY: The Haworth Press.

Wood, G. and Middleman, R. (1989). *The structural approach to direct practice in social work*. New York: Columbia.

Chapter 3

The Meaning, Scope, and Context of the Concept of Social Justice in Social Work with Groups

Alex Gitterman

In small groups, as in systems of all sizes, justice or fairness is the highest virtue of democratic life. In a just system, notions of fairness and equity determine distribution of resources, rewards, and punishments. In unjust systems, people with power economically, socially, psychologically, and physically dominate and exploit others for personal gain. They enslave others in the service of their selves. On a societal level, poverty and all its ills—hunger, homelessness, crime, and incarceration—are consequences of coercively established and maintained injustices (Gill, 1998). In examining the concept and subconcepts of social justice and injustice, there are two realities—at times congruent and other times discrepant. One reality is the actual objective distribution of resources and rewards; the other reality is subjective judgment about what is fair and unfair. The focus of this chapter is more on the subjective and less on the objective realities. Social judgments and attributions about fairness have a profound effect on interpersonal behavior. These judgments are made in three areas: distributive justice, procedural justice, and retributive justice. Each concept will be discussed and its relevance for group work illustrated.

DISTRIBUTIVE JUSTICE

A conception of social justice provides a standard for assessing the distributive aspects of society's basic structures (Rawls, 1971). On a macro level "distributive justice is generally associated with the goal of alleviating economic deprivation and with the methods of policy-making and social reform" (Wakefield, 1988, p. 189). On a micro level, distributive justice refers to the extent of satisfaction or dissatisfaction people experience with the distribution of resources. Weighing what they have in comparison to what they believe they should or ought to have activates these social judgments. Judgments about the fairness and unfairness of distributed resources are primarily based on the evaluation of one's relative contributions in comparison to others in a reference group. We experience a sense of *relative deprivation* when we perceive inequity in relation to others in our own reference group. For example, research has shown limited association between objective living standards and extent of satisfaction with achieved resources. Objectively, economically advantaged people are often more unhappy with their resources than are less-advantaged people. They socially compare themselves to other economically advantaged peers and find themselves lacking (Tyler et al., 1997).

For another example, some women receive lower salaries than men for comparable work. Women in higher-status positions resent the salary differences much more than do women in lower-status employment. The higher-salaried women feel more deprived than lower-salaried women because they have male colleagues with whom they can compare salaries (Tyler et al., 1997). Similarly, secretaries are much more distressed by small differences among one another than by significant differences between them and their managers (Tyler et al., 1997). As previously stated, the standard is primarily established by *social comparisons* within one's reference group. This is a major reason that employers discourage the sharing of information about salaries: knowledge provides leverage and leverage increases bargaining power.

In applying the concepts of equity and relative deprivation to small groups, we must keep in mind that people's experience of social justice and injustice is not limited to distribution of material goods and services, "but also a fair allocation of non material socially produced 'goods' such as opportunity, power and the social bases of self respect" (Wakefield, 1988, p. 193). Affection, status, and recognition are also essential justice resources.

In practice, a worker had difficulty when a group member would complain about being treated unfairly: "Hey, Billy has one more potato chip than I do—it ain't fair." Or, "Hey, John took one more foul shot than me—it ain't fair." Responding undefensively was difficult for the worker. Proving that he was fair by counting potato chips or foul shots never achieved hoped-for results. The worker did not sufficiently appreciate that group members were referring to certain intangibles. They felt unfairness in the distribution of affective resources when they made social comparison. They probably picked up subtleties in the worker's distribution of praise and emotional support. Even though the worker was beyond reproach in the distribution of potato chips and foul shots, he did respond differently to youngsters who seemed more vulnerable and needy. To other group members, however, the additional support that these peers received was yet another example of distributive injustice.

In our practice, we must make more conscious use of the concept of distributive justice and injustice by involving members in processing whether the worker's and members' behaviors are fair or unfair as well as their experiences with other systems. Whether the work begins with what is happening inside the group or with what is happening outside the group, the issue of fairness or justice is extremely important for us to pursue. If group members' perceptions of internal and external social injustices remain unexplored, their distrust and resentment will severely inhibit mutual aid because "distrust and resentment corrode the ties of civility" (Rawls, 1971, p. 6). Some group members will withdraw and become apathetic, some will displace and externalize their pain, and still others will engage in self-destructive behaviors. All these behaviors sap energy from mutual aid and diminish the members' abilities to take individual and/or collective action against distributive injustices.

Members must experience their group as a distributively fair and safe place before they will undertake effective collective action. Making a difference in one's group is a prerequisite for attempting to make a difference in the larger environment. We may have insufficiently appreciated this connection. In fact, research has found three factors must be in place before members will be committed to collective action. First, members must feel that they can make a difference. Second and third, respectively, members must feel that the group can make a difference and that their participation is needed in the collective effort (Azzi, 1992). Confidence in oneself, confidence in the group, and confidence in one's role in making a difference is acquired by actually making a difference within one's own group, which is by members being involved and owning their group processes.

For members to experience making a difference in their own groups, workers must simultaneously focus on group process and tasks. In other words, group processes and group tasks must be integrated. Group process cannot be sacrificed to accomplish group tasks; nor can group tasks be ignored for the sake of overdone process. By championing one at the expense of the other, inevitably both are sacrificed.

An additional thought about group collective action: Since people make their comparisons primarily within their own social context, the less fortunate tend not to define themselves as victims of unjust distribution of resources. They are likely to perceive their disadvantaged position as their place in life based on limited education and other circumstances. As long as people have individual perspectives on the distribution of resources, they are unlikely to engage in social protests. However, if they view inequities in terms of collective rather than individual deprivation, they are much more likely to engage in social and political action.* For this very reason, several group work educators, Breton (1989, 1990, 1995), Gitterman (1996), Gutiérrez (1990), Gutiérrez and Lewis (1999), and Lee (1991, 2001), have eloquently written about the importance of consciousness raising to empowerment practice. Consciousness raising aims to help group members shift from individual to collective definitions. This shift is essential to social engagement.

PROCEDURAL JUSTICE

People also make judgments about whether decisions are made fairly. The U.S. public supported President Clinton, in spite of his outrageous behavior with Ms. Lewinsky, because of a strong reaction to Congress's procedural injustices. Procedural justice refers to the extent of fairness or unfairness people experience in resolving differences, conflicts, and grievances. Research indicates that people are

---

*Tyler et al. (1997, p. 27) review numerous studies to support the association between perception of collective inequities rather than individual and engagement in social and political action.

more attuned to procedural justice issues than actual social policies (Tyler et al., 1997). For example, even when people favor capital punishment, their support wanes when they learn of class and race unfairness in legal representation and recourse.

In small groups, members require procedures for interacting and decision making. These procedures, rules, and norms create the structure for members to evaluate the extent of procedural justice. In making judgments about the worker's procedural fairness, members judge whether the worker's application of rules are consistent or whether he or she has favorites. Members are vigilant about whether the worker embodies fairness in decision making. A blatantly procedurally unfair worker invites internal group strife; a subtly procedurally unfair worker invites constant testing.

A social work intern punished her after-school group for an individual member's misdeed by canceling the subsequent two meetings. The group howled with indignation. When she met with her field instructor, the intern informed him that she felt very bad about her action. However, she was concerned that she would be perceived as too weak if she changed her mind. The field instructor responded that it was her decision, but he thought that members would intuitively know that it took strength to admit a mistake and that members would feel they had a fair worker rather than a weak one. The intern implemented her field instructor's suggestion and found that group members marveled that an adult could and would say, "I am sorry, I made a mistake." She had learned much from that experience about being authentic, and the group members learned from a wonderful role model about what it means to be procedurally fair.

RETRIBUTIVE JUSTICE

People expect that there will be consequences for not following established procedures or rules. Retributive justice refers to the extent of fairness or unfairness people experience with the consequences for breaking social rules. If people feel that rules are broken without any consequences, they either withdraw, begin to break the rules themselves, or seek personal vengeance. Of course, rule breaking and personal vengeance eventually spiral out of control.

To diminish personal retribution and rule breaking, societies institutionalize consequences for rule infractions through a system of laws, police enforcers, and court adjudicators. We have developed the principle that the punishment should fit the crime to establish the fairness of the retribution. The primary function of the punishment is for the victim and observers of the infraction to feel that retributive justice has taken place, and not for the rehabilitation of the rule breaker (Tyler et al., 1997).

I wish I had understood this distinction when I directed a program for adolescents in a settlement house. I organized a youth council whose functions included: developing program policies, procedures, and rules; acting as a peer court; and establishing consequences for rule breaking. The president of the council was a very bright gang leader in whom I invested a great deal of time and energy. He became active in the agency, brought in other gang members, and found the setting a wonderful vehicle for his leadership skills. One might say he was doing too well.

At a Saturday night dance he violated established procedure by sneaking in alcohol and marijuana. He came before the youth council and was confronted by his peers. This was very courageous for the youngsters to do as many were younger and of a lower status than he was. The members felt that he should be suspended from the settlement for two months. I was concerned that without the agency's support, he would regress in his behavior. Thus, I advocated for a lesser consequence. This was a horrific mistake, because I had undermined the collectivity's sense of the punishment fitting the crime and their pro-social view of distributive justice. Those relatively unsophisticated youngsters made a vital distinction—a distinction that unfortunately escaped me. Namely, they were upset by the fact that his wrongdoing was premeditated—that he willfully planned to break the rules and that he showed no remorse.* This was extremely threatening to their new sense of governance and therefore required a harsher response. Instead, I focused on rehabilitation. Unfortunately, I lost the other youngsters, and the youth council never regained its spirit and independence.

---

*Tyler et al. (1997, pp. 129-130) point out that intentional wrongdoing threatens the social order and, therefore, evokes intense reactions. Showing remorse restores some balance to the social order and equity in the victim.

CONCLUSION

In the United States, some distributive social justice policies such as Social Security and minimum wage have acquired broad public support. Other social policies such as affirmative action, public assistance, and universal health insurance have received significantly less acceptance. In these latter instances, macro social justice principles are incongruent with micro social justice perceptions. To more effectively advocate on behalf of the poor and disenfranchised, we need to find ways to improve the fit between macro social justice polices and micro perceptions.

For example, Rank (1999) reports on a 1993 study conducted by Blank who found during a thirteen-year period that at some point 25 percent of the white population in the United Sates experienced poverty. During the same period, nearly 70 percent of the black population experienced poverty. Moreover, 67 percent of the whites were below the poverty line for three years or less as compared to only 30 percent of blacks. In other words, 70 percent of the black population in the United States experienced poverty for more than three years during the time of the study. This is a glaring example of distributive injustice. Yet because of micro perceptions that the concept of a safety net is an unfair social distributive policy, we have been unable to convince the public of its social justice value. We have to promote social welfare programs differently to the public. Micro perceptions and macro social distributive polices will be more congruent if we reconceptualize these programs to be more inclusive.

In relation to poverty, an association exists not only between race and poverty, and single parenthood and poverty, but also between age and poverty. By examining the association between age and poverty, we learn that poverty is not a rare event affecting only a small minority of the U.S. population. Rather, a clear majority of U.S. citizens at some point during their lives will have to deal with being poor. Life tables suggest a U pattern for poverty—high rates at childhood, a drop in the thirties and forties, and a rapid increase from ages sixty-five and older. Children and older people are extremely vulnerable to poverty (Rank, 1999).

By age sixty-five, over 50 percent of the American population will have lived in poverty for at least one year and by age eighty-five, the percent will increase to nearly 70 percent. By advocating for safety-net programs for children and older adults, we are more likely to win over public support. By winning public support, we will be helping single mothers and people of color. For example, by age seventy-five, 91 percent of black Americans will have experienced poverty for at least one year, and 68 percent chronic poverty (Rank, 1999).

One might make a similar argument for affirmative action. Micro perceptions reflect opposition to favoring one group over another. The policy generates reactions of distributive injustice rather than justice. People feel left out; they feel that some are gaining at the expense of others. They do not focus on the racism in society and the stacked deck confronting people of color in the United States. A more effective strategy might be to advocate for affirmative action for all people who experience barriers: all poor people, disabled people, single parents, recent immigrants, as well as people of color. By being more inclusive, we might acquire greater support for this social distributive policy. Certainly, black and Latino poor confront greater barriers than their white counterparts. However, by developing more inclusive distributive policies, affirmative action might not be in jeopardy.

REFERENCES

Azzi, A. 1992. Procedural justice and the allocation of power in intergroup relations: Studies in the United States and South Africa. *Personality and Social Psychology Bulletin*. 18:736-747.

Breton, M. 1989. Liberation theology, group work, and the right of the poor and oppressed to participate in the life of the community. *Social Work with Groups*. 12(3):5-18.

Breton, M. 1990. Learning from social group work traditions. *Social Work with Groups*. 13(3):21-34.

Breton, M. 1995. The potential for social action in groups. *Social Work with Groups*. 18(2/3):5-14.

Gill, D. G. 1998. *Confronting injustice and oppression*. New York: Columbia University Press.

Gitterman, A. and Germain, C. B. 1996. *The life model of social work practice: Advances in knowledge and practice*. New York: Columbia University Press.

Gutiérrez, L. 1990. Working with women of color: An empowerment perspective. *Social Work*. 35(2):149-153.

Gutiérrez, L. and Lewis, E. 1999. *Empowering women of color*. New York: Columbia University Press.

Lee, J. A. B. 1991. Empowerment through mutual aid groups: A practice-grounded conceptual framework. *Groupwork*. 4(1):5-21.

Lee, J. A. B. 2001. *The empowerment approach to social work practice: Building the beloved community*. New York: Columbia University Press.

Rank, M. R. 1999. The likelihood of poverty across the American adult life span. *Social Work*. 44(3):201-216.

Rawls, J. 1971. *A theory of justice*. Cambridge, MA: Harvard University Press.

Tyler, T. R., Boeckman, R. J., Smith, H. J., and Huo, Y. J. 1997. *Social justice in a diverse society*. Boulder, CO: Westview Press.

Wakefield, J. C. 1988. Psychotherapy, distributive justice, and social work. Part 1: Distributive justice as a conceptual framework for social work. *Social Service Review*. 62(2):187-210.

Chapter 4

Current Innovations in Social Work with Groups to Address Issues of Social Justice

Paule McNicoll

I'd like to start with a quote from Ruby B. Pernell, who reminds us that social work with groups is also involved with the promotion of engaged citizenship: "A good society lies in the work of small groups" (R. B. Pernell, personal communication, June 10, 2000). The task given to me for this chapter was to do a retrospective of recent practices of social work with groups toward social justice and possibly make some theoretical linkages. I have added some thoughts about what I perceive are barriers for social workers to expand their work beyond the clinical realm, an analysis of the current context to identify opportunities for change, and ideas of actions we can take to make it easier for all of us to develop group work practice for social justice.

My first task was to look around, in the literature and in my environment, to make an inventory of actions in social justice originating from group work practice. Charles Garvin (1991) states that "we have no indication of how frequently social action does occur in social group work" (p. 66). I think we still do not know. There are, however, many inspiring examples of groups for social justice and they are not, by far, the exclusive domain of professional social work. I will present social work examples first, but I will go on to mention the contributions of other professionals and social work students.

EXAMPLES OF INNOVATIVE PRACTICE

By Professional Social Workers

The literature presents in detail many group work experiences that led to social action, in particular with one of the most vulnerable populations, homeless persons. For example, the work of Margot Breton (1989), Ruth Crammond (1989), and Toby Berman-Rossi and Marcia Cohen (1989). Many of these examples have been readily available and since there are a multitude of less-documented, undocumented, or very recently documented examples, I will present the latter group here.

The first example is researcher Maria Christina Salazar (Salazar, 1991) from the University of Columbia, and six social workers who decided to do something about child labor in the poor suburban areas of Bogotá, Colombia. At the beginning, the seven social workers spent a lot of time with the youth, something they called the "vivencia" attitude. Once basic trust was established, they asked the youth to talk about their daily working lives. The children talked about their heavy work schedule, the long distance they had to travel to and from work, and environmental conditions. The social workers used sociodramas, autobiographies, puppet shows, pantomime, mud sculptures, stories, and theatre performances. Together, the youth and the workers produced an illustrated booklet on child labor problems, with pictures and photographs the children made or collected. It was also a two-way process: social workers brought information about human rights and local, national, and ethnic history, and wove it into the process as questions were raised. They believed this helped alleviate inferiority complexes and brought self-respect and self-esteem to group members.

The results of the project included the provision of job training in useful skills such as breadmaking, mechanics, and carpentry, and the creation of four bakeries and one carpentry shop employing 150 youth and operating on a basis of self-determination and workers' control. At the individual level, the youth had gained self-esteem, confidence, and hope. They also learned skills for expressing their own views. At the group level, they had tasted their own collective strength and resourcefulness. They knew that they could plan and successfully conduct actions to transform their social reality.

The hardest challenge the workers encountered was the initial resistance of the youth to engage. The youth were expecting orders, not freedom. At first, they showed discomfort at the openness of the group structure. Using artistic forms of expression helped the group workers to acclimatize the youth to democratic and egalitarian relationships. A challenge they expected but did not encounter was censorship by the government funders. In particular, it was clear that when they first talked to government officials about "participation," the social workers and the officials had two very different takes on the concept. At many points during the process, some education and clarifications were necessary. But there was never a clampdown on the radical participatory approach the workers advocated. The social workers found that there was a margin of freedom for innovative action; however, they knew it was fragile and could be taken back at any point.

Another good example of this type of group work was written about by Nuala Lordan (2000) in an article published in the *Journal of Progressive Social Work*. In Ireland, as in many other countries, people with disabilities are one of the most marginalized groups of society. A particularity of Ireland is that services to people with disabilities are mostly funded through charity, a fact that provides an excuse for the state to abdicate its responsibilities toward this segment of the population. It also means that individuals with disabilities are dependent on the goodwill of volunteers and charitable institutions, a very humiliating position to be in. Access to the services they need is *not* perceived as a right.

Six people, some with disabilities, others professionals frustrated with the lack of genuine social action about disabilities, started a mutual aid support group. The first task they chose was to liberate the voices of the disabled so they could be heard. When looking together for resources that might help them make an impact, they became aware of an educational program that was developed in the United Kingdom—the Disability Equality Training. The philosophy of this university-level training can be summed up by a quote from French (1993, in Lordan, 2000): "The way to reduce disability is to adjust the social and physical environment to ensure that the needs and rights of people with impairments are met, rather than attempting to change disabled people to fit the existing environment" (p. 52).

They decided to organize to bring this training program to Ireland on a permanent basis and to make sure that people with disabilities could take the training and find employment later. The work on making the training available to people with disabilities was two-pronged. The easier part was to advocate and obtain the necessary physical changes (e.g., ramps, toilet access). A more challenging part was to prepare the students of the training program to accept that people with disabilities had the capacity to take charge of the project, be trained, and teach.

As in the previous example, group process was very important. Creating a space of safety, comfort, and freedom to explore new ways of thinking took a while. One particular example was the introduction of people with disabilities as trainers. There was resentment of these trainers at first, which had to be dealt with. Eventually, most students realized that people with disabilities were the ones with the knowledge.

By Other Professionals

Group work for social justice happens outside of social work settings. This is the case of group work in a nongovernmental agency, End Legislated Poverty in Vancouver, which runs an open-ended group called the "Wages and Welfare Group." Every month, eighteen to twenty-five people who are living in poverty attend. They talk about issues affecting their lives, try to understand the reasons there is such a thing as poverty in a rich country, plan action to either raise community consciousness or make the laws fairer, and join together in action. Sometimes action is lobbying the politicians, which the facilitator, Linda Moreau, states "they love," while she does not consider it a very effective action. Other times, the group members contribute an article to the End Legislated Poverty newspaper, *The Long Haul,* or a letter to the *Vancouver Sun,* with the idea of making linkages with allies from the middle class. Not long ago they organized a demonstration about the lack of decent and affordable housing. Members also engage in mutual aid and sharing of information and resources. Many also state that the group makes them feel whole, alive, healthy, and not demoralized as they were when they first joined.

I also found people from different professional backgrounds who work with groups that aim at greater social justice. In Australia, Jim

Mienczakowski (1994) works with various oppressed groups. His approach is to ask people what they need to say to their oppressors, and write and mount a play with them. Many such plays have been written and performed: *Syncing Out Loud: A Journey into Illness* (1994), with people with schizophrenia, a play denouncing the medical processes and community attitudes; and *Busting: The Challenge of the Drought Spirit* (1993), with people who were undergoing alcohol detoxification. Mienczakowski calls his work critical ethnography.

In Vancouver, David Diamond (1993), an actor and director, considers that "good theatre is a search for truth" (p. 36). He is a friend and student of Augusto Boal, the Brazilian actor who created the concept of "theatre of the oppressed," which is directly based on the work of Paolo Freire (1970). Diamond directs/facilitates interactive performances on different aspects of oppression.

I went to a performance of David Diamond and the topic was "corporation in my head," an important topic if one considers globalization the new form of colonialism. Three people were invited to share one instance in which they became aware of the influence of corporations in their lives. The audience voted to work on the story that had the most relevance to them at this point in time. The following story was chosen. A woman stated that she was in a grocery store and wanted to buy tomatoes. There were two choices: pink tomatoes that were a bit hard and, she knew from experience, tasted nothing like the real fruit, and vine-ripened tomatoes, which were perfectly round, red, and very expensive. She remembered reading an article in the newspaper about these greenhouse tomatoes, informing her that they may be genetically modified and were grown in greenhouses that occupy the best land in the province, but make no use of that rich soil as they are hydroponically grown. She pondered the issue for awhile and finally left the store without buying tomatoes.

As she told her story, David Diamond noticed that the woman blinked a lot at one point, a sign of complex thinking to him, and asked her to identify the many confusing messages she was processing. She identified three messages that could have come from different corporations: a voice of seduction ("Look at this gorgeous apple!"), a voice of isolation ("Do not listen to negative people"), and a voice of coercion ("You do not have the choice really. I own both kinds of tomatoes, and soon I will own all tomatoes"). People in the audience were invited to play each voice. There was discussion about the meanings of these voices. Then each voice was played by an actor, and the woman was invited to respond and stand up to these voices. Later, it was the turn of audience members who came to play out their strategies of resistance. Some strategies failed, and others were successful. There was a general debriefing about why this is so, and what needs to be done. The evening ended late, as people continued engaging in discussion long after the performance was over.

I would agree that this is a one-session group, and that fact may limit the strength of its impact; but I also want to stress that it addresses, within three hours, what is a problem in people's lives, why this problem exists, and how to address it. The performance was also powerful because it touched more than just the intellect: the new knowledge gained was inscribed in the body and it also involved people's imaginations. There was a live connection between those who played out roles (about ten people in all), and the members of the audience. I am personally very inspired by this work and find in it many ideas I would like to integrate into my work. I also think that there is good potential for an alliance between actors and social workers, and for common work on specific issues.

The final example I will provide in this category is shown in a video on participatory action research titled *From the Field: Participatory Action Research for Change* (Laszlo and Norris, 1993). The video relates the experience of an exchange between a community of campesinos and farmers from the province of Alberta. The site of the action is rural Mexico.

I will provide a vignette from this video as an example of the work done. A few families of Canadian farmers are living with the campesinos. There are regular meetings between the campesinos and the farmers. These meetings are facilitated by a popular educator, Arturo Ornelas, and cover events of daily life, decisions to be made by the whole community, and reflections about the outcome of these decisions. On one of his daily walks, one Albertan farmer discovers an abandoned and broken tractor. He brings the issue to the meeting and asks why people are not using this tractor, since there are obvious chores for which this tractor could be very useful. He was told that this tractor was given by a foreign government to people of this area, but it had been kept by an official of the local government who had used it for a couple of years and then abandoned it when it broke down. The Albertan suggested they go together to get this tractor right away, but the campesinos decided they should think about it. Many weeks later, when the Albertans had given up on a possible action, they were visited by a group of campesinos who said, "Tonight we decided to get the tractor. We now realize it really belongs to us." They retrieved the tractor, repaired it, and put it to use.

This example shows that knowledge of group process is an important tool for those who are working toward social change. I am referring, in this true story, to the tension between those who want to act and those who want to reflect, to the recognition and respect of different standpoints in the group, and to the importance of time and timing. Also necessary in this case were cultural sensitivity and an analysis of the power imbalances.

By Social Work Students

A very pleasant surprise for me was how much group work and social action was done by our students. The following are two examples.

Christine, who had lost a leg to amputation, started a group with people who had just had a limb amputated. She did it in a rehab hospital for her practicum and her work challenged the type of group work usually done there. Usually, such groups focus on grief work, but Christine approached it differently. She addressed the issue of grief when it arose, but she also opened up the field to do some direct advocacy for better prostheses (there are a lot of painful difficulties in this area) by having the group meet and give feedback to the engineers who devise the prostheses. That was just the beginning, of course. Empowered by this first action, the members also started to talk about the way they were treated in the hospital and so on.

Since it was Christine's practicum, the field coordinator, knowing what Christine was planning, ensured that she worked with supervisors who would be supportive and who would have the clout to protect her if there were strong reactions to her empowering work. At the end of her successful experience, Christine mentioned that, besides gaining advocacy and community development skills, she also learned some useful clinical skills (something in which she did not much believe at the onset of the practicum).

Sue, another student, got interested in social work when she organized a group of parents of children with cerebral palsy to advocate for more and better services. During the trials and tribulations of this advocacy work, she met many social workers who were supportive of her work and she decided to become a social worker. She is now starting another group of students who are also parents. In British Columbia, under the tax subsidies regulations, student loans are considered "income." For parents who study and need day care for their children, this means that they have to forgo subsidy and pay full price for day care. Members of her group think that student loans, which have to be paid back, are debt, not income. The group is just starting, so the actions are not yet planned.

There is something more to tell about Sue. She is in the final year of her master's degree and is looking for a job. She wants to do advocacy work. The chance of getting a job such as that, which would be well paid, is remote in Vancouver. It exists, but it is at most 1 percent of the social work job market. Sue is not the first student trained to work for social justice and social change who will end up finding employment in a traditional agency setting. As new employees, these former students find few opportunities to use their community development skills and are encouraged to take workshops and other training to beef up their clinical skills. I could name a dozen such students who graduated in the past few years.

Sue's example made me realize that the current job market in social work offers few opportunities to those who are training to work in social action. This situation also makes it very hard to build capacity in group work that addresses issues of social justice, i.e., supervisors for trainees, administrators who would create jobs for this kind of work. I decided, therefore, to address the issue of barriers to group work for social justice.

BARRIERS

When I developed the following ideas of barriers, I had not yet made a connection with Charles Garvin's excellent article on the same topic published in 1991. So, although my ideas were developed independently, I would like to acknowledge Charles Garvin's work, because what he wrote over ten years ago is still valid today.

At least three factors contribute to the general lack of social work support for social justice groups: a medical model of social services, entrenched habits of social workers, and isolation of people who work toward social justice.

Medical Model of Social Services

In our current system, most people have to label themselves as "patients" or "clients," meaning persons with a problem, before they can access social services. The labeling exercise having happened at the individual level, it follows that the work would also be done at the individual level. The logic for this system has to do with our view of scarcity of resources and, therefore, our decision to focus on problems, rather than on the whole person, contrary to Margot Breton's admonition to listen to lessons from the past. Breton wrote in 1990, "A group can be structured so that only the hurt, broken, troubled part of the person is invited, but it can also be structured so that the whole person in each member is invited" (p. 27).

I think it is still possible to invite the whole person in the present system, but it is more difficult because it involves intentionally changing the tacit contract existing between institution and client. Besides being reductionistic in scope, the medical model is also reductionistic in terms of time. I remember working in a psychiatric hospital and trying to do radical social work based on a model developed by Jeffrey Galper. Long before a person I was working with individually and in group was ready for consciousness raising, this person was discharged. As Judith Lee (1997) puts it, I found it "unethical to 'treat' victims clinically or interpersonally without attempting to help them raise consciousness, throw their oppressor off their backs, and become victors" (p. 18). In the context of the hospital in which I was working, my goal of working toward emancipation was laughable. It is even more so now than it was then, with the introduction of brief intervention models.

Entrenched Habits of Social Workers

Our own habits of work constitute a second barrier to social justice work. In 1993, I was in a position to design a group for older people who had immigrated from Vietnam (McNicoll and Christensen, 1995). I was collaborating with a committee of Vietnamese professionals. My first task was to devise a group format, discuss it with the committee, make changes, and implement it. Informed and inspired by the literature, I planned a closed support group of eight to twelve older people that would meet for eight weeks. The group would be conducted in English and Vietnamese, and people would be invited to share issues from their present life and past history.

The Vietnamese committee was not impressed. We had stormy sessions about this plan. At this point, however, they stated it was preposterous to hold the meetings partly in English, which would mean that only the facilitators would be able to participate. They also said that it would be silly to believe that these Vietnamese elders were going to share their individual problems.

To make a long story short, we ended up changing the model and the group developed into a large group (up to ninety people) held weekly for five hours per session. A program was designed in collaboration with the elders that included health screening (eyes, blood pressure, pharmacist, etc.), gentle exercises, socialization time, English classes for those who wanted them (classes of about twenty people), lecture and discussion, or a field trip or a visit. Most lectures were on a topic of interest about Canadian society and were followed by a group discussion (in Vietnamese). The field trips were to places of power (e.g., Parliament in Victoria, Court House to see a trial), or places where the Vietnamese seniors could enjoy themselves. Occasionally, the Vietnamese group visited or received people from other groups (e.g., a class from the local secondary school or a group of Japanese-Canadian elders).

Actions have developed from this program. The older people obtained a grant to make a video on the life of Vietnamese refugees. They had their own consultation at city hall about how they saw the Vancouver of the future. (At that point, with some support, they were able to do it in English.) They organized a co-op for getting funeral services at rates they could afford, and successfully lobbied city planners to have this type of group offered in other centres. I owe a lot to my Vietnamese colleagues. Without their input and tenacity, I would have just followed my habit and created yet another individually focused group.

I did some reflecting. Groups such as the one I was planning are the standard in other places. Why, I wondered, would it not work with this population? Then I realized that, unlike most clients who approach a social services agency individually, after having labeled themselves "in need of help," the Vietnamese I worked with saw themselves as a collectivity of citizens. Therefore, they would not take "individualizing" from me. Good for them!

Isolation of People Who Do Social Justice Work

Isolation of people who do social justice work constitutes the third barrier. In one of my classes, a group of students doing community development in five different contexts decided to start their own support group. Meeting with the students weekly, I heard them talk about how useful it was for them to work together because they felt so isolated and had no one to consult when the process became difficult in their work.

I invited them to attend the group workers' network being organized in Vancouver. Those who came were a bit confused by the therapeutic language of the majority of attendees. It is an issue that will need to be addressed, obviously. We may decide to alternate the focus of our meetings: one meeting on work based originally on social change, the next meeting on work that starts from the remedial approach.

OPPORTUNITIES

I perceive a quickening of activity in developing theory for social justice groups. Of course the theoretical basis of social justice work is not new. We owe thanks to Paolo Freire (1970), Elizabeth Lewis (1991), Ruby Pernell (1986), and many others. But there seems to be a new level of theoretical activity for empowerment, social justice, and emancipation.

In 1990, Margot Breton reconnected group work practice to its emancipatory origins by giving us a summary lesson on group work traditions: from the settlement movement, from the recreation movement, and from the progressive education movement.

In 1991, Audrey Mullender and Dave Ward defined "self-directed groups" that addressed the three following questions: What are the problems in your life? Why do these problems exist? How can you address these problems to make some change? These authors also proposed five practice principles: refuse labels, focus on the rights of people, base your intervention on a critical analysis, use the group approach as a tool to build collective power, and take a facilitator rather than a leader stance.

In 1994, Judith Lee introduced the "fifocal vision" that includes a historical understanding, an ecological view, an ethnicity-class analysis, a feminist approach, and a critical perspective. Lee now suggests that we can forget the word *fifocal,* as it is now multifocal because she added two new dimensions: a cultural focus and a globalization focus.

In 1998, Ruth Parsons, Lorraine Gutierrez, and Enid Opal Cox clarified the concept of empowerment practice. They identified four components necessary for personal and group empowerment: belief in self-efficacy, validation through collective experience, knowledge and skills for critical thinking and action, and reflective action.

In 1999, Marcia Cohen and Audrey Mullender published an article posing that our current classification of group work may be problematic. If we define a group as "remedial," are we not limiting it? Isn't it the basis for a social work agency to hold that, because it is doing remedial work, it cannot be called to work toward social justice?

In 2000, Margot Breton, Enid Opal Cox, and Susan Taylor presented a new configuration of the connections between the different modalities of social work with groups. The traditional distinction between the micro, meso, and macro types of groups vanishes. All groups are now called to be effective at all levels, whatever the original point of entry might have been. There is no limit on how politically active a remedial group can become, and there is recognition that social action groups can have huge positive impacts at the personal level. If you agree there is momentum, join the ride and the theoretical debates to come.

A second opportunity is the new legitimacy of participatory action research (PAR), which is based on Paolo Freire's work. An elegant way of describing PAR is that it is "a natural process of growth." In this definition, "natural" means that nothing is forced in, that the worker starts where people are and believes in the strengths of the members. Process is the never-ending succession of discovering, taking action, reflecting, and doing it again and again together. The final product is a spiraling cycle of "growth" that happens at many levels: individual, group, social, and political. Arturo Ornelas (in Laszlo and

Norris, 1993), the facilitator in the PAR project I described earlier, said:

> Participatory action research is about movement for personal and social transformation. It permits us, little by little, to discover the reality of our lives. When we as a group investigate our situation and make decisions to take power and create justice, we transform our reality. In so doing, we also are transformed— losing fear and gaining self-esteem. We build knowledge: the wisdom of the people. (p. 16)

A third opportunity in certain countries is the emergence of the health promotion model. In Canada and some other countries around the world, the medical model is under challenge where it hurts the most: in the health system. Health promotion emphasizes community over individuals, focuses equally on the strengths and on the problems, and encourages community participation and mutual aid (Epp, 1986).

Health promotion has been the official basis for health policy in Canada since 1986. It is also the official health policy of the World Health Organization (WHO). Of course, the policy and the current reality have very little in common. But I perceive an opportunity there. The mission statements of hospitals and community health centres are based on health promotion. We can use these statements to back up arguments to do different types of groups and work in more progressive ways. Some British authors (Drysdale and Purcell, 1999; Reverand and Levy, 2000) have also noted the place made for group work by the health promotion model.

The fourth and last opportunity is the activity of the theatre of the oppressed in many urban centers. It is called Theatre for Liberation in Seattle, and Theatre for Living in Vancouver. It also is very active in Toronto. Many of the innovative examples I have listed use various artistic techniques to motivate and deepen the level of consciousness. I think we could learn from "jokers," which is the name facilitators of the theatre of the oppressed call themselves. Besides learning from them, we could join forces with the jokers to create groups and events that foster social justice.

WHAT'S TO BE DONE?

The following are preliminary suggestions. I know better than to try to set an agenda by myself, but here are some ideas worth considering. First, let's identify those who are facilitating groups for social justice in our community and invite them to join our chapter and make space for them. Second, we should be on the lookout for all activities that end up promoting social justice. There may be ideas to glean from these experiences. For instance, in the Indian state of Kerala, Meera Nanda (1997), a biologist, wrote about science groups that are the basis for emancipatory views of the world, such as challenges of the traditional views that women or persons of certain castes are inferior. Third, let's do our part to change the job market for social workers. Some of us here may be in positions of power in agencies or have enough clout to have an influence. I would think that it would be time very well spent. Although it is desirable that social workers share with other citizens the task of creating a just society, it is problematic to find barriers to social justice work in the very profession that claims social change as its speciality and ultimate goal. Finally, let's think of ways to take advantage of the opportunities I have mentioned earlier, such as moving from a medical model to a health-promotion one, albeit not uncritically.

To conclude, I will borrow a quote attributed to Margaret Mead (2001) to remind us of the centrality of group work in the fight toward a better society: "Never doubt that a small group of thoughtful, committed citizens can change the world. Indeed, it is the only thing that ever has."

REFERENCES

Berman-Rossi, T. and Cohen, M. (1989). Group development and shared decision making working with homeless mentally ill women. In Lee, J. A. B. (Ed.), *Group work with the poor and oppressed.* Binghamton, NY: The Haworth Press: 63-78.

Breton, M. (1989). The need for mutual-aid groups in a drop-in for homeless women: The *Sistering* case. In Lee, J. A. B. (Ed.), *Group work with the poor and oppressed.* Binghamton, NY: The Haworth Press: 47-61.

Breton, M. (1990). Learning from social group work traditions. *Social Work with Groups, 13*(3): 21-34.

Breton, M. (1999). The relevance of the structural approach to group work with immigrant and refugee women. *Social Work with Groups, 22*(2/3): 11-29.

Breton, M., Opal, E., and Taylor, S. (2000). Social justice, social policy, and social work with groups: Securing the connections. Paper presented at the 22nd International Symposium of the Association for the Advancement of Social Work with Groups, Toronto, October.

Cohen, M. and Mullender, A. (1999). The personal in the political: Exploring the group work continuum from individual to social change goals. *Social Work with Groups, 22*(1): 13-31.

Crammond, R. (1989). Social group work and community development: Complementary methods of social work practice with homeless and socially isolated adults. In *Proceedings of the 11th Symposium of the Association for the Advancement of Social Work with Groups.* Montreal, Quebec: 119-144.

Diamond, D. (1993). Out of the silence: Headlines Theatre and power plays. In Schutzman, M. and Cohen-Cruz, J. (Eds.), *Playing boal: Theatre, therapy, activism.* London: Routledge: 35-52.

Drysdale, J. and Purcell, R. (1999). Breaking the culture of silence: Groupwork and community development. *Groupwork, 11*(3): 70-87.

Epp, J. (1986). Achieving health for all: A framework for health promotion. *Canadian Journal of Public Health, 77:* 393-430.

Freire, P. (1970). Pedagogy of the oppressed. New York: Seabury Press. In Lee, J. A. B. (Ed.), *Group work with the poor and oppressed.* Binghamton, NY: The Haworth Press: 63-78.

French, S. (1993). Disability, impairment or something in between? In Swain, J., Finkelstein, V., French, S., and Oliver, M. (Eds.), *Disabling barriers, enabling environments.* London: Sage Publications: 17-25.

Galper, J. (1976). Introduction of radical theory and practice in social work education: Social policy. *Journal of Education for Social Work, 12*(2): 3-9.

Garvin, C. (1991). Barriers to effective social action by groups. *Social Work with Groups, 14*(3/4): 65-75.

Laszlo, U. and Norris, J. (1993). *From the field: Participatory action research for change.* Calgary: The PAR Trust.

Lee, J. A. B. (1994). *The empowerment approach to social work practice.* New York: Columbia University Press.

Lee, J. A. B. (1997). The empowerment group: The heart of empowerment approach and an antidote to injustice. In Parry, J. K. (Ed.), *From prevention to wellness through group work.* Binghamton, NY: The Haworth Press: 15-32.

Lewis, E. (1991). Social change and citizen action: A philosophical exploration for modern social group work. In Vinik, A. and Levin, M. (Eds.), *Social action in group work.* Binghamton, NY: The Haworth Press: 23-34.

Lordan, N. (2000). Finding a voice: Empowerment of people with disabilities in Ireland. *Journal of Progressive Human Services, 11*(1): 49-69.

McNicoll, P. and Christensen, C. P. (1995). Making changes and making sense: Social work with groups with Vietnamese older people. In Salmon, R. (Ed.), *Group work practice in a troubled society: Problems and opportunities.* Binghamton, NY: The Haworth Press: 101-116.

Mead, M. (2001). Retrieved October 24, 2001, from <http://www.mead2001.org/faq_page.htm#quote>.

Mienczakowski, J. (1994). *Syncing out loud: A journey into illness. A research report,* Second edition. Gold Coast, Australia: Griffith University Reprographics.

Mullender, A. and Ward, D. (1991). *Self-directed groupwork: Users take action for empowerment.* London: Whiting and Birch.

Nanda, M. (1997). Against social de(con)struction of science: Cautionary tales from the third world. *Monthly Review, 48*(March): 1-20.

Parsons, R., Guttierrez, L., and Cox, E. (1998). *Empowerment in social work practice: A sourcebook.* Pacific Grove, CA: Brooks/Cole.

Pernell, R. B. (1986). Empowerment and social group work. In Parnes, M. (Ed.), *Innovations in social group work: Feedback from practice to theory.* Binghamton, NY: The Haworth Press: 107-118.

Reverand, E. E. and Levy, L. B. (2000). Developing the professionals: Groupwork for health promotion. *Groupwork, 12*(1): 42-57.

Salazar, M. C. (1991). Young laborers in Bogotá: Breaking authoritarian ramparts. In Fals-Borda, O. and Rahman, M. A. (Eds.), *Action and knowledge: Breaking the monopoly with participatory action-research.* New York: The Apex Press: 54-63.

SECTION II:
SOCIAL JUSTICE IN THEORY
FOR SOCIAL WORK WITH GROUPS

Chapter 5

Group Work and Social Justice: Rhetoric or Action?

George S. Getzel

"Justice, justice you shall pursue so that you thrive . . ." is the exhortation of the Hebrew Bible (Plaut, 1981). The double emphasis reminds us of the urgency of justice as a central goal of a Good Society. We might ask, "Justice, justice where are you in group work practice and theory?", a question prompted by the dearth of attention to the concept of justice to be found in group work texts (Northen, 1988; Toseland and Rivas, 1998; Shulman, 1999; Gitterman and Shulman, 1994).

Fear not, this chapter will not be a prophetic outburst about the sins of omission of scholars but rather an argument for the explicit inclusion of a justice concept that is compatible with group work theory and practice. Possible reasons for the lack of attention to the concept of justice and the current social scene will be examined. John Rawls's (1971) definition of social justice provides a starting point to examine implications of a *justice-centered group work* approach. Examples from different settings will illustrate the implementation and action potential of such an approach. Finally, scapegoating is identified as a special case that allows the group worker to move past surface concerns and to plumb deeper matters of empowerment and social justice. One powerful tool toward these ends is the invention of transforming images by the group-as-a-whole.

STATE OF THE ART

This chapter benefits and builds on the empowerment concepts carefully defined and used by a number of social work and group work theorists. Simon (1990) calls empowerment "a reflexive activity and a process capable of being initiated and sustained by those who seek power and self-determination" (p. 32). It seems there has been a disproportionate emphasis on the negative, yet necessary, concept of "oppression," and not a corresponding attention to the positive concepts of empowerment and justice in social work practice. In addition, we suffer from sloppy definitions of empowerment that confuse, abetting the potential for empowerment of people with the highly condescending and omnipotent claim of *empowering people,* something human beings can do only for themselves (Lee, 1994; Simon, 1990). This confusion between means and ends spells disaster.

Judith Lee (1994) identifies the particular connection between groups and empowerment:

> Groups are . . . the optimum medium for empowerment on all levels. However, the empowering potentialities of groups are only realized by the worker's skills in defining empowerment as group purpose, challenging obstacles to the work, and enhancing the group process that develops the group's power as a group. This relates to the worker's knowledge of group process and to the particular form or approach used. (p. 209)

The dichotomy between personal healing versus social change has been noted as specious and deleterious for effective use of groups (Schwartz, 1969; Breton, 1995; Middleman and Wood, 1994; Cohen and Mullender, 1999). Breton (1995) argues that social science findings strongly suggest that personal healing and social change are dialectically related and therefore interactive and inseparable. Sadly, the bias of individual assessment and moral uplift, whose origins actually preceded professional social work, is still assumed by some social workers to be the predicates for collective action and social change.

HISTORICAL CONTEXT

William Schwartz (1959), in his classic examination of the historical origins and development of group work, contends that the goal and scope of social group work in the United States was shaped definitively during the Progressive Era between the 1890s and turn of the twentieth century, a period that featured two economic depressions, the start of the modern labor movement, and the political activation of farmers, workers, and their sympathizers. Schwartz writes that progressive voices such as Jane Addams and Lillian Wald remonstrated that

> a true democratic freedom could not be built on the hopes of a propertied elite and the promise of static evolutionism . . . [but rather on] a system of cooperative and interdependent relationships designed to raise the level of existence for all men. (p. 204)

Small groups in the form of clubs, discussion groups, and community associations, begun in the earlier social settlements, provided ample proof to these pioneer social workers with groups that cooperative relationships among diverse people in communities were as powerful as or more significant than individuals competing in the marketplace and elsewhere as visualized by the social Darwinists. Mutual-aid activities and other cooperative structures indicated the capacity of human beings to engage in effective social action and self-governance. Cooperation was identified as the source of power for ordinary people who do not have favored access to money, influence, and coercive power. In short, most human beings have an underrecognized and undervalued source of strength in their acquired skills to cooperate socially, economically, and politically. There actually can be a competitive advantage to individual citizens coming together to further what they see as their collective benefit.

THE DEBATE AND ARGUMENTS

Unfortunately, some social workers continue to perpetuate a disguised variant of social Darwinism which advances the idea that mutual aid and cooperative activities are not serious or effective strategies of social action (Specht and Courtney, 1994). Although this belief may serve some polemical purpose, it unfortunately promotes insufficient recognition of how social change actually occurs on a day-in, day-out basis in the actual lives of people.

The close relationship between cooperative activities within a group and group members' ability to act outside their usual boundaries is a crucial understanding for social workers. We cannot continue to maintain the practice divide between the personal problems of group members and the public issues they reveal (Schwartz, 1969).

An analogy by the late Hy Weiner of Columbia University may be useful in this regard. Picture the social worker as a lifeguard at the river's edge. After bravely and fearlessly saving innumerable drowning people in the group, when does the question occur to the social worker: Who is throwing people into the river?

The image of people being thrown into the river can arise into awareness in moments of quiet reflection that precede hopelessness and desperation. Such reviving images open new modes of action for the worker and group members; their field of perception broadens beyond the otherwise fixed boundaries of the group. In short, the social worker with the group identifies new images that transform the conditions of oppression, thereby expanding the idea of social justice.

THE CURRENT SOCIAL SCENE

There are many people drowning in the river, which makes it a very daunting and interesting time to be working with groups. We live in a period of rapid social change abetted by technological breakthroughs, as exemplified by the Internet and the identification of the components of human genome. The globalization of trade and human resources is occurring rapidly, in a world becoming increasingly smaller and interdependent. These developments have and will continue to create considerable dislocations, problems, and possibilities for nation-states and regions of the world.

In the past two decades, the concept of social justice embodied in legislation, which are the building blocks of the welfare state in North America and Europe, has been harshly attacked. In the United States, the very word *entitlement* in reference to basic health, education, and income supports has acquired pejorative connotations. Efforts to privatize public education, social services, and health care exist alongside millions of people without health insurance, deteriorating urban schools, the underfinancing of public higher education, nonrational or nonexistent federal policies for the halt of the spread of HIV/AIDS, the mass incarceration of male youth of color, and a spreading epidemic of substance abuse affecting all social classes and geographic regions. The list of ills seems endless and all reflect serious value conflicts and questions of social justice.

UNIVERSALITY OF SOCIAL JUSTICE

Our inchoate sense of justice typically arises when we experience injustice. Although the sense of justice and injustice is widespread and inherent in the lives of ordinary people, it typically flows out of the negative conditions of deprivation and oppression.

In the West we may share biblical images of justice that reflect the injunctions of God elaborated by prophetic passion and universalized for all of humankind. The example of Jesus, as well as his parables, leaves a strong example of social justice. Islam offers well-developed ideas of equality and justice (Armstrong, 2000). Within different traditions of Buddhism, reflection on the impermanence of human existence registers in believers deep compassion and concern for all beings, reflected in living nonviolently and acknowledging the dignity and the equality of all (Batchelor, 1997). Now for more than fifty years, a majority of the nations of the world have adopted the Universal Declaration of Human Rights, a lofty document, daunting to implement on a planet rife with discord, oppression, and physical violence (Glendon, 2001). All social workers must have a grounded understanding of the deeply rooted efforts of humankind to develop a just society across the eons and in different cultures. It may be argued that what makes us human beings is the capacity to transcend immediate urges and to develop an abstract notion of justice for ourselves and others.

TOWARD A DEFINITION OF JUSTICE

John Rawls (1971) provides a heuristic for thinking about social justice in its application to the conditions of people interacting in large social institutions. Rawls's concepts are quite congruent with group workers' sense of social justice and fit well with the problems that arise in small groups.

Rawls sees justice as related to a priori principles that rational persons could agree upon and apply in their cooperative social and economic activities based on the assumption that certain benefits or goods should be distributed fairly if not equally. These principles would apply to specified fields of action in public and private life, but not to every aspect of living, agreed upon whenever possible in advance. This social contract idea of justice is dynamic and subject to renegotiation based on changing circumstances and a new consensus.

Rawls's initial two principles of justice are a good starting point for the exploration of social justice and group work practice. The first principle asserts "each person is to have an equal right to the most extensive basic liberty compatible with a similar liberty for others" (p. 60). The second principle accounts for morally grounded exceptions to the fairness advocated in the first principle: "social and economic inequalities are to be arranged so that they are both (a) reasonably expected to be to everyone's advantage, and (b) attached to positions and offices open to all" (p. 60).

The first principle focuses on basic liberties that are related to areas specified in the U.S. Bill of Rights and similar rights specified in the Universal Declaration of Human Rights—freedom of expression and thought, due process of law, protection of personal property, freedom of assembly, and other political rights or freedoms. The second principle focuses on the inequality of social and economic status that is assumed to be found even in a just society, which gives effective advantages to a small group of citizens, possibly at the expense of many other people. Such inequalities are justified if the unequal shares benefit everyone in some larger sense. For example, physicians may have a higher income than others, if as a consequence the brightest and most skilled among them are recruited to work with poor and wealthy alike. The universal good of such an unequal distribution of income to doctors would be the reduction of physical and psychic pain in the society. Members of a society may rationally and thoughtfully make such a choice, weighing their judgments and values to the conditions of everyday life and in conformance to the aforementioned principles of social justice.

These principles correspond to the choices group members might make with the help of a social worker in a group. For example, a group of adolescent males of color may debate whether their club should have officers or forgo such formalities in obeisance to group cohesion and amity. The downside of no formal leadership may be inefficiencies in accomplishing certain instrumental tasks important to them as a group, such as being notified of a change of time or location of meetings. The application of the principles of social justice for a group may extend outside its usual boundaries, when one member tells irate and frightened peers that he was a victim of racial profiling resulting in physical and psychological harassment. The group members have choices based on their evolving concept of social justice. Their choice as a group might be to support the aggrieved member as he fills out a complaint against the police, or for the group-as-a-whole to join a coalition advocating an independent, civilian complaint commission. They may defer any type of action based on the volatility of emotions in the group and the neighborhood. Quite clearly, any action would involve the group worker with the politics of his or her social agency. Systematic interactions of the justice-centered group work approach are not simple, but are dynamic, incremental, and evolving.

VALUE PREMISES OF SOCIAL JUSTICE

A concept of social justice of necessity entails the identification and operationalization of predicate values that are shared by all those who pursue the practical virtue of social justice in a locality, a nation-state, or a small group. The following value premises for reciprocity among human beings are offered as predicate and intrinsically related to an evolving sense of social justice:

1. The human beings' health, development, and social solidarity are of ultimate value. Neither money, belief systems, nor ideology may threaten or undermine the right to health, growth, and belonging. Human beings are first and foremost an end in themselves and not a means to some narrow end.
2. Human personal and cultural diversity should be affirmed and supported. The rich diversity of cultural groups and individual perspectives is intrinsic to all, now as in the past.
3. Human beings have the need and the right to question received knowledge and beliefs in each generation and in different historical moments.
4. All human beings are equal in their basic needs (health, development, and social solidarity), and have certain responsibilities and obligations to each other.
5. Human beings' individual and group conditions find highest fulfillment in nonviolent activities and conditions.
6. Human beings have a right to freedom of expression and thought in all dimensions of their existence.

VALUES IN CONFLICT

For a group worker working with different populations in small groups, value conflicts are not abstruse, remote issues, but are strongly displayed in group behaviors and emotions. Underlying the conflict, controversy, and contradictions in any group are the playing out of concerns related to the enumerated value premises. Members of a group may differ in their knowledge and understanding of certain value premises, because of historic or current conditions, situations, and opportunities. The group becomes the context and the means to examine value premises and an emerging concept of social justice.

Illustration

In a support group for parents of children who have been murdered, there is frequent arguing among participants, over whether mothers are the most traumatized party after the event. Mothers must take care of spouses and surviving children, and are unable to express their own profound sense of loss. In this frustrating discussion are the hurt feelings of both mothers and fathers who find themselves casting implicit if not actual blame on each other for their tragedy. Such cross accusation does not give relief, and members do not effectively deal with the issue of culpability and justice.

Slowly and carefully, not favoring one side or the other, the social worker encourages discussion about the conflict that is occurring. Fairness in sharing domestic tasks within the family is examined. There is agreement that fathers should do a greater share of household tasks, and mothers should be more direct in expressing demands to their husbands. Shortly after this conflict is addressed, group members begin to express angry feelings over the failure of the district attorney and the court personnel to keep them informed of arraignments and trial dates. They note that society did not protect their children from violent death and the criminal justice system denies them information and opportunities to participate in what is perceived as a defective and immoral system.

SCAPEGOATING

A telltale indication of a significant issue of social justice is found in scapegoating incidents that occur in groups. Below the surface of scapegoat interaction is latent content of injustice in the external environment.

There has been increased interest in the phenomenon of scapegoating in society and in small groups (Colman, 1995; Douglas, 1995). Scapegoating is a ubiquitous element of group life and, for that matter, of organizations and social institutions. Scapegoating is widespread and predictable; Colman refers to scapegoating as a collective archetype.

The occurrence of scapegoating typically points to a practical crisis that is rife with value dilemmas, and is the underlying question of social justice for a group. To the extent that scapegoating is a displacement of a negative attribute of some group members onto one of its members, the principles of social justice become salient. Scapegoating, by its unidimensional accounting of blame, speaks to a concept of rude justice by the many against the few, the strong against the weak, or "the survival of the fittest." The scapegoating situation is understood as a group-level societal reenactment and as such can open up the small group to consider actions that focus on redistributional justice.

The following event occurred in a group of people with HIV/AIDS engaged in scapegoating one member. The worker assisted the group in discussing the intricacies of the scapegoating process together that point to broader issues of social justice.

Illustration

In a group of people with HIV/AIDS, there has been a good deal of discussion about the possibility of going back to work, as members see their health and vital energy improving from new drugs. The expense of these medications is enormous and growing. Members are reluctant to go off medical entitlements or publicly subsidized insurance for health care and medications. A job would mean more expensive health insurance policies with large co-payment requirements.

John, a depressed and pessimistic group participant, has been the butt of other members' humorous asides for being a "whining queen" who just wants attention and sympathy. When this pattern of scapegoating is noted by the group worker, its impact is minimized, even by John. The group begins a diffuse and somewhat elliptical discussion about most people without HIV/AIDS thinking the epidemic is over, while *they* are still very vulnerable. Members lament that the epidemic has not ended for them, and they are envious of their friends and lovers who predeceased them—"At least they don't have to fret over how they will pay for medication. The dead are finished worrying about 'when the other shoe will drop.' "

TRANSFORMING IMAGES

Ruth Middleman (1985) reminds social workers that images with rich sensory potential are valuable products of group interaction. An image takes the rich complexities of human experience and simplifies its essence, so it can be apprehended in its nuances with enriched perception and sensory awareness. An effective image mobilizes the observer through enhanced understanding of action choices. To be human is to invent and reinvent images related to behavioral interactions that guide and direct our multilayered contacts with others in the environment. Examples of strong, useful images may be *lame ducks, shit hitting the fan,* or *one step at a time.*

The potency of a good image at the right time and place cannot be overemphasized. For example, early in the AIDS epidemic a group of people newly diagnosed with the disease rejected the terminology *AIDS victim* or *AIDS sufferer,* insisting instead that AIDS organizations and the press describe them as *people with AIDS*—first and foremost human beings, not to be wholly defined by the disease or be seen as its hapless victims.

The following example points to the special power of images to provoke understanding and activity in a group. The worker validates group images and encourages their creation as a shared group experience, when a potent image occurred in the group of people diagnosed with AIDS who were struggling to stay healthy, but were frustrated that employment would mean the loss of life-preserving medical treatment and medicines:

> After going around in circles about working or not working, group members become alternately angry and sad about their plight, even envying those who have died of complications of AIDS who were spared this conflict. The group worker shares the image that all their discussion seems to be about: *giving power to the virus and letting it make all decisions.* This comment with its ludicrous cartoon figure of a bossy microbe invokes laughter and puzzlement among group members. The discussion that follows is about seeking legal advocacy and advice about keeping benefits while taking on a job. Group members show interest in joining a lobbying effort to pass legislation allowing people with AIDS to retain publicly subsidized benefits while working.

Another example of imaging occurred in the group of parents of children who were victims of homicide. The mothers asked for a separate group to address their specific concerns as oppressed survivors of a horrific tragedy. Over time they identified with a central image within the group and it later moved them to engage government representatives.

There is frequent discussion in the group of how their children's bodies looked after the murder. Some mothers suffer because they were unable to have their children in open caskets. A Latina mother wanted to rub the body of her son with alcohol and dress it, but could not. These conversations are strongly emotional and the mothers tenderly support one another.

They begin to self-identify as *Mothers of Murdered Children*, which invokes powerful images of the special relation between the mother and the dead child. This group name resonates with richly textured images of the *Pieta* and *Stabat Mater* (Mary and her son, Jesus). This central group image of mothers of murdered children gives courage to the women to offer testimony before the state legislature. They succeed in getting the legislature to pass an appropriation subsidizing mental health services to family survivors of homicide. The mothers argue that this is reparation for the government's failure to protect their children.

CONCLUSION

A justice-centered group work approach gives direction and hope to the people we serve. The argument has been made that a justice-centered practice is not for special groups made of special people interested in social change, but is an intrinsic possibility for all groups served by conscientious practitioners.

The centrality of social justice for all people was eloquently stated by Eleanor Roosevelt, the architect of the Universal Declaration of Human Rights:

> Where, after all, do universal human rights begin? In small places, close to home—so close and so small that they can't be seen on any maps of the world. Yet they are the world of individual peoples; the neighborhood he lives in. The school or college he attends; the factory, farm or office. . . . Such are the places where every man, woman and child seeks equal justice, equal opportunity, equal dignity without discrimination. (Lash, 1972, p. 81)

In the years ahead, let the practice of group work be synonymous with the concept of social justice. Without broad participation in the quest for social justice, personal healing and human solidarity will wither and die. So let us enliven and renew our knowledge and understanding of human rights for all people. No greater challenge confronts social workers with groups today.

REFERENCES

Armstrong, K. (2000). *Islam: A Short History.* New York: Modern Library.

Batchelor, S. (1997). *Buddhism without Belief: A Contemporary Guide to Awakening.* New York: Riverhead Publishing.

Breton, M. (1995). The potential for social action in groups. *Social Work with Groups, 18*(2/3), 5-13.

Cohen, M.B. and Mullender, A. (1999). The personal in the political: Exploring the group work continuum from individual to social change goals. *Social Work with Groups, 22*(1), 13-31.

Colman, A.D. (1995). *Up from Scapegoating: Awakening Consciousness in Groups.* Whelmed, IL: Chiron Publications.

Douglas, T. (1995). *Scapegoats: Transferring Blame.* London: Routledge.

Gitterman, A. and Shulman, L. (Eds.) (1994). *Mutual Aid Groups, Vulnerable Populations and the Life Cycle,* Second Edition. New York: Columbia.

Glendon, M.A. (2001). *The World Made New: Eleanor Roosevelt and the Universal Declaration of Human Rights.* New York: Random House.

Lash, J.P. (1972). *Eleanor: The Years Alone.* New York: W.W. Norton.

Lee, J.A.B. (1994). *The Empowerment Approach to Social Work Practice.* New York: Columbia.

Middleman, R.R. (1985). Maybe It's a Priest or a Lady with a Hat with a Tree on It, or Is It a Bumble Bee: Teaching Group Workers to See. In M. Parnes (Ed.), *Innovations in Social Group Work: Feedback from Theory to Theory.* Binghamton, NY: The Haworth Press, pp. 29-42.

Middleman, R.R. and Wood, G.G. (1990). *Skills for Direct Practice in Social Work.* New York: Columbia.

Northen, H. (1988). *Social Work with Groups,* Second Edition. New York: Columbia University Press.

Plaut, G. (Ed.) (1981). *The Torah: A Modern Commentary.* New York: Union of American Hebrew Congregations, pp. 1455-1463.

Rawls, J. (1971). *A Theory of Justice.* Cambridge, MA: Harvard.

Schwartz, W. (1959). Group work and the social scene. In A.J. Kahn (Ed.), *Issues in American Social Work.* New York: Columbia, pp. 11-13.

Schwartz, W. (1969). Private troubles and public issues: One job or two? *Social Welfare Forum.* New York: Columbia University Press, pp. 22-43.

Shulman, L. (1999). *The Skills of Helping Individuals, Families, Groups, and Communities,* Fourth Edition. Itasca, IL: F.E. Peacock Publishers, Inc.

Simon, B.L. (1990). Rethinking empowerment. *Journal of Progressive Human Services, 1*(1), 27-39.

Specht, H. and Courtney, M. (1994). *Unfaithful Angels: How Social Work Has Abandoned Its Mission.* New York: Free Press.

Toseland, R.W. and Rivas, R.F. (1998). *An Introduction to Group Work Practice,* Third Edition. Boston: Allyn & Bacon.

Chapter 6

Social Group Work, Social Justice

Sue Henry

The premises of this chapter are that social justice is social justice, and that small group experiences in and through social group work are the prototype of social justice encounters. Social justice is an elusive phenomenon. Social work espouses it as a much-desired state of human affairs, but it seems always to be beyond our grasp. The search for evidence to uphold the assertion that social justice is social justice, regardless of the size or complexity of the social system in which it exists, whether large-order social units or small-order social units, such as the small groups with which social group workers work, created the need for characterizations of social justice and of social group work that could be shown to be of parallel construction.

The contours of the term *social justice* will be traced first, followed by a discussion of a model of social group work that is analogous to it, and then illustrations of practice that demonstrate the correspondence will be presented.

THE MEANINGS OF SOCIAL JUSTICE IN SOCIAL WORK

A search for the social work connotation of the term *social justice* led to a wide variety of social work sources, from the encyclopedia (NASW, 1995), to the dictionary (Barker, 1999), to social policy texts (Karger and Stoesz, 1994), to large-system practice texts (Haynes and Mickelson, 1991). What turned up were illustrations of social justice, but nothing in terms of how to bring it into being. Remarkably, nothing in social work sources showed social justice operating in social units smaller than neighborhood entities.

Reference to a couple of sources reveals the nature of social justice as it is portrayed in social work literature. DuBois and Miley (1996) state:

> Ideally, social justice is the social condition in which all members of a society share equally in the rights and opportunities afforded by society and in the responsibilities and obligations incurred by membership in society. Full participation in society means that individuals have access to the social benefits of society to realize their own life's aspirations and contribute to societal well-being. (p. 49)

Elsewhere, their explication of social justice is specific to the citizenry of a society rather than to the state of being of the society itself:

> all members of a society share the same rights to participation in the society . . . opportunities for development, responsibility for social order, and access to social benefits. Social justice prevails when all members of a society share equally in the social order . . . [and] . . . secure an equitable consideration of resources and opportunities. (p. 13)

Haynes and Mickelson (1991) make a contribution to the possibility that the scope of social justice is not necessarily limited to large order societal concerns. In a closely reasoned argument, they construct the following position:

> there seems to be little disagreement that the founding principle of social work is related to social justice: To the extent that this is and has been true, it represents a posture that redirects and reallocates resources toward a more "just" distribution. . . . Generally, social work has ascribed to the principle that inequities in power . . . should not exist unless they work to the benefit of all. (p. 42)

From the previous depictions of social justice, a set of ideas may be deduced. They stand as value statements or social value assertions:

- Social justice is a condition of equal sharing in rights and opportunities; that is, the same rights to participation, to protection, to opportunities for development, and to access to social benefits.

• Social justice is a condition of equal sharing in responsibilities and obligations; that is, responsibility for social order, for an equitable consideration of resources, and for full participation.

No discussion of how to bring about social justice was found in the literature. The challenge for social work and social group work is to demonstrate that socially just experiences in social work groups mirror social justice and have the potential to be preparatory to achieving social justice in the wider society.

Coyle, an early theorist, asserted the link between social group work and social action (Coyle, 1937a,b, 1939, 1947). The term employed today to refer to the end state, "achieving social justice," is a plausible and practicable expression of earlier terms.

Incidentally, when "social change" is heard, people often translate it as "*societal* change." They may or may not be the same. Think, rather, of social change taken to mean change in social functioning, social relationships, the social environment, social institutions, and change in social systems.

How do we demonstrate the equivalence between social justice and social group work? The first task is to identify *which* social group work is referred to. Fortunately for the present enterprise, Papell and Rothman (1966) partitioned the concept, social group work, and named models: social goals model, remedial model, and the reciprocal model. Here, it should be noted that Lang (1972) points out that the three models are not conceptualized on the same partitioning basis. Two models refer to an end result (social goals and remedial), and the other to the means of work (reciprocal). There is, nonetheless, some virtue in turning to the original sources of a group work method for light on today's challenges.

THE SOCIAL GOALS MODEL

The settlement house movement and later social movements are the roots of the social goals model, but the model has its origins in such endeavors as the labor union movement and the women's movements of the 1930s. It is social work's oldest group method. Although Cohen and Mullender (1999) assert that the social goals model is "[r]eferred to in recent literature as social action group work" (p. 16), they provide no documentation of that. It is a limiting characterization to say that "the central goals of this model are social change and the empowerment of oppressed populations" (p. 16). Perhaps Cohen and Mullender wish to associate it to empowerment-oriented social work but, without demonstration of the fit with the originally conceived model, that point is left unmade.

The social goals model stands squarely on social science, small group, and group dynamics theories but it stands more strongly on an avowed social values stance. Social science theories were fully explicated and developed for social work chiefly by Grace Coyle and Margaret Hartford (Coyle, 1930, 1947, 1958; Hartford, 1972; Alissi, 1980b). Practice theories that followed were elaborated by a number of group workers over the years: Coyle (1948); Phillips (1951); Hartford (1972); Blum (1964); Lang (1972); Henry (1992); as well as others cited by Papell and Rothman (1966).

Following is the representation that Papell and Rothman (1966) make of two central assumptions of the social goals model:

> The model assumes . . . a unity between social action and individual psychological health. Every individual is seen as potentially capable . . . of meaningful participation in the mainstream of society. . . . [T]he social goals model approaches every group as possessing a potential for effecting social change. Program development moves toward uncovering this strength. . . . This . . . derives from the assumption that collective . . . action represents individual social competence. (p. 68)

In her own words, Coyle, the first theoretician of this form of social group work, espouses these tenets:

> Group workers have from the beginning been interested in the use of group experience as a preparation for the responsible participation of members of groups as citizens. . . . Experience in the small . . . group . . . provides experience in the pursuit of common goals, in the . . . accomplishment of deferred common ends, in . . . the learning of leadership skills, i.e., in the experience of the democratic process . . .
>
> A second way in which group workers use group experience as preparation for citizenship is by . . . discussion of various kinds of social issues . . .

A third way in which group work services have been used to contribute to socially desirable attitudes lies in the use of planned group experience to deal with . . . tensions especially in interracial or interethnic group situations. (Coyle, 1959, in Alissi, 1980a, pp. 42-43)

Further on in the same paper, Coyle says:

> The . . . values which . . . are available through properly trained group work leadership show two interacting functions, one related to the meeting of individual need through a variety of group experience, the other a contribution to society itself through developing habits and skill in democratic participation and the social attitudes and concerns which make for healthy community life. (p. 45)

So, of what is this practice made? Coyle points in that direction:

> the primary skill is the ability to establish a relationship with a group as a group . . . and to be able to perceive both individual behavior and its collective manifestations . . .
> This establishment of a relationship with the group rests in part on an intellectual understanding of the dynamics of individual behavior and a rational system of ideas for the diagnosis of group behavior within its social setting . . .
> Among the essential skills of the group worker is the necessary knowledge about program activities . . . [resting] . . . on the recognition that various group experiences have different values . . .
> A third major aspect of the group worker's role lies in his [sic] ability to deal with values and the conflicts of values he [sic] may encounter . . .
> The group worker needs also certain knowledge and skills which are common to all social workers. (Coyle, 1959, in Alissi, 1980a, pp. 46-48)

If we deduce principles from these statements, as we did from the characterizations of social justice, we come to the following as the knowledge, skills, and values requisite for social group work practice.

Knowledge

- Dynamics of individual behavior
- Individual behavior and its collective manifestations
- System of ideas for understanding group behavior
- Program activities of interest to a particular group, based on the knowledge that different group experiences have different values to particular individuals or at particular times in life
- Knowledge common to all social workers: how to help those who need more help than a group experience; how to recognize symptomatic behavior; referral sources; community services

Skills

- Diagnosis of group behavior within its social setting
- Establishment of a relationship with the group as a group
- Dealing with values and conflicts of values
- Recognition of symptomatic behavior
- Giving and taking referrals
- Making appropriate assignment to specific groups
- Provision of necessary social services

Values/Attitudes

- Identification with the social work profession
- Collective action for the collective good
- Group experiences as the setting for learning citizen participation and democratic values
- Rights and opportunities are balanced with responsibilities and obligations
- Provision of group services for addressing social and societal problems taking precedence over provision of group services for addressing individual problems

What does practice look like, then, in this perspective which joins social group work and social justice? The following are two practice examples, with interpretive comments. The first example comes from indirect practice, with a social group worker staffing an agency committee of adult women involved in public affairs studies. The second comes from a long-term residential facility for adolescents ages fifteen to eighteen.

PRACTICE EXAMPLES

The Public Affairs Committee and a Hispanic Freedom Movement

The YWCA in a metropolitan area in the Rocky Mountain West had a central administrative and program facility and twelve decentralized program centers for women and their preschool children. Part of the mission of a YWCA is to provide leadership opportunities and leadership-skills training for members. One avenue for these widening leadership occasions is membership on various central committees of the agency. It was not unusual for a female program participant to be noticed for her leadership qualities and subsequently elected as a member of the central body's board of directors; conceivably, she might be elected an officer of the organization, and later become a leader in the voluntary, nonprofit sector in the community. In the specific instance discussed here, working on social justice issues from within the organization led directly to working on social justice issues in the wider community. A social group worker provided staff service to the central Public Affairs Committee and it was her duty to share study resources and national agency policy positions, prepare members of the committee for their representative function, and provide leadership training.

In this case a Hispanic freedom movement was forming in the community for the purpose of creating an alternative "charter school" and a cultural community center. The charter school was meant not only to teach children in Spanish, but was also to expose them to knowledge of the centuries of oppression experienced by indigenous peoples at the hands of whites.

But the Hispanic freedom movement was lacking financial resources to realize its aims, lacking some organizational skills to move toward its goals, and lacking some degree of widespread community understanding and support to take on the work. Leaders of the movement received planning assistance from the local council of churches, and the council put out a call to a meeting among agencies known for their support of social issues.

A meeting was held at the temporary headquarters of the Hispanic freedom movement, to which representatives of some thirty voluntary social service agencies were invited. The social group worker accompanied one of the members of the central Public Affairs Committee from one of the decentralized program sites. The purpose of the staff person was to provide support; the purpose of the volunteer was to gather information, take the information back to the central Public Affairs Committee for discussion, and to refer the discussion information to the decentralized program sites for further discussion. Using the representative mechanism employed by the agency, a report would come to the next month's committee meeting and policy-action recommendations would be made to the board of directors.

Prior to the meeting at the Hispanic freedom movement facility, the group worker met with the designated representative, giving orientation to the movement, to the council of churches' role in bringing things to that moment, suggesting to her the scope of assurances that she could give at the meeting, and explaining the representative role.

Although the committee member later expressed uneasiness with her role and with traveling into the area of town where the meeting was held—a low-income area with three public housing projects for the Spanish-speaking population and an area where the volunteer had never been—the committee member performed her representative service admirably. In subsequent meetings of the committee and of the board, the volunteer was able to be persuasive in favor of support for the freedom movement, and the YWCA became one of the strongest advocates for that venture. Perhaps not so incidentally, the volunteer subsequently became a member of the state social legislation coalition, the agency board of directors, president of the board, and a member of the local United Way Allocations Committee.

The Hispanic freedom movement became a firmly established and well-regarded player in the cultural and political scene of the metropolitan area. Some years later, school board members, state legislature members, and city council members have emerged from the movement.

Analysis

The structure of the organization was designed to provide for collective action. The centralized/decentralized program arrangement was intended to use a variety of kinds of groups as tools for facilitating social participation. Personal and social growth opportunities were available to agency participants, headed toward taking increasing leadership roles. The worker behavior consisted of understanding the woman's uneasiness in taking the representative role and in going into a part of town with which she was unfamiliar. The worker provided information in the form of orientation and in identifying the scope of her role performance relative to the meeting. Clearly, the focus was not on individual problems; fully capable adult functioning was assumed and, based on that, was achieved on behalf of social change and, ultimately, social justice. The example reinforces Coyle's observation that "social services are rooted in the sense of responsibility which a democratic society has for making provision by collective effort for the needs which society itself produces or which it comes to recognize" (Coyle, 1959, in Alissi, 1980a, pp. 36-37).

Independent-Living Skills in an Adolescent Residential Facility

The initial purpose of the group at the residential facility for youth ages fifteen to eighteen was to teach and learn independent-living skills that would stand the group members in good stead when they were living on their own. Some examples of skills to be worked on, as envisaged by the staff at the home, were: job searching and interviewing, budgeting and saving money, renting an apartment and taking care of it, living comfortably with others in a neighborhood, etc. This was a facility in which daily groups were the order of the day. One would assume that a basic group for such a facility would improve upon life skills, but all the groups in existence at that time were highly treatment oriented. This was one of the reasons the idea of a different type of group caught so much attention within the small group home; it was a change. The residents all attended the nearby high school, which had the uncommon policy of requiring every student to participate in some schoolwide activity, which could range from music groups to student government to academic subject interest groups. The policy was not especially popular with the adolescents in the residential facility; they thought it was "nerds and geeks" who were involved in school activities, but it was a graduation requirement so they felt stuck. The group work staff decided this could be capitalized on to achieve two aims: first, to involve the residents in acquiring a skill fostering their future independent-living and citizenship roles; and, second, the staff thought that house self-government could be an outcome, thereby supporting the adolescent developmental task of exercising control over decisions that affect their lives. The residents of the home had a certain reputation within the student body at the high school and they worked to maintain the perception of their difference. In their style of dress, body piercings, hair color, slang, choice of music, and "inside" vocabulary (inside the residential facility, that is), the adolescents communicated insider/outsider mores. Although their bravado indicated that they were self-satisfied with that state of affairs, the staff wanted to work with the residents to make more productive choices.

A brief description of the possible self-government group was mentioned at a whole house meeting. Six of the sixteen residents indicated an interest in the nonmandatory group. This indication was followed by a pregroup interview where their individual goals and aims were specified and particularized. The group work staff shared with the residents, in the pregroup interview, their hope that the experiences of the house self-government group could be transferable to the high school experience. Although this was met with some degree of doubt, the workers left their hope as an optimistic aim and the residents left it "on the table," but not as a high priority.

Following the pregroup interviews, it was mutually decided that all six were suitable for group membership. Together, at the first meeting of the self-government group, the residents and co-workers fashioned a group-oriented contract having to do with group rules, agreement to adhere to group rules, and the consequences for violating them. The matter of formal leadership roles was determined by using a rotating system for each meeting (decided at the end of the previous meeting) and order would be maintained in meetings by raising hands and being called upon by the leader for the day and fines being levied when this rule was broken. At the beginning of each meeting, the leader for the day asked for agenda items from each member, and the group, together, decided the sequence in which items would be taken up.

Within a very short period of time, other residents began to suggest issues that they felt affected the shared-living experience and other residents began to lobby for the self-government group to be opened up to become the house "council." The idea was taken to an all-house "community meeting" where it was debated and discussed over the period of a month and, ultimately, put in place. Representatives were selected (by election, by consensus, or by volunteering) from each wing of each floor of the house, making six members in all.

Prior to each meeting, one of the co-workers would meet with the designated meeting leader and help him or her rehearse skills for meeting management. After each meeting, the co-worker would debrief the session with the leader and help him or her assess performance and identify what he or she could work on for the next time.

Remarkably, when the high school student-government group was chosen at the next election, one of the adolescent girls from the residential facility was picked to represent sophomore girls. The student-government sponsor reported to the group work staff at the house that the performance of the resident was wonderfully mature and responsible. The idea of taking others into account, working on behalf of all, reflecting a positive point of view on rights and responsibilities, and showing understanding of sharing and turn-taking were all skills that the student council sponsor attributed to the sophomore resident of the facility in her role at the high school.

Analysis

This practice example is a clear reflection of the truth that "collective group action represents individual social competence" (Papell and Rothman, 1966, p. 68). One could add that meaningful participation and individual *social* health are part of the unity of this approach to social group work. Adolescents *can* assume a high degree of control over decisions that affect their lives, *can* take on functions that produce effective results on behalf of themselves and others, *can* exercise a range of leadership skills, and *can* receive recognition and approval for all of those ways of integrating themselves into the adult world. The willingness of the group workers to introduce flexibility into the design of group services in the residence was a strong start in that direction. The opportunity for adolescents to grow from a feeling of being marginalized, placed out of their families of origin (perhaps several times), to a point of taking responsibility for governing their own living situation by being elected to school government, is one that fully fits with the possibility of progress toward working on social justice.

The two practice examples portray social justice as being realized through social group work practice. We know a great deal about social justice and we know a great deal about social group work. What we do not know a great deal about is how to *do* social justice. The practice processes illustrated here rest on a set of assumptions. First, the presence of a group worker with the group is assumed. Second, it is assumed that members of the group are capable of what Lang (1972) terms "autonomous" functioning—capable of taking decisions over matters under their control and those that affect their lives, capable of participating in deliberations and decision-making occasions with full recognition of their status relative to that of others, and capable of surrendering some degree of self-interest for the sake of others achieving their goals. Beyond those, several practice principles inferred from the previous discussion are offered here:

- Social distance between worker (or the worker person) and group members must be reduced from the outset and remain so through the experience. A group-level contract, negotiated between and among the members and the worker, is a very useful device for assuring reciprocity of roles and relationships.
- Leadership must be fostered and distributed among members; the worker person is not "the leader." Leadership is or ought to be a widely available resource.
- The group as a social unit must operate on the basis of an equal and equitable distribution of resources and benefits.
- There really *is* unity between social action (toward social justice, I would add) and individual psychological health.
- Practice is always value driven and must be openly so.

SUMMARY

This chapter considered various presentations of social justice in the social work literature. A model of social group work was discussed that was identified nearly thirty-five years ago as the social goals model but the practice itself is more than sixty-five years old. The precepts of that model were outlined. The knowledge, skills, and values derived from the historic and classical formulation of the social goals model were cataloged and discussed. Two examples were shown of practice from the social goals model perspective and an analysis of each was furnished to demonstrate working toward social justice.

REFERENCES

Alissi, A.S. (Ed.) (1980a). *Perspectives on social group work practice.* New York: The Free Press.

Alissi, A. (1980b). Social group work; Commitments and perspectives. In A. Alissi (Ed.), *Perspectives on social group work practice,* (pp. 5-35). New York: Free Press.

Barker, R. (1999) *The social work dictionary,* Fourth edition. Washington, DC: NASW Press.

Blum, A. (1964). "The social group work method: One view." *A conceptual framework for the teaching of the social group work method in the classroom.* Paper presented on Faculty Conference Day, 12th Annual APM of CSWE, New York: Council on Social Work Education.

Cohen, M.B. and Mullender, A. (1999). "The personal in the political: Exploring the group work continuum from individual to social change goals." *Social Work with Groups,* 22(1), 13-32.

Coyle, G.L. (1930). *Social process in organized groups.* New York: R.R. Smith.

Coyle, G.L. (1935). "Group work and social change." *Proceedings of the national conference of social work, 1935.* Chicago: University of Chicago Press, pp. 393-405.

Coyle, G.L. (1937a). "Social work and social action." *Social Work Today* (November).

Coyle, G.L. (Ed.) (1937b). *Studies in group behavior.* New York: Harper and Brothers.

Coyle, G.L. (1939). "Education for social action." In *New trends in group work,* J. Lieberman (Ed.) (pp. 1-14). New York: Association Press.

Coyle, G.L. (1947). *Group experience and democratic values.* New York: Women's Press.

Coyle, G.L. (1948). *Group work with American youth: A guide to the practice of leadership.* New York: Harper.

Coyle, G.L. (1958). *Social process in the community and group: Significant areas of content in a social work curriculum, a study of group process.* New York: Council on Social Work Education.

Coyle, G.L. (1959). "Some basic assumptions about social group work." In M. Murphy (Ed.), *The social group work method in social work education.* Volume XI. A project report of the curriculum study (pp. 88-105). New York: Council on Social Work Education.

DuBois, B. and Miley, K. (1996). *Social work: An empowering profession.* Boston: Allyn & Bacon.

Hartford, M.E. (1972). *Groups in social work.* New York: Columbia University Press.

Haynes, K.S. and Mickelson, J.S. (1991). *Affecting change: Social workers in the political arena,* Second edition. New York: Longman Publishers.

Henry, S. (1992). *Group skills in social work: A four-dimensional approach,* Second edition. Pacific Grove, CA: Brooks/Cole Publishing.

Karger, H.J. and Stoesz, D. (1994). *American social welfare policy: A pluralist approach,* Second edition. New York: Longman Publishers.

Lang, N. (1972). "A broad range model of practice in the social work group." *Social Service Review* 46(1) (March), 76-89.

National Association of Social Workers (1995). *Encyclopedia of social work.* Washington, DC: NASW Press.

Papell, C. and Rothman, B. (1966). "Social group work models: Possession and heritage." *Education for Social Work,* 2(Fall), 66-77.

Phillips, H.U. (1951). *Essentials of social group work skill.* New York: Association Press.

Chapter 7

Culturally Grounded Approaches to Social Justice Through Social Work with Groups

Flavio Francisco Marsiglia

INTRODUCTION

Our profession in general and group work in particular have a long tradition of promoting a social justice agenda. In the United States, for example, many social workers identify the settlement house movement to reaffirm minimal distributive justice as the essential mission of social work (Haynes and White, 1999; Wakefield, 1998). The movement is not only known for responding effectively to the social needs of immigrants and migrants in large cities, but also for actively advocating needed policy and structural changes. It emerged out of the need to respond to population and economic changes produced by industrialization in the first half of the twentieth century. In these postindustrial times, our profession is once again challenged to respond to the much debated effects of globalization.

The ideological climate in the early twenty-first century, however, is remarkably different from the one in which the settlement house movement flourished. There has been an ideological switch that does not necessarily match a classic social work agenda. Our professional value base has been defined as a "theory of caring based on values of justice, independence and freedom, the importance of community life, client self-determination, and social change" (Appleby, Colon, and Hamilton, 2001, p. 10). The values of mainstream global society are often at odds with these humanitarian and egalitarian ideals. Increased levels of individualism and consumerism have resulted as an intended or unintended consequence of globalization. Social work is interfacing with a society that is becoming increasingly global in its economic output but ethnocentric, classist, and xenophobic in its attitudes and social policies.

The described mismatch has produced some soul-searching and tension within the profession (van Wormer and Boes, 1999). Notions of fairness, social justice, and achieving community well-being through the principles of equality, freedom, and autonomy for individuals are being questioned (Valentine, 1999). Social work is being pressured to become more global. In order to maintain its professional relevance, social work needs to reassess its value base and the impact of globalization on social work policy and practice (Abbott, 1999). Our profession is working with some individuals, groups, and communities benefitting from the global economy and with others coping with the negative consequences of their participation or exclusion. Tension will undoubtedly emerge as traditionally oppressed and marginalized communities are called to become global, often at the expense of the social supports present in their traditional cultural milieu. This chapter revisits the principle of social justice in the context of our global times and proposes the use of culturally grounded group work as one approach to responding to the current challenges presented by globalization.

GLOBALIZATION, SOCIAL JUSTICE, AND SOCIAL WORK

The global economy has legitimated economic rationalism and classic liberalism by determining the value of individuals solely by their contribution to the economy (Valentine, 1999). These and related ideas have inspired social policy in the United States and in other countries under its influence with the consequence of allowing market forces to structure social relations. Under economic rationalism, social workers are forced to deliver services in an environment that seems to exacerbate inequalities and does nothing to further social justice (Sherman, 1999). Globalization appears to have accentuated socioeconomic differences, with those in the lower sectors of society benefitting less than those with more privileged backgrounds. The World Bank calculates that one-third to one-fourth of the world's people still live in severe poverty—these calculations are based on minimal wage rates of one dollar to two dollars a day (Madrick,

2001). The globalization of capital is transforming not only economic relations but also social and political institutions. Some have argued for the need to allow local social conditions to play a stronger role in deciding the future of communities as a means to balance the influence of international institutions with universal formulas (Wade and Rodrik, 1999). People struggling to survive in this atmosphere are developing new forms of interaction and organization, both locally and transnationally (Whitmore and Wilson, 1999). These efforts aim at countervailing the negative effects of certain aspects of the market economy by advocating a more equitable distribution of resources and social justice. As a result, in spite of the apparent prosperity, there has been a surprisingly strong resurgence of a social justice agenda.

In part as a reaction to globalization, environmental concerns, and third-world debt, different voices are calling for change in the name of social justice. The emergence of a politics of difference (i.e., socioeconomic status, ethnicity identity, gender identity, sexual orientation) has also contributed to the resurgence of a social justice discourse (Smith, 2000). The argument proceeds from the recognition of morally significant aspects of human sameness, through the identification of human needs and the case of associated rights, to an egalitarian conception of social justice.

The institutional approach to social justice favored by John Rawls (1999) can be useful in explaining these renewed efforts toward social change. From a Rawlsian sense of justice, society has a special obligation to ensure that the basic terms of people's daily human interactions are just (Mandle, 2000). Following a social justice objective implies changing social institutions and organizations in order to actively support the protection of basic human rights and socioeconomic needs (Schoeny and Warfield, 2000).

Current global and national trends toward a market-oriented economy and its corresponding social policies are making us reexamine not only social work practice but social work education and research. As a result there have been specific calls for the profession to take actions, such as:

• Assume a courageous stance in reclaiming its own voice in order to realize its commitment to human transformation and social justice (Weick, 1999)

- Embrace compassion, solidarity, and empowerment in order to promote social justice among those who are marginalized (Coleman, 1999)
- Stand for service to "the least among us," diversifying social work's professional workforce, and promoting community engagement (Haynes and White, 1999)
- Take a position on human rights and social justice, weighing conceptual, cultural, and political aspects (George, 1999)

These are major challenges for a profession faced with increasing political influence but with limited access to the major brokers in global centers of power. In the best social work tradition, it is at the local level that the profession can best influence the aforementioned global challenges. In this process, social work defines feasible strategies by balancing its internal tendencies between idealism and pragmatism, and between universalism and relativism (George, 1999). A generalist practice connects the local, regional, national, and transnational efforts toward social justice. These linkages are specific and political, with the profession exercising its moral authority against forces working against its social justice agenda.

The proximity to the real world and social phenomena—the natural settings—has been a traditional source of nonscientific moral authority for the profession, one that strengthened its ability to speak up and advocate for social change and social justice. In the past fifty years the trend has been toward seeking knowledge gained at a distance (Weick, 1999). Integrating the social sciences into the profession provided legitimacy to traditional advocacy efforts, but it may have also silenced social work. There is a need to find a synthesis by grounding social work research and teaching in the profession's value focus, and decades of rich practice experience (Weick, 1999). Culturally grounded practice and research are made possible through our profession's historical applied approach.

A CULTURALLY GROUNDED APPROACH

Globalization is producing a homogeneous culture based on consumerism at the expense of unique local cultures, the environment, and other contextual differences. Social work practice promoting social justice needs to be grounded on the cultures of the participating communities. Recognizing and celebrating the centrality of culture is a means of resisting the homogeneity and oppression resulting from a consumer society. Culture, however, can be an elusive concept to operationalize by its defenders and can be easily labeled as an effort toward Balkanization by those opposing a culturally grounded approach to social justice. The elusive nature of culture can be explained in part because it is an outcome and a process that arises through the meaningful activity of people. As action becomes meaningful, members of a culture develop expectations about the activities of its members (Bantz, 1993). These expectations become resources and strengths that nurture, protect, and inspire group members toward participation.

It has been suggested that social identities, social representations, and shared power are crucial elements for constructing a social psychology of participation (Campbell and Jovchelovitch, 2000). Communities cannot, however, defend their unique social identities and worldviews if they are not aware of them. This is the reason that interventions promoting social justice often need to start at the cultural awareness level or with *conscientization* efforts (Freire, 1995). It is from this perspective that we support a culturally grounded approach to group work as a means to resist oppression and promote social justice in these times of globalization.

Grounding social work interventions in the culture of the group members has been described by using different terms such as *indigenization* (Narayan, 2000), *ethnoculturalism* (Anderson, 1997), or *empowerment* (Lee, 1994). Independent of the terminology used, these efforts tend to be closely linked to Freire's core concept of "critical consciousness." Through group participation, individuals who have been alienated from their culture are encouraged to identify, examine, and act on the root causes of their oppression (Gutierrez and Lewis, 1998). This process involves a gradual and cyclical action-reflection-action chain of group behaviors, which Freire terms *praxis,* involving dialogue and action (Freire, 1995).

Although praxis as a concept and a method was developed and extensively tested in South America and later in Africa, it has been identified as a useful approach in the United States, Canada, and Mexico to aid in the creation of more just social structures and more caring communities (Duncan, 2000). Social work scholars have specifically identified praxis as a means to continue the social justice-social diversity mission that is central to our profession (Nagda and Gutierrez, 2000).

Praxis implies that group members identify issues, define or "name" them, and look for common solutions. The role of the group facilitator is to help the group become aware of its power to act and to transform. The group becomes a laboratory of democracy where all opinions count, but where empty words quickly become discouraged.

In becoming a transforming force, the group initially decides on small action steps, develops plans, and implements them. Once the course of action is implemented, the group reflects on its accomplishments and shortcomings, relates the outcome to the larger social phenomena they are concerned about, and starts planning the next action step. Group members become more capable of challenging and rejecting messages from the larger society that says nothing can be changed. They connect personal problems to political issues (Gutierrez and Lewis, 1998), and their personal and group-defined issues to larger societal issues such as racism, sexism, and heterosexism. They continue to take steps to overcome them. Together they become better dreamers and aim at other steps such as promoting social justice (Marsiglia and Zorita, 1996).

It is not the role of the social worker to define what social justice is or to suggest steps to make it tangible, but neither is it our role to remain neutral. "Claiming neutrality does not constitute neutrality; quite the contrary, it helps maintain the status quo" (Freire, 1995, p. 141). Social workers become more openly political as the group becomes political by starting to take a position on human rights and social justice, and weighing conceptual, cultural, and political aspects (George, 1999).

The workers' worldviews, beliefs, and values strongly influence their practice and comfort with groups (Kurland and Salmon, 1999). Thus, praxis becomes a compass not only for the group members but also for the workers. It helps them find a balance between the needs of the group, their worldviews, and the profession's code of ethics. The group with its equalitarian force neutralizes the power and potential oppression of the worker. In a circle, the worker becomes one more member, but with a professional role. Behaviors and attitudes promoting a social justice and equality agenda are defined, rehearsed, and modeled in group. Once the group engages in praxis, the lessons learned are universalized.

GROUP WORK

Group work epitomizes the profession's most important principles and ethics (Knight, 2000). As such, group work is a natural venue to involve members of oppressed communities in their own liberation (Freire, 1995). Culturally grounded group work utilizes the culture of the group members as a precious resource and as an experiential tool for critical consciousness.

From a social justice perspective, individuals and communities should be allowed to be who they are at the same time that they access the economic benefits of globalization. This is a dynamic process that eventually will lead to a bicultural stance for the minority client. Biculturalism, however, recognizes the two worlds and aims at retaining what is of value from the culture of origin as individuals adopt what is of value from majority culture. These exercises on identity development are made easier with the support of the group, where members learn from one another and take risks together.

Clients who find their culture reflected and recognized in the substance and the format of the group are more likely to be motivated to participate and to benefit from the experience (Kuykendall, 1992). Natural helping and traditional social networks must be recognized as needed resources in assisting minority clients in their transition process into the new economy (Patterson and Marsiglia, 2000). Culturally grounded group work rescues, validates, and integrates community-based narratives and practices as natural, indigenous, and transforming ways of helping.

Culturally grounded group work highlights and supports the resiliency factors present in the evolving cultural narratives and actions coming from the members' communities. Following the tradition of the settlement house movement, culturally grounded group work promotes social justice from a grassroots perspective. Social justice is defined by the group members at the local level and is based on their own unique biographies. Once the group members accomplish the purpose they set for their group they project themselves into other larger circles. Social justice is accomplished in personal ways as a means of resisting a progressively global and anonymous society.

Culturally Grounded Group Work
with Ethnic-Minority Youth

Ethnic-minority youth often encounter difficulties in their quest to develop a sense of identity and social competency in an increasingly global society (Spencer and Markstrom-Adams, 1990). Competing elements such as bicultural status, racial inequality, nonminority peers, and a stereotypical media figure prominently in their psychosocial development (Peeks, 1999). Younger members of communities are often more directly exposed to the effects of globalization and consumerism than their parents. Tensions and conflicts such as internalized oppression emerging from different acculturation statuses need to be identified, named, and addressed (Marsiglia, Kulis, and Hecht, 2001).

Group work with children and youth through the use of mutual aid can be an effective counterforce to devaluing the other (Malekoff and Laser, 1999). Group members are encouraged to participate in group activities that connect them to their cultural roots and in turn speak about it or reflect about what happened and how the activity relates to their lives at home and in the community. This approach maximizes the potential of the members' narrative legacies, and their commonalities become explicit (Marsiglia and Zorita, 1996).

The application of this culturally grounded perspective with youth follows an identity-development approach as it focuses on individuals who become strongly aware of their identity issues and oppression due to their cultural background (Garvin, 1997). Group facilitators educate themselves about historical traditions, beliefs, and community norms; assess the members' level of assimilation into the dominant culture; and understand what any loss of culture may represent (Williams and Ellison, 1996). Youth groups can assist their members by enhancing their awareness of changes in their norms, values, and traditions. Resources from the culture can be creatively and respectfully used to support this process. Group members from ethnic-minority communities can share and support each other in their challenges as members of "two worlds" represented in minority and majority communities (Marsiglia, Cross, and Mitchell, 1998; Marsiglia and Johnson, 1997; Gutierrez and Ortega, 1991). Issues of prejudice and internalized prejudice need to be addressed, as they constitute barriers to social justice.

Case Study

The described culturally grounded approach was used in working with youth in a large city in the Southwest United States. One of the many consequences of globalization in the borderland region is an economic and demographic explosion. As they are once more becoming a numerical majority in many communities throughout the region, Mexican/Mexican-American youth often encounter prejudice and discrimination, such as stereotypes that they use drugs or are involved in drug trafficking. The National Institute on Drug Abuse awarded a research grant to develop and test a culturally grounded drug-prevention program to reach these youths.

Two small groups of high school students, majority Mexican/Mexican American, were involved in the development of a drug abuse-prevention program for their younger middle-school peers. Different steps were taken to identify the protective factors present within the culture to resist drugs and to use those strengths to develop a citywide prevention program.

1. Narratives from middle-school students on ways they typically refuse drugs were collected by university trained ethnographers from the School of Social Work.
2. Their narratives were analyzed and a set of resistance strategies was identified. Differences were found between the ethnic groups represented in the sample.
3. Three sets (Latino, non-Latino, and mixed) of four video scripts were developed by the high school students for each of the most commonly used strategies. They conducted the casting, and filmed and edited the videos with the support of professional film directors. Throughout the process they met in group and discussed the process (praxis) with professional group facilitators.
4. A prevention curriculum was developed around the student-produced videos. Teachers were trained on how to teach the curriculum. The program was implemented at forty-two schools, reaching more than 6,000 middle-school students.
5. A three-year-long comprehensive evaluation showed positive results. When compared to the control group, participants in the program significantly reduced their use of alcohol and other drugs and changed their attitudes in the desired direction between the pretest and the three follow-up posttests.

Classrooms were treated as groups. Teachers received training on group facilitation and culturally grounded approaches to communication. Social workers facilitated small groups at all the participating schools with students referred by their teachers as needing more support. The small groups followed a culturally grounded narrative approach. Stories were shared and they were acted out, and "scripts" were changed by the students to reflect healthier behaviors. Cultural dif-

ferences were celebrated in the group. Drug trafficking and drug use in the bor-
derlands were discussed from cultural, health, educational, and political perspectives.

Middle-school students reacted positively to a program that reflected them in its content and format. The strategies they learned
were coming from the experiences of youth such as them, and the
prevention messages were packaged by youth such as them. These
programmatic features were conducive to open communication and
dialogue in group. One of the female group participants commented
during the final session of her small group: "I liked how we could be
open and say what we wanted to without being laughed at."

Small groups were at the core of the whole effort. Although the
adults participating in the project encouraged the youths to take control, at the beginning of the process students did not know how to be
in charge. Similar difficulties were encountered by ethnic-minority
students when they were asked to produce materials that reflected
their culture. During the initial sessions students avoided any cultural
content and later relied on majority culture's stereotypes about their
ethnic community. It was through praxis that they became aware of
these initial behaviors and attitudes and in group gained the confidence necessary to celebrate and express their own sense of self.

REFERENCES

Abbott, A.A. (1999). Measuring social work values: A cross-cultural challenge for
    global practice. *International Social Work, 42*(4), 455-470.
Anderson, J. (1997). *Social work with groups: A process approach.* New York:
    Longman.
Appleby, G.A., Colon, E., and Hamilton, J. (2001). *Diversity, oppression and social
    functioning.* Boston, MA: Allyn & Bacon.
Bantz, C.R. (1993). *Understanding organizations: Interpreting organizational
    communication cultures.* Columbia: University of South Carolina Press.
Campbell, C. and Jovchelovitch, S. (2000). Health, community and development:
    Towards a social psychology of participation. *Journal of Community and Ap-
    plied Social Psychology, 10*(4), 255-270.
Coleman, J.A. (1999). Compassion, solidarity and empowerment: The ethical con-
    tribution of religion to society. *Social Thought, 19*(2), 7-20.
Duncan, G.A. (2000). Race and human rights violations in the United States; con-
    siderations for human rights and moral educators. *Journal of Moral Education,*
    29(2), 183-201.

Freire, P. (1995). *Pedagogy of the oppressed.* New York: Continuum.

Garvin, C. (1997). *Contemporary group work.* Boston: Allyn & Bacon.

George, J. (1999). Conceptual muddle, practical dilemma: Human rights, social development and social work education. *International Social Work, 42*(1), 15-26.

Gutierrez, L. and Lewis, E. (1998). A feminist perspective on organizing with women of color. In F. Rivera and J. Erlich (Eds.), *Community organizing in a diverse society* (Third edition) (pp. 97-106). Boston: Allyn & Bacon.

Gutierrez, L.M. and Ortega, R. (1991). Developing methods to empower Latinos: The importance of groups. *Social Work with Groups, 14,* 16-32.

Haynes, D.T. and White, B.W. (1999). Will the "real" social work please stand up? A call to stand for professional unity. *Social Work, 44*(4), 385-391.

Knight, C. (2000). Critical content on group work for the undergraduate social work practice curriculum. *The Journal of Baccalaureate Social Work, 5*(2), 93-111.

Kurland, R. and Salmon, R. (1999). Education for the group worker's reality: The special qualities and world view of those drawn to work with groups. *Journal of Teaching Social Work, 19*(1/2), 123-137.

Kuykendall, C. (1992). *From rage to hope: Strategies for reclaiming black and Hispanic students.* Bloomington, IN: National Educational Service.

Lee, J.A.B. (1994). *The empowerment approach to social work practice.* New York: Columbia University Press.

Madrick, J. (2001). The mainstream can't or won't recognize some basic facts about world poverty. *The New York Times,* August 2, p. C2.

Malekoff, A. and Laser, M. (1999). Addressing difference in group work with children and young adolescents. *Social Work with Groups, 21*(4), 23-34.

Mandle, J. (2000). Globalization and justice. *The Annals of the American Academy of Political and Social Science, 570,* 126-139.

Marsiglia, F. F., Cross, S., and Mitchell, V. (1998). Culturally grounded group work with adolescent American Indian students. *Social Work with Groups, 21*(1/2), 89-102.

Marsiglia, F.F. and Johnson, M. (1997). Social work with groups and the performing arts in the schools. *Social Work in Education, 18*(1), 53-59.

Marsiglia, F.F., Kulis, S., and Hecht, M.L. (2001). Ethnic labels and ethnic identity as predictors of drug use and drug exposure among middle school students in the Southwest. *Journal of Research on Adolescence, 11*(1), 21-48.

Marsiglia, F.F. and Zorita, P. (1996). Narratives as a means to support Latino/a students in higher education. *Reflections, 2*(1), 54-62.

Nagda, B.A. and Gutierrez, L.M. (2000). A praxis and research agenda for multicultural services organizations. *International Journal of Social Welfare, 9*(1), 43-52.

Narayan, L. (2000). Freire and Gandhi: Their relevance for social work education. *International Social Work, 43*(2), 193-204.

Patterson, S. and Marsiglia, F. F. (2000). "Mi casa es su casa": A beginning exploration of Mexican Americans' natural helping. *Families in Society, 81*(1), 22-31.

Peeks, A.L. (1999). Conducting a social skills group with Latina adolescents. *Journal of Child and Adolescent Group Therapy, 9*(3), 139-153.

Rawls, J. (1999). *A theory of justice.* Cambridge, MA: Belknap Press of Harvard University Press.

Schoeny, M. and Warfield, W. (2000). Reconnecting systems maintenance with social justice: A critical role for the conflict resolution. *Negotiation Journal on the Process of Dispute Settlement, 16*(3), 253-268.

Sherman, C. (1999). Alice in social work wonderland: Reflections on disability policy and services during student placement. *Australian Social Work, 52*(3), 57-61.

Smith, D.M. (2000). Social justice revisited. *Environment and Planning, 32*(7), 1149-1162.

Spencer, M. and Markstrom-Adams, C. (1990). Identity processes among racial and ethnic minority children in America. *Child Development, 61*, 290-310.

Valentine, B. (1999). National competition policy: Legitimating economic rationalism. *Australian Social Work, 52*(1), 26-31.

van Wormer, K. and Boes, M. (1999). Social work, corrections, and the strengths approach. *Canadian Social Work, 1*(1), 98-111.

Wade, R. and Rodrik, D. (1999). *The new global economy and developing countries: Making oneness work.* Washington, DC: Overseas Development Council.

Wakefield, J.C. (1998). Psychotherapy, distributive justice, and social work revisited. *Smith College Studies in Social Work, 69*(1), 25-59.

Weick, A. (1999). Guilty knowledge. *Families in Society, 80*(4), 327-332.

Whitmore, E. and Wilson, M. (1999). Research on popular movements: Igniting "seeds of fire." *Social Development Issues, 21*(1), 19-28.

Williams, E. and Ellison, F. (1996). Culturally informed social work practice with American Indian clients: Guidelines for non-Indian social workers. *Social Work, 41*(2), 147-151.

Chapter 8

Social Work with Groups, Mutual Aid, and Social Justice

Dominique Moyse-Steinberg

The purpose of this chapter is to visit the intersection of mutual aid and social justice in social work with groups. It is clear that to visit this intersection is to revisit a juncture that came into existence with the birth of social group work (Breton, 1990, 1995, 1999; Coyle, 1949; Garland, 1986; Glassman and Kates, 1990; Hartford, 1964; Middleman and Wood, 1989, 1990; Newstetter, 1935; Northen, 1988; Papell, 1997; Schwartz, 1961, 1971, 1985/1986).

In 1956, Joseph Eaton likened social work to a "rambling historic building, redecorated sporadically by many subtenants, with a new management bent on modernizing it to serve a more integrated purpose as fast as it can get around to do the job" (Papell, 1997, p. 7). As Papell argues, however, group work has paid a price for the privilege of pulling "its share of the work for professional defining and methodological development" (p. 7) over the last half-century as a subtenant in that building. That price has been such extensive micro-defining of the stuff of social work that some of the fundamental connections among group workers are not always so evident. A question for group work, however, is the extent to which it can serve an integrated purpose, if that is the case.

To qualify as *social* work, practice must, among other things, focus on enabling people to "do" for themselves in all arenas of life so that whenever and wherever the need arises, they will be better at that "doing." Thoughts of mutual aid commonly lead group workers to think of "doing" in small groups, however, and the term *social justice* often leads to visions of "doing" on some broad sociopolitical scale. In fact, mutual aid *is* a form of social action and inevitably creates social justice. It encompasses all efforts, large or small, intended to advance quality of life, and social justice is the result of all efforts, large or small, intended to advance quality of life. Mutual aid and social justice go hand in hand, are joined at the hip, reflect two sides of one coin. Whichever the metaphor, the concepts are inexorably connected—the latter denoting a state of respect and the former denoting a process of respect. Requiring a blend of honesty and empathy, mutual aid encourages people to see the relationship between their personal and interpersonal good and to understand that personal good can only be advanced *in tandem* with, not *at the expense* or *regardless* of, others. Catalyzing mutual aid, therefore, is the "doing" of social work practice with groups—the use of professional skill to help people appreciate the inherent personal and social value of collectivism and collaboration.

All major mandates for advancing civilization understand the intersection between mutual aid and social justice. Social scientist Petr Kropotkin (1908) stated it well when he wrote:

> Don't compete!—competition is always injurious to the species, and you have plenty of resources to avoid it! That is the tendency of nature, not always realized in full, but always present . . . the watchword which comes to us from the bush, the forest, the river, the ocean. Therefore "combine—practise [sic] mutual aid! That is the surest means for giving to each and to all the greatest safety, the best guarantee of existence and progress, bodily, intellectual, and moral. (p. 75)

At its best, parliamentary procedure is an excellent example of mutual aid. Defined as "a meeting about national concerns" (*American Heritage Dictionary,* 1992, p. 1317), the term *parliament* comes from the French word, *parler,* which means "to talk"; and when it takes place, it does so with the intent of identifying common ground and of addressing issues of common interest. As a verb, "talk" is defined in over a dozen ways (*American Heritage Dictionary,* 1992, p. 1831). Each definition, however, connotes some form of communication. In other words, to really talk is to communicate, and when people no longer engage in real talk the process of helping one another search for common ground breaks down and the advancement of social justice comes to a halt. The intent is no longer one of engaging in real talk about real things (Steinberg, 1997), or finding commonality. Rather, it is to preach or to hear the sound of one's own voice or to fill some uncomfortable silence or to protect against the nature, meaning, and implications of other feelings, other attitudes, other viewpoints. Whichever reason, however, mutual aid is no longer taking place. Social justice is no longer being advanced.

For example, to the extent that she initiates real talk, when Margaret Sanger, founder of the birth control movement (Katz, 2001), promotes a dialogue about women's rights to practice contraception, she catalyzes mutual aid and advances social justice. People think about, talk about, and compare their real feelings and attitudes toward sex, sexuality, marriage, parenthood, gender roles, and countless other related factors. Issues are identified and clarified, and implications of being and doing one way or another are made visible, tangible, and personal; as a result, society recognizes the right of women to exercise personal sovereignty over one of their most fundamental roles.

When some attorneys in Illinois who represent thirteen men on death row in that state speak out against capital punishment, they catalyze mutual aid and advance social justice. People think about, talk about, and compare their real feelings and attitudes toward crime and punishment. Issues are identified and clarified and implications of being and doing one way or another are made visible, tangible, and personal; as a result of this dialogue capital punishment is overturned in one more state.

When the concern by the rabbinical leadership of a community that a local music festival might promote anti-Semitism is met with an invitation by the management of that festival to an evening of discussion, mutual aid is initiated and social justice advanced. Needs, desires, concerns, and attitudes are exchanged, explored, understood, and respected.

Modern technology and the facility of travel have moved social work increasingly toward specialization in the past fifty years. Specialization feels right to social workers, who are taught and trained to manage the "wicked" problems of today by partializing them into "bites" and chewing those bites one by one (e.g., eating the proverbial elephant). In fact, specialization may even be pragmatically useful (Middleman and Wood, 1990). One of its side effects, however, is that it creates the potential for disconnection.

For example, it is not uncommon today to hear that some forms of social work with groups advance social justice and others do not, or that mutual aid applies only to some group work. Not only must group work be based on the intent to catalyze mutual aid in order to qualify as *social* work, mutual aid *always* takes place in social work with groups. In other words, the intent to catalyze mutual aid is a constant, a core of practice.

It is not the point of this chapter to suggest that there is no room for diversity of effort in social work or within social work with groups. Rather, it is to suggest that labeling some efforts but not others as social action may cause professional nearsightedness. The ultimate intent of social work practice with groups is to advance social justice—and whatever its label, it does so. It is a mistake, therefore, to see the catalysis of mutual aid as a *step* toward social action rather than as a *reflection* of social action. Wherever and whenever mutual aid is catalyzed, social justice is advanced both immediately and exponentially. Similar to a pebble thrown into water that causes increasingly large concentric circles of motion, mutual aid has an inevitable ripple effect.

Consider a group that refers to itself as the Livingroom Dialogue Group. This group is composed of Jewish and Palestinian men and women who left Israel several years ago. The members of this group all live in the same city in California, and the group has met over 100 times in the past few years. The purpose of the group, as one member said recently in a television broadcast, is to help its members maintain empathy for one another, particularly in times of great social stress. Not only is it impossible to believe that the mutual aid in this group has no effect on their near and immediate quality of life, it is impossible to believe that it does not in some way advance social justice in Israel, thousands of miles away.

Clearly, there is always the potential to catalyze *more* mutual aid and to advance *more* social justice. For instance, a group was formed in an agency in Toronto, Canada, in the early 1980s to help immigrant Hispanic women who lived in the community (Breton, 1999). The workers in that group could have decided, as Breton describes, to frame its purpose in terms of helping members find ways to cope with depression and could have catalyzed mutual aid to that end. Instead, they remained open in their thinking about needs, desires, potential, and capacity, and as a result the group defined its mission as one of changing some of the systemic barriers in the community. That is, the group used its internal mutual-aid muscle to flex its external muscle. Simply by virtue of catalyzing mutual aid, however, the practitioners advanced social justice by helping members think things through (the nature of those things), by helping them express themselves, by helping them listen to one another, by encouraging them to respect their differences, and by helping them reach for and harness their common ground. Had the intent of practice been and its actions done nothing other than that, it would still have advanced social justice.

When a practitioner based in a New York City high school began to work with a group called the Young Men's Club (Malekoff, 1999), she did not know that the mutual aid catalyzed in that group would ultimately lead to improved conditions in the boys' bathroom. Yet that is exactly what happened. As with the practitioners in the previous example, she too could have decided to frame her job in terms of helping members cope or "do" with the way things were. Instead, however, she chose to remain open in her thinking about needs and goals, and as a result the mutual aid that evolved in the group led it to become an advocate for better school bathroom conditions. Again, however, had her intent been and actions done nothing other than to help members talk and listen to one another with respect, she would have advanced social justice.

Therefore, when a social work intern decided to provide to the British-style High Tea Group (with which she was working at a New York City day treatment center) some real plates, cups, and silverware after learning that members had never eaten from other than paper and plastic, she too advanced social justice by offering a taste of and cultivating a taste for respect along with tea (Newmann, 1999). As the title of the paper indicates, there is no doubt that the dignity that was brought to group process produced a remarkable change for the better. Holding the teacups, pouring the tea, passing around plates—all of these actions became deliberate, thoughtful, and careful. Along with growing awareness of and sensitivity to that process came a growing awareness and sensitivity in other areas: to the nature of dialogue, to the quality of interaction, to the meaning of group membership, to the look and feel of helping and being helped. Mutual aid was catalyzed, social action took place, and social justice was advanced.

Paradoxically enough, even as group work struggles to stay afloat in increasingly generic waters, then, by constantly highlighting what it has to offer that is separate and distinct from casework, it would be useful for group work to think less in terms of labels or even models and more in terms of common ground.

Clara Kaiser (1958) argues that social work with groups is more a question of approach to practice than it is one of setting or characteristics of members. In other words, there is a great deal of "wiggle room" for shaping practice in spite of the formal ideologies that surround it. An excellent example of using "wiggle room" can be found in social work research, which has over recent years increasingly recognized the legitimacy of qualitative study (Padgett, 1998), and even more recently, participatory action research (de Roux, 1991). It was not that long ago that neither of these forms of inquiry were considered methodologically sound ways of practising research.

There is always some way in which mutual aid can be introduced into practice so that it reflects a social work process and, by reflecting social work, advances social justice. Providing real china is an example of one way. Sharing some degree of responsibility over the group's affairs is another. Helping people express themselves in a way that can be heard is another. Asking them to listen carefully is another. Encouraging them to share their own stories and to look for the common threads in those stories is yet another.

The label *social goals* is often used to connote an overt agenda of social action in group work. If social justice is a state of respect, however, and social action is about taking steps toward such a state, then to the extent that it catalyzes mutual aid, practice is always one of social goals. Labels such as *remedial, reciprocal,* and *social goals* may be used to provide a kind of shorthand language to give a quick sense of things. As with sound bites, they do not necessarily accurately portray the substance of things. They can be misleading, and can cause people to lose sight of connections and of common ground. Thus, some labels suggest that mutual aid is more applicable to one form of social work with groups than it is to another, and some suggest that one type of group or one model of practice reflects social action more than does another.

Perhaps labels are a useful pragmatic tool. In the spirit of professional connection, however, it may be helpful at this point to slow down the use of labels in talking about social work practice with groups. Not only do they easily cause professional nearsightedness, no label other than *social work* can truly reflect the complexities of practice (Garland, 1986). As Hans Falck (1988) proposes, it would be useful to think in terms of membership. Eyes that focus on membership focus on connection, and eyes that focus on connection cannot lose sight of what is connected. They must move beyond labels in search of substantive common ground.

To be effective, every system needs to have some degree of common ground between or among its parts, and it needs to recognize that common ground. Why? Common ground creates necessary connections, and the recognition of those connections advances the system's welfare. In social work with groups, that common ground is the intersection of—or connection between—mutual aid and social justice, and for the advancement of social work with groups, it is necessary for group workers to recognize that there is always this intersection in social work practice—that it is at this intersection that all group workers meet. It may be useful for group work as a system, then, to move from the well-known mandate of dual focus to one of multifocus, or *hard eye/soft eye,* a term that comes from the world of dressage and refers to guiding a horse through complex maneuvers by slight body movements. The rider keeps an eye on the distant and indirect (soft eye) as well as on the near and immediate (hard eye), and by doing so, keeps all grounds and views in sight, related, connected.

One way to translate the concept of *hard eye/soft eye* to social work with groups is to apply it to actual practice. For instance, the practitioners in the Hispanic Women's Group (Breton, 1999) previously discussed exercised hard eye/soft eye in their work with that group by paying attention to a multitude of factors: the presence of each individual in the group; the presence of the group as a system; the needs, desires, and concerns of members; their own perceptions; the quantity and quality of relationships among members; the potential relationships between "personal" and "interpersonal"; the nature, meaning, and impact of context; the potential in and out of the group; and capacity—theirs, that of each individual in the group, of the group, of the organization, of the immediate community, and of larger society. That is more than dual focus! Remaining open to differences in problem definition is practising with hard eye/soft eye vision. Helping happen what needs to happen, even if it is not quite what was expected to happen, is practising with hard eye/soft eye. Extending a conversation about the value of collective responsibility in such a way that it helps members translate its value outside the group is practising with hard eye/soft eye. Another way of practising hard eye/

soft eye vision, however, is to see the intersection between mutual aid and social justice in all work with groups that is social work.

The theoretical connections between mutual aid and social justice are strong, even between models of practice that stereotypically reflect opposite ends of the specialization spectrum (Cohen and Mullender, 1999). In effect, even when practice is conceptualized as "treatment," social justice is advanced if mutual aid guides the process. People who share some degree of power over their treatment by participating in its delivery always receive it more effectively. To suggest that of the three models that seem to dominate practice today (remedial, reciprocal, and social goals), only social goals groups pursue social change (Cohen and Mullender, 1999) may be to misunderstand the inherent capacity of mutual aid to advance social justice wherever and whenever it is catalyzed. Personal growth is never just personal in impact. Regardless of context, helping people listen to others even as they express their own feelings and attitudes, helping them appreciate the views and rights of others even as they assert their own, and helping them reach for empathy when they are having a difficult time understanding one another cannot help but advance quality of life.

Are there really ever any forms of personal distress that are so internally caused that they have absolutely no connection to the social for which including the recognition of that connection would be irrelevant? So-called individual problem solving in a group is much less "individual" than it sounds when it relies on mutual aid (Steinberg, 1997). Much of what is conceptualized as "personal distress," therefore, also may be less personal than it sounds and occasions in which it exists rare; and using a hard eye/soft eye approach to practice would help make that evident. It may make the possibilities for "doing" endless, but the special strength of social group workers is their ability to catalyze mutual aid in order to help people sort through those possibilities.

At the same time, exercising hard eye/soft eye can help to keep the intersection between social work with groups and social justice more evident. How? It reveals that the existence of a social goals group connotes the existence of a "nonsocial goals" group, which is, from the perspective of social work, simply an oxymoron. When social work takes place, mutual aid must take place, and when mutual aid takes place, social goals are realized. William Schwartz (1971) argues that social workers are only incidents in the lives of group members. As with a butterfly whose tiny flapping wings have an impact on global weather patterns, group workers can and do have an impact on social justice wherever and whenever they practice.

Where does this kind of thinking lead group work? In effect, it leads to the rediscovery of something that group workers have always known: that choice and diversity apply to many aspects of social work practice, but not to intent or result; that labels do little to accurately portray the substance of practice and much to make the common ground of social work with groups vague (Breton, 1995, 1999); and that wherever and whenever there is an intent to catalyze mutual aid, basic human needs are met, social work takes place, and social justice is advanced.

REFERENCES

American Heritage Dictionary. (1992). Boston: Houghton Mifflin Company.

Breton, M. (1990). Learning from social group work traditions. *Social Work with Groups,* 13(3), pp. 21-34.

Breton, M. (1995). The potential for social action in groups. *Social Work with Groups,* 18(2/3), pp. 5-13.

Breton, M. (1999). The relevance of the structural approach to group work with immigrant and refugee women. *Social Work with Groups,* 22(2/3), pp. 11-29.

Cohen, M. B. and Mullender, A. (1999). The personal in the political: Exploring the group work continuum from individual to social change goals. *Social Work with Groups,* 22(1), pp. 3-31.

Coyle, G. (1949). Definition of the function of the group worker. *The Group,* 11(3), pp. 11-13.

de Roux, G. I. (1991). Together against the computer: PAR and the struggle of Afro Colombians for public service. In O. Fals-Borda and M. A. Rahman (Eds.), *Action and knowledge: Breaking the monopoly with participatory-action research* (pp. 33-55). NY: Apex Press.

Eaton, J. W. (1956). Whence and whither social work? A sociological analysis. *Social Work,* 1(1), pp. 11-26.

Falck, H. (1988). *Social work: The membership perspective.* New York: Springer Publishing Company.

Garland, J. (1986). The relationship between social group work and group therapy: Can a group therapist be a social group worker, too? In M. Parnes (Ed.), *Innovations in social group work: Feedback from practice to theory* (pp. 17-28). Binghamton, NY: The Haworth Press.

Glassman, U. and Kates, L. (1990). *Group work: A humanistic approach.* Newbury Park, CA: Sage Publications.

Hartford, M. (Ed.). (1964). Frame of reference for social group work. *Working papers toward a frame of reference for social group work* (pp. 4-10). New York: NASW Press.

Kaiser, C. (1958). The social group work process. *Social Work,* 3(2), pp. 67-75.

Katz, E. (2001). Bio of Margaret Sanger. *Margaret Sanger Papers Project.* Retrieved October 26, 2001: <http://www.nyu.edu/projects/sanger/ms-bio.htm>.

Kropotkin, P. (1908). *Mutual aid: A factor of evolution.* London: William Heinemann.

Malekoff. A. (1999). Pink soap and stall doors. *Families in Society,* May/June, pp. 219-220.

Middleman, R. and Wood, G. G. (1989). *The structural approach to direct practice in social work.* New York: Columbia University Press.

Middleman, R. and Wood, G. G. (1990). From social group work to social work with groups. *Social Work with Groups,* 13(3), pp. 3-20.

Newmann, E. (1999). High tea anyone? Bringing dignity to social work practice. Unpublished paper, Hunter College School of Social Work, New York, NY.

Newstetter, W. (1935). What is social group work? In *Proceedings of the national conference of social work* (pp. 291-299). Chicago: University of Chicago Press.

Northen, H. (1988). *Social work with groups.* Second edition. New York: Columbia University Press.

Padgett, D. K. (1998). *Qualitative methods in social work research: Challenges and rewards.* CA: Sage Publications.

Papell, C. (1997). Thinking about thinking about group work: Thirty years later. *Social Work with Groups,* 20(4), pp. 5-17.

Papell, C. and Rothman, B. (1980). Relating the mainstream model of social work with groups to group psychotherapy and the structured group approach. *Social Work with Groups,* 3(2), pp. 5-23.

Schwartz, W. (1961). The social worker in the group. *The social welfare forum.* New York: Columbia University Press.

Schwartz, W. (1971). On the use of groups in social work practice. In W. Schwartz and S. R. Zalba (Eds.), *The practice of group work* (pp. 3-24). New York: Columbia University Press.

Schwartz, W. (1985/1986). The group work tradition and social work practice. *Social Work with Groups,* 8(4), pp. 7-27.

Steinberg, D. M. (1997). *The mutual-aid approach to working with groups: Helping people help each other.* NJ: Jason Aronson, Inc.

SECTION III:
SOCIAL JUSTICE IN THE PRACTICE
OF SOCIAL WORK WITH GROUPS

Chapter 9

Meet Them in The Lab:
Using Hip-Hop Music Therapy Groups
with Adolescents in Residential Settings

Susan Ciardiello

Adolescence is a stage of development plagued by turbulence and rebellion, and it is especially challenging for youth in residential settings (Brown, 1986). Traumas that led them into care, such as abuse, rejection, and abandonment, have left them with a mistrustful and negative lens through which to view the world. These experiences have conditioned the residents to react to people and situations in ways that cause further rejection and disapproval. Their lives are also compounded by the daily stress inherent in residential programs. Residents have no control over the simplest areas of life, such as when they eat, sleep, and where and when they can go out (Schnekenberger, 1995). Strict rules and rigid expectations permeate these homes and set many of them up for failure rather than provide a helpful structural environment. Residents often test authority in angry or passive-aggressive ways, resulting in more restrictions on their freedom (Casey and Cantor, 1983).

Many of these agencies also maintain problem-focused therapeutic programming where the adolescents are expected to attend individual or verbal group therapy (Gold and Kolodny, 1978). Programs that emphasize pathology often create barriers for adolescents. The social stigma of therapy, and the expectations that they will have to talk about their character flaws and problem behaviors, often repels them from this type of treatment (Brown, 1986). Studies have discovered that more than 50 percent of all teenagers referred to treatment drop out after their first few sessions (Katch, 1988). Refusal to attend therapy is termed by a vast number of mental health professionals as "resistance," and phrases such as "adolescent is resistant to therapy" can be found in many agency progress notes and/or psychosocial reports. However, are they "resistant," or are we failing to engage them in treatment?

Gitterman (1983) addresses this question in his assertion that "labeling a client's behavior as resistant often enables workers to avoid confronting deficiencies in their agencies and themselves" (p. 127), which relieves them of looking into their inadequate methods of engagement. As a result, residents in care are often left without therapeutic support, vulnerable to repeating their own or their families' undesirable behaviors that often precipitated their placements. It seems the traditional problem-focused approach to treatment is not helping many adolescents in care (Garland, 1992). It is suggested that workers consider adolescents' therapeutic needs and interests in order to learn how to engage them (Kurland, 1978; Malekoff, 1997).

THE NEEDS OF ADOLESCENTS IN CARE

Adolescents in care have a strong need to initiate and maintain some autonomy and control in their lives (Casey and Cantor, 1983). They need a safe place where their feelings, views, and strengths can be expressed, attended to, and nurtured (Malekoff, 1997). Residents need to learn how to contain and rechannel their strong emotions in safer ways, and they need help connecting past experiences with current undesirable behaviors. They also need to develop trusting relationships with adults and the peers with whom they reside (Resnick, 1978). Residents often assert their need for more freedom and meaningful activity. Thus, they are in need of legitimate social outlets during after-school hours.

When considering their needs, it appears that a more cooperative and empowering approach to treatment is warranted. A group work approach that includes the residents' interests can serve this purpose.

THE USE OF GROUP MEMBERS' INTERESTS IN PROGRAMMING

Many group work scholars agree that using activities based on members' interests is an effective way to engage adolescent clients

(Gold and Kolodny, 1978; Middleman, 1980; Casey and Canter, 1983; Brown, 1986; Malekoff, 1997). Gold and Kolodny (1978) propose that success is more likely when group members' interests are used as the medium for working on interpersonal challenges. Additional benefits to the use of members' interests in programming include a decrease in adolescent anxiety levels and high levels of engagement and commitment among members (Casey and Cantor, 1983). Furthermore, when group members initiate and suggest the activities that are used in programming, they are given a chance to exercise some control in their lives (Brown, 1986). Meeting this need is a key factor to connecting and working with adolescents (Casey and Cantor, 1983). Finally, including the residents' interests creates an environment of comfort and openness without the stigma that accompanies programs organized around specific problems (Brown, 1986). Thus, in order to create an engaging therapeutic program, workers must identify and learn what the members enjoy and find interesting.

With this objective in mind and the challenging task of engaging group home residents into a therapeutic program, I "met them" in their group homes, and asked a simple question, "What do you enjoy?" The residents identified hip-hop or rap music. So, I learned the culture of hip-hop.

HIP-HOP CULTURE

Hip-hop is a contemporary culture that includes music, dance, film, graffiti art, dress, language, and expressions. In 1976, hip-hop was born in the Bronx, when a group of disc jockeys (DJs) began throwing free parties in parks, creating open-air community centers in neighborhoods where there were none. Each DJ had a master of ceremony (emcee) who would talk to the crowd and tell them to "get up and dance." Eventually, the emcees started to tell stories about life in the ghetto in rhymes over the DJ's music. A few years later, emcees started to record their own music.

The music began to saturate urban streets and homes all across the country (Brewster and Broughton, 1999). The real-life portrayals of the complexities of urban life hit home to many urban dwellers. It empowered them to create a culture that reflected their plight. Hip-hop music replicates and reimagines the experiences of urban life with talk of gang wars, street violence, drugs, prostitution, domestic violence, parental abandonment, and economic stagnation. Such urban realities leap out of hip-hop lyrics, sounds, and themes (Fernando, 1994). Its popularity grew rapidly and now, over twenty years later, hip-hop is the largest music industry in the world (Brewster and Broughton, 1999).

Hip-hip music serves as an outlet for adolescents. They listen to the rappers' life struggles and identify with them. For adolescents in care who are overwhelmed with feelings of loss, rejection, and abandonment, the music fits into their world because many hip-hop songs are flooded with similar life challenges. The Lab is a group work program that uses activities based on the residents' interest in hip-hop culture as the medium for change. The following is a deeper look into the program model, to illuminate the different theoretical frameworks that are at work in The Lab.

THE LAB GROUP WORK PROGRAM MODEL: ACTIVITY-CENTERED THERAPY (ACT)

The theoretical framework for The Lab is what I refer to as activity-centered therapy (ACT) programming. The ACT program model can be described as a therapeutic melting pot because there are a number of theoretical frameworks that are integrated into its philosophy. These include sociorecreation (the activities); psychotherapy (group discussions of life themes, worker as observer and interpreter); cognitive-behavioral principles (peer models and reward system); and psychoeducation (skill development).

Sociorecreation

Sociorecreation, or the use of activities in group work, is a central component of ACT group programming. The Lab uses the group members' interest in hip-hop music and integrates it into a therapeutic activity (Casey and Cantor, 1983; Middleman, 1980; Rose, 1998). Using activities in groups can tap into members' strengths and foster their creativity in problem solving and self-expression (Malekoff, 1997). Activities such as games, arts and crafts, music, and/or drama are integrated into therapeutic groups and are the primary medium in which feelings are expressed (Middleman, 1980; Malekoff, 1997; Garvin, 1997; Rose, 1998). In The Lab, activities include decorating the program room(s); listening to, writing about, and discussing song lyrics; and creating original music. Regarding the activity of decorating the program room(s), The Lab is presented to the members as their place to decorate and make their own. They are invited to paint murals on the walls, use graffiti art, and arrange wall hangings or posters as they wish. This offers them some ownership and control of the program. I found that this ownership process sets off internal controls within the residents that makes them more protective of the equipment and makes stealing and property destruction a rarity. It seems what they feel they own, they treat better.

Psychotherapy

Listening to and discussing song lyrics incorporates the psychotherapeutic process into the program model. This activity is also referred to as Hip-Hop therapy (HHT). HHT is a nonjudgmental approach that uses hip-hop music to provoke discussion and the critical analysis of issues, ideas, and events that impact youth (Tyson, 1998). Lyrical analysis activates buried emotions and experiences and brings them to the surface for discussion (Mazza and Price, 1985). There is empirical support for the use of popular music as a therapeutic group technique (Arnold, 1980; Mazza and Price, 1985; Lyons, 2000). Music enhances early engagement through a non-threatening medium and facilitates group process. It breaks down resistance and allows workers to reach affect and behaviors that might not be as accessible through traditional modes of group work (Mazza and Price, 1985; Garvin, 1997). Furthermore, music has been used in group work with adolescents (Tyson, 1998). Songs universalize many of the adolescents' feelings and experiences and help them to feel less alone. Lyrical analysis helps stimulate group discussions about their presenting problems and how such challenges came into existence (Mazza and Price, 1985).

In The Lab, HHT is implemented in the following way. In an hour-long group session, the members first listen to a hip-hop song as they read the lyrics. The worker can look up the lyrics on the Internet, print them out, and then make copies for the members to read as they listen to the songs. Once the song is over, the members quietly write their reactions in their journals. Writing their reactions down promotes self-expression in a nonthreatening way (Schnekenberger, 1995). Furthermore, the inclusion of journal writing allows the members to self-disclose at their own pace and comfort levels.

Next, the members are invited to share their reactions with the group. Talking about difficult issues in the third person also helps members feel more comfortable to disclose at their own pace. Specifically, lyrics reveal hip-hop artists' experiences and views, which allow the members to discuss anxiety-producing issues in the third person. This is important because adolescents vary in their ability to tolerate anxiety during emotionally charged discussions (Levine, 1978). Discussing issues in the third person is safer, less threatening, and allows anxiety and tension to be regulated and maintained (Hurley, 1984). Malekoff (1991) adds, "Experiences and feelings which seem otherwise inaccessible emerge more readily in the third person context" (p. 110). This use of the third person also helps mitigate the likelihood of acting-out behavior that is often a result of overwhelming feelings of anxiety and tension.

The hip-hop songs used in The Lab are consistent with themes and experiences familiar to the group (see Table 9.1). The worker selects songs according to the developmental stage of the group. In the beginning phase of group work, songs with less emotionally charged issues are used (e.g., first love experiences or faith in God). Once mutual trust and cohesion have been established during the middle phase, songs with more powerful and sensitive themes are used (e.g., familial abuse or out-of-home placement).

In The Lab, Middleman's (1978) worker skills are put into practice. More specifically, the worker uses two reaching skills: reaching for a feeling link and reaching for an information link to maximize group process. The worker reaches for a feeling link by asking members to identify and connect their emotions with the feelings expressed in the songs and by the other members. The worker reaches for an information link by asking the members to connect their ideas, opinions, and beliefs with those expressed by the hip-hop artist and one another. Reaching for stories in the group members helps the worker bridge the gap between them (Schnekenberger, 1995).

TABLE 9.1. Hip-Hop Songs Used to Engage NYC Group Home Residents

Hip-Hip Artist	Album	Song Title	Relevant Life Issue/Struggle
1. DMX	*It's Dark and Hell Is Hot*	"The Convo"	Faith in the face of adversity
		"Prayer"	Faith in God
2. Eve	*Let There Be Eve . . . Ruff Ryders First Lady*	"Love Is Blind"	Domestic violence/relationship abuse
3. Eminem	*The Marshall Mathers LP*	"Stan"	Paternal loss and abandonment, relationship abuse
4. LL Cool J	*Phenomenon*	"Father"	Domestic abuse, paternal drug use and abandonment
5. Janet Jackson	*Janet*	"If"	Trust jaded by heartbreak
6. Notorious B.I.G.	*Life After Death*	"What's Beef"	Street violence
		"Ten Crack Commandments"	Drug dealing
7. Brand Nubian	*Foundation*	"I'm Black and I'm Proud"	Black pride, faith in God
8. Tupac Shakur	*Me Against the World*	"So Many Tears"	Street violence, loss, depression
9. Tupac Shakur	*R U Still Down?*	"Hold On, Be Strong"	Encouragement through difficult times
10. Xzibit	*At the Speed of Life*	"Carry the Weight"	Alcoholism, abuse, group home placement

Cognitive-Behavioral Principles

The cognitive-behavioral principles of peer modeling and positive reinforcement are also integrated into The Lab. When forming the HHT groups, a balance of personality types is used so members have peer models with whom they can identify. Such a mix might include adolescents who are aggressive, peaceful problem solvers, followers, outgoing leaders, and those that are withdrawn. The inclusion of peer models allows the undesirable behaviors of others to be recognized, challenged, and changed. After this learning occurs, the members practice new socialization skills and develop new roles and relationships with each other (Rose, 1998).

In addition to the principle of peer modeling, adolescents are in need of a continual system of recognition and reinforcement if they are to succeed despite numerous emotional, social, biological, and familial barriers (Malekoff, 1997). In The Lab, a reward system is integrated following the residents' participation in the HHT group. Specifically, the group breaks up into subgroups of two to three members and they are rewarded with thirty minutes of "DJ time," or free time to use the music equipment. During their DJ time, residents can create their own mix tapes from the albums available to them in The Lab. They can also write their own lyrics, sample beats from records to create original background music, and then put them together to create their own songs. With a group of nine adolescents, two-and-a-half hours of worker time are needed. However, each member only stays in The Lab for ninety minutes.

Psychoeducation

There is also a psychoeducational or skill-development component to ACT programming. In The Lab, members learn and practice DJ skills, which can become a marketable skill. In addition, many of the members choose to write and record their own lyrics, which encourages them to practice and strengthen their creative-writing skills. For youth prone to acting out, writing out feelings and experiences provides the necessary boundaries to channel confusing and powerful feelings (Mazza and Price, 1985).

In summary, the ACT program model combines sociorecreational, psychotherapeutic, cognitive-behavioral, and psychoeducational techniques into one theoretical framework. This model is a therapeutic melting pot that provides youth with corrective emotional and behavioral group experiences.

SETTING UP THE LAB

In The Lab, a therapy room is transformed into a miniature music studio with a budget of approximately $400 to $600. The equipment includes two turntables, a mixer, two speakers, an amp, a tape recorder, two to three microphones, one set of headphones, and a collection of albums by the members' favorite hip-hop artists. Blank tapes can be bought as needed for the members to record their music. A more advanced setup would include a sample machine and a drum machine for the residents to sample beats from records to create their own music. Regarding the purchasing of supplies, it has been my experience that music companies are more than willing to support such an important cause by donating hip-hop music. In addition, not-for-profit agencies can get a significant discount on music equipment when purchasing through large sales distributors such as Sam Ash

Music in New York City. Such businesses have educational coordinators that work with schools and not-for-profit agencies to help them with supplies and equipment for music programs. Also, used equipment can be found through listings in newspapers and city/town circulars at reasonable prices.

If the worker has little or no budget with which to work, The Lab is set up somewhat differently. The worker can bring in a portable cassette/CD player and ask the members to bring in tapes or CDs of their favorite songs. If The Lab is set up in this way, the HHT groups can be facilitated once or twice a week for one hour. During the first group, members can brainstorm together inexpensive or free ways they can be rewarded for their attendance and participation (e.g., trips to the park, cultural fairs, exhibits, concerts, etc.). The worker can consult with his or her supervisor to determine how often the members can be rewarded for their efforts.

Regarding issues of safety, the worker must be inflexible about his or her role of assuring that the members of the group are safe (Levine, 1978). Members cannot hurt themselves or others, or come to the program if they have been using illegal substances. Limits are acceptable to the group when they are presented and understood in this concrete way (Casey and Cantor, 1983). All other rules on behavior are left to the group to identify and monitor (Levine, 1978). I found that because the program is of value to the members, they feel strongly about adhering to the rules and quickly challenge those who break them. The worker then supports the corrective peer effort while clarifying the struggle for them (Casey and Cantor, 1983).

The involvement of the agency administrators is essential. They must be committed to the group work method and provide the supports needed if the program is to be successful (Birnbaum et al., 1989). It must be understood that the program is given as a part of the agency's commitment to the residents' therapeutic needs (Cantor and Casey, 1983), and thus cannot be used as a form of punishment. Members cannot be prevented from attending the program if they have broken rules in their residential setting. This should be reviewed with child care staff and agency administrators before the program is implemented to assure member continuity in the program and the agency's investment in it.

Finally, before attempting to create The Lab, the worker should assess the agency's level of comfort with using hip-hop songs that have profanity and sexual references. According to Malekoff (1997), "the banter, the language, the posturing, the styles—it's all a part of a culture that they are familiar and comfortable with. For adolescents to be expected to adjust to some standard held by adults is a mistake" (p. 127). When the worker is tolerant of swearing within the therapeutic milieu, a new process begins. The worker watches for opportunities to help the members examine how they view the world they live in, how it fits into the hip-hop artists' views, and if this lens will help the members achieve what they want for themselves (Irizarry and Appel, 1994). If using hip-hop music helps create a comfortable place for residents to share their life stories and challenge each others' undesirable behaviors, then it is worth accepting profanity and objectionable song lyrics. Furthermore, adolescents are listening to these songs anyway, and The Lab offers them the opportunity to reflect, talk about, and understand the songs on a deeper, more personal level.

WHO IS IN THE LAB?

There should be a mix of no more than nine adolescents of both genders in The Lab. Coed groups are used because the gender mix is beneficial to the group process. Female adolescents tend to be less critical of each other in the presence of male adolescents. This makes them more apt to establish closer relationships, which builds group cohesion. Furthermore, adolescent boys seem to respond better to female confrontation. This may be related to their need to feel attractive to the opposite sex. Levine (1978) informs us "coed groups with older adolescents are often especially useful to boys, who are more likely to deal with feelings with the help of the girls of the same age group" (p. 189).

ACT groups are open-ended, which allows for such uncontrollable factors as clients moving in or out of placement or the adoption of new cases with adolescents in need of corrective group experiences. Adolescents are accepted into the program if there is room and if the group environment is a good therapeutic fit for them. Furthermore, group workers must be mindful of where new members stand in relation to group development. Workers should talk to the group about the normal feelings of resistance and apprehension that accompany changes in group composition (Galinsky and Schopler, 1989).

THE LAB IN ACTION

The following is an excerpt from The Lab program created with group residents from five New York City group homes. The members listened to the song "Love Is Blind," by the hip-hop artist Eve. The song involves the theme of relationship abuse and the consequential murder of Eve's best friend, who was the victim of her boyfriend's rage. The song opened the members up and helped them express their feelings, experiences, beliefs, and observations about difficult issues such as domestic violence, murder, revenge, and the codes of the street.

During the song, the residents made comments and body movements that suggested to the worker the lyrics had aroused strong emotions in them (e.g., "Oh that's ****ed up"). Some members became more sullen, suggesting they were identifying with the lyricist's story in some way. After the residents listened to the song, they wrote in their journals. Once everyone seemed to be done writing, one of the members initiated the discussion.

DONALD: [Eighteen y.o. resident whose parents are both deceased; in the foster care system since early childhood. He is a gang member of the Bloods, although The Lab program has seemed to replace the gang with its provision of a leadership role.] That's ****ed up, I would never lay a hand on a girl, never have; they should be respected and treated right. That's ****ed up—he went and killed the mother of his children.

EDWARDO: [Fifteen y.o. resident placed into care with his three brothers because of maternal neglect and mental illness. He holds a follower role in the group— acceptance by his peers seems vital to his self-esteem.] My mom gets beat up like that by my stepdad—it makes me mad.

TYQUASIA (TY): [Nineteen y.o. resident suffering from a degenerative illness. Parents are deceased. Ty hopes to be a music producer someday and has become quite invested in the program. She is a strong leader and is respected by group members. However, she has yet to disclose any personal traumas with the group. Ty was noticeably sullen while the song was being played. At this point a few members looked at her. Her hazy glaring into space and her atypical quietness seemed to unsettle them.]

GEE: [Seventeen y.o. resident whose parents are deceased. Both he and his younger brother have been in care for most of their adolescence. He lived with his aunt who now only allows his brother to visit because he is less volatile than Gee.] Ty, what's wrong? [She says nothing.]

TERRANCE: [Sixteen y.o. resident who has been in care since he was nine. His mother is dying of a degenerative illness and is pregnant. He has sporadic contact with his father. Domestic violence plagued his family for years. He writes poetry and song lyrics and has a strong appreciation for the program.] Maybe she doesn't feel like talking, Gee. [He attempts to protect her with his words, which in some way may also serve to protect his own anxiety about the issue. His mother stabbed his father in the neck in front of him when he was a child.]

RUBIN: [Seventeen y.o. resident who has been in care most of his life. His mother is also dying of a degenerative illness. His father-figure was his uncle, who was shot and killed in front of him when Rubin was eight years old. He is a quiet member who rarely shares his feelings and opinions.] Yeah, let her be. [He knows how it feels to need silence.]

JESSICA: [Eighteen y.o. resident who has been in care for three years and has a rocky relationship with her mother. Her father has never been involved in her life.] I've been there—well, I was abused by my ex-boyfriend's words— sometimes I wonder if words are worse than getting beat down. He used to tell me I was ugly and no good, worth nothing.

DONALD: That's not true.

GEE: That's ****ed up.

JESSICA: Yeah I know. My mother was beat down, too, like Ed's mom, sometimes I wonder if getting beat down like her would have been better. [Ty looks up—it seems as if their self-disclosures have made it safer for her to share her own abusive demons. She takes a risk.]

TY: I lived that story.

And for the first time since the group started five months previously, Ty let down her defenses and reached out to the group for comfort and support. She let go of her need to preserve a strong and self-protective stance and allowed herself to become vulnerable. She shared her story with the group: After her mother died, when Ty was thirteen years old, she lived with a twenty-eight-year-old man who served as her "boyfriend." He gave her money and bought her clothes; but the price she had to pay for those things was a violent one. She talked about how she felt trapped, and how hard it was to leave him because she had nowhere else to go ("my home died with my mother"). The group also talked about the age difference between Ty and her ex-boyfriend, and how under the law what he did was statutory rape. She shared feelings of wanting to seek revenge on him, as in the song when Eve shot her friend's boyfriend, but reflects how he wasn't worth a life in jail. This leads to a group conversation about the proverb "an eye for an eye," and how gangs rigidly follow it on the street.

The previous excerpt shows how listening to song lyrics can bring to the surface strong feelings and painful life experiences, as well as bring the group members closer together.

Membership in The Lab seemed to have a profound impact on the number of AWOLs (absent without leave) of group-home residents. During the course of nine months, twenty group-home residents were active participants in The Lab. A retrospective analysis of their quarterly reports indicated that the total number of AWOLs for program participants dropped from thirty-two (first quarter total) at the start of the program to nine (last quarter total) at the end of the program.

Moreover, during the course of the program, eleven out of twenty of the residents went AWOL less often over time and eight of the residents never went AWOL at all. Although these results were not gathered within a controlled experimental design, they are encouraging. Future research is needed that follows a more structured empirical approach to the study of this type of group work program.

Initially, The Lab was facilitated with an hour of HHT group followed by DJ time for the members. Over time it was transformed into a program rich with other initiatives that seemed to flow from the members' strengths, creative energy, and interests. Groups that utilize program activities based on the interests of the members seem to open the members up to their natural, creative gifts, and they begin to have the courage to innovate (Malekoff, 1997). The Lab program members began to celebrate holidays together and planned events such as a Halloween party where some of them volunteered to DJ. The program members also created the agency's first resident magazine, *The Real Deal: Kids Keepin' It Real*. The magazine was rich with pages of the members' art, photography, poetry, and articles about family and agency life. The magazine also included a section called "Rhymes and Reason," which included the lyrics from two hip-hop songs to help agency personnel and family members understand the music for what it was—the reality of many of their lives. These unexpected program outgrowths are the transformations that help the group develop to its full potential (Middleman, 1980). This use of program transformed itself into its own unique entity that had never before been in existence within the agency (Malekoff, 1997).

CONCLUSION

The Lab is a group work program that uses the lyrics from hip-hop songs as a way to encourage adolescents in residential settings to talk about their experiences of survival, strength, and suffering. Many people have a negative view about hip-hop or rap music, without exploring why so many adolescents in residential care embrace it. Hip-hop music represents the residents' reality; their life histories are as uncensored as the songs. Therefore, it seems inevitable that group workers should embrace the music as well and use it to engage their adolescent clients into a therapeutic milieu. Once their interests are embraced, walls of resistance fall, and they begin to explore their life struggles, both past and present, and the issues that led them into care. Group workers are encouraged to take the first step and "meet them in The Lab," where there are many opportunities to help the residents take themselves where they need to be.

REFERENCES

Arnold, R.J. (1980). They're Playing Our Song: The Use of Popular Music in Confronting the Loneliness of the Alcoholic. *Social Work with Groups, 3*(2), 53-63.

Birnbaum, M.L., Catalina, J., Nisinzweig, S. and Abrams, V. (1989). Institutionalization of a Group Service in an Individual-Oriented Agency. *Social Casework, 70*(10), 495-501.

Brewster, B. and Broughton, F. (1999). *Last Night a DJ Saved My Life.* New York: Headline Books.

Brown, L.N. (1986). Mobilizing Community Services for Adolescents in Trouble. *Social Work with Groups, 9*(1), 107-119.

Casey, R.D. and Cantor, L. (1983). Group Work with Hard-to-Reach Adolescents: The Use of Member-Initiated Program Selection. *Social Work with Groups, 6*(1), 9-22.

Fernando, S.H. (1994). *Exploring Music, Culture, and Attitudes of Hip-Hop.* New York: Anchor Books.

Galinsky, M.J. and Schopler, J.H. (1989). Developmental Patterns of Open-Ended Groups. *Social Work with Groups, 12*(2), 99-114.

Garland, J. (1992). Developing and Sustaining Group Work Services: A Systemic and Systematic View. *Social Work with Groups, 15*(4), 89-98.

Garvin, C. (1997). *Contemporary Group Work* (Third Edition). Needham Heights, MA: Allyn & Bacon.

Gitterman, A. (1983). Use of Resistance: A Transactional View. *Social Work, 28*(2), 127-131.

Gold, J. A. and Kolodny, R.L. (1978). Group Treatment of Socially Dispossessed Youth: An Activity/Discussion Approach. *Social Work with Groups, 1*(2), 145-159.

Hurley, D.J. (1984). Resistance and Work in Adolescent Groups. *Social Work with Groups, 7*(1), 71-81.

Irizarry, C. and Appel, Y.H. (1994). In Double Jeopardy: Preadolescents in the Inner City. In A. Gitterman and L. Shulman (Eds.), *Mutual Aid Groups, Vulnerable Populations, and the Life Cycle* (pp. 119-149). New York: Columbia University Press.

Katch, M. (1988). Acting Out Adolescents: The Engagement Process. *Child and Adolescent Social Work, (5)*1, 30-40.

Kurland, R. (1978). Planning: The Neglected Component of Group Development. *Social Work with Groups, 1*(2), 173-178.

Levine, B. (1978). Reflections on Group Psychotherapy with Adolescents, with Some Implications for Residential Treatment. *Social Work with Groups, 1*(2), 179-193.

Lyons, S.N. (2000). "Make, Make, Make Some Music": Social Group Work with Mothers and Babies Together. *Social Work with Groups, 23*(2), 37-54.

Malekoff, A. (1991). Difference, Acceptance, and Belonging: A Reverie. *Social Work with Groups, 14*(1), 105-112.

Malekoff, A. (1997). *Group Work with Adolescents.* New York: The Guilford Press.

Malekoff, A. (1999). Pink Soap and Stall Doors. *Families in Society,* May-June, 219-220.

Mazza, N. and Price, B.D. (1985). When Time Counts: Poetry and Music in Short-Term Group Treatment. *Social Work with Groups, 8*(2), 53-66.

Middleman, R.R. (1978). Returning Group Process to Group Work. *Social Work with Groups, 1*(1), 15-26.

Middleman, R.R. (1980). The Use of Program: Review and Update. *Social Work with Groups, 3*(3), 5-23.

Resnick, D. (1978). Utilizing Group Treatment Concepts in a Residential Treatment Center. *Social Work with Groups, 1*(4), 381-388.

Rose, S.D. (1998). *Group Therapy with Troubled Youth.* Thousand Oaks, CA: Sage Publications.

Schnekenberger, E. (1995). Waking the Heart Up: A Writing Group's Story. *Social Work with Groups, 18*(4), 19-40.

Tyson, E.H. (1998, October). Hip Hop Therapy: An Innovative Therapeutic Synergy Between Biblio-Therapy and Music Therapy in Group Work with At-Risk and Delinquent Youth. In T. Berman-Rossi (Chair), *Strengthening Resiliency Through Group Work.* Paper presented at the 20th Annual Symposium for the Association for the Advancement of Social Work with Groups, Miami, Florida.

Chapter 10

Talking Circles:
A Traditional Form of Group Work

Arielle Dylan

Everything an Indian does is in a circle, and that is because nature always works in circles, and everything tries to be round.

Black Elk
Black Elk Speaks

The past few decades have presented an intensification of former social problems and new challenges in the topology of human suffering requiring attention from social workers. As a result, the popularity of group practice in the field of social work has increased due to both cost-effectiveness and methodological efficacy (Gitterman, 1989; Middleman and Goldberg Wood, 1990). Groups, especially mutual aid groups, are "entities with many helpers," where the group process is benefited by the power residing within the group-as-a-whole, an entitative force that surpasses the sum power of the individuals constituting the group (Middleman and Goldberg Wood, 1990, p. 92). First Nations have always been group oriented, valuing as they do the collective over the individual; but it is only during the past thirty years, in an attempt to recover from the incalculable cultural devastation wrought by colonialism and Eurocentrism, that the talking circle has experienced a renaissance (Marsiglia, Cross, and Mitchell-Enos, 1998; Dufrene and Coleman, 1992). The unshakable determination First Nations have regarding traditional healing practices is directly related to the success of culturally based treatment; and the talking circle, a traditional group process, bears a sufficient resemblance to non-Aboriginal group work to warrant comparison.

When attempting to place talking circles in the context of social work with groups, many structural, phasic, processual, and temporal commonalities are evident, yet there remain considerable distinctions between the two types of groups, largely attributable to the differing philosophical views and cultural beliefs held by Western and First Nations societies.

In order to proceed with an examination of the talking circle as a group process apropos the social work paradigm, a description of its formulation is necessary. Although it is difficult to find literature written by First Nations people on the actual method of the talking circle, I did manage to obtain an oral description of the ceremony from an employee of the Native Women's Resource Centre (NWRC) in Toronto. There are descriptions of talking circles written by non-Aboriginal people that are helpful but not as thorough or as traditionally imbued as the operational definition I received from the supervisor at the NWRC. The entrance to a talking circle "faces east, whence comes the light of day, and warmth. It signifies revelations of Light" (Gall Eagle, 1997, p. 38). People enter the circle, walk one full revolution around its inner boundary, and sit down. The seating is side by side; nobody is in front and nobody is behind, a symbol of equality. Any one of four traditional medicines will be used in the healing circle for the purpose of cleansing the spirit: these are sage, sweet grass, tobacco, and cedar. Each of the participants in the circle will smudge with the medicine selected. Smudging is the process whereby the group leader, an elder (a First Nations person recognized by the community as having significant spiritual attainment and traditional wisdom), will set fire to one of the medicines and go around the circle passing the smoke in front of each of the group members' bodies. Participants collect the smoke with their hands and wipe it over their bodies, particularly over the heart and eyes. As a person is smudging, she is asking the Creator to help her keep an open mind and heart, so she will not judge. As the smoke is passed over the eyes, the participant asks the Creator for assistance with seeing clearly. The smoke cleanses the spirit and releases negativity. Spiralling upward, the smoke carries away spiritual contaminants.

Once the smudging is finished, the elder sits down and the talking segment of the circle begins. The elder picks up an eagle feather (or some other sacred object) and begins the verbal piece with a prayer or traditional song. Following this, the elder expresses issues she deems worthy of consideration by group members: these are usually gleanings the elder has gained through the smudging segment. Everybody else sits in silence, for only the person holding the eagle feather is allowed to speak. When the elder is finished speaking, the feather is passed in a clockwise direction, imitating the path of the sun, moving from the east to the west, as each person has a chance to speak. The person who holds the sacred object speaks without interruption, and others listen respectfully, sending prayers to the speaker. While holding the feather, a person may choose not to speak and pass the sacred object to the left. After the object has made its way around the circle several times, it is put in the centre of the circle, and anyone who has anything further to say is entitled to pick up the feather and speak. When nobody picks up the eagle feather, and it is clear that members have finished speaking, the elder will close the talking circle with a prayer. What is helpful to the circle members is taken away, and what is negative or irrelevant is left behind. All participants understand that "what is said in the circle remains in the circle to demonstrate respect for all members and to protect the sacredness of the experience" (Walkingstick Garrett and Osborne, 1995, p. 38).

The seating arrangement in talking circles resembles that of most social work groups. Groups that focus on talking reflect the spirit of inclusion by having members sit in a circle. This deliberate physical organization of members is nonhierarchical, where all members are at the same level and in plain view of one another (Shulman, 1992). But in talking circles the seating arrangement signifies more than egalitarianism; there is a potent tautology at work. The circle is "central to Native life": it is a sacred institution, the heart of First Nations ceremonies, representing interrelationship, the movement of life, wholeness and strength, and the totality of the universe (Ross and Ross, 1992; Walkingstick Garrett and Osborne, 1995; Brady, 1995; Regnier, 1994). Even the sequential ordering of group members' verbal expressions pays homage to the sacred circle. Although some would argue that this round-robin approach interferes with member-to-member communication and the natural development of the group, the question of what is natural and for whom must be considered (Duffy, 1994). For First Nations people involved in group situations that are not simply social, it is "necessary to wait until the other person [has] fully completed speaking before offering [one's] own words" (Ross, 1996, p. 88). Moreover, it is better still to leave a "period of silence before [responding] to show that you [are] giving serious thought to what the other person said" (p. 88). Having people speak in turn in the circle is a reminder that everybody has a place and provides an opportunity for all to speak. Toward the end of the talking circle when the eagle feather is placed in the circle's centre and members can choose to pick up the feather and speak, there is the possibility for member-to-member communication. The tremendous respect and attentiveness central to talking circles coupled with the tautological circular movement and the spiritual component transform what could otherwise be a series of monologues into a multilogue. Because interrelatedness is intrinsic to the talking circle, members' words, despite the round-robin structure, become palpably and intuitively interactive.

Talking circles can be either open- or closed-ended, and, as with social work groups, membership will vary, depending on the purpose of the circle. Circles that are designed for more serious issues, for example sexual or substance abuse, will typically have a screening process to assess suitability for participation. On the other end of the continuum are weekly open-ended circles where membership criteria do not exist. Although talking circles can serve a variety of populations, only the elements of composition, number of meetings, and open/closed-endedness are subject to change. The basic form of the talking circle itself is immutable. Because circles are highly formalized, the initial stress that typically exists in social work groups, due to lack of structure or norms (Berman-Rossi, 1992), is usually negligible. Members understand the procedure in advance, and the fear of performance anxiety is minimized by the injunction to be nonjudgmental and the right to relay the eagle feather without having spoken a word. Although the approach-avoidance dilemma of the preaffiliation stage, and the power and control stage, conceptualized by Garland, Jones, and Kolodny (1973), generally do not pertain to developmental phases in talking circles because of the sophisticated structure and the role of the elder, the stages of intimacy, differentiation, and separation certainly do occur. Circle participants experience the burgeoning of trust; mutual exploration, sharing, and support; and positive departure.

Although the "group interaction process" does not range "freely . . . and spontaneously both with respect to how people communicate . . . and to the variety of means and routes the group may use to process its goals" (Lang, 1979, p. 210), it would be an error to deem the talking circle a narrow model with extremely limited application. In the elaborateness, the redundancy, the mosaic ritualism of the talking circle there is a funneling of possibilities to an ostensibly narrow band; but through this very locus of seeming narrowness, comes a gyroscopic reversal that gives rise to expansiveness.

I experienced the potency of the talking circle in a support group I initiated for *consumer/survivors*. In our seventh session, I suggested that we try a modified version of the talking circle (i.e., without the smudging and elder) the following week. Everybody agreed to participate, so I brought in my eagle feather for the eighth session. The response was remarkable. Members who had been consistently quiet and diffident, despite my "reaching for feeling and information links," (Middleman and Goldberg Wood, 1990) found their voice in the talking circle: holding the eagle feather, they spoke confidently and frankly, expressing their thoughts and feelings. When we debriefed afterward for the purpose of ascertaining how members felt about participating in the talking circle, everybody described feeling enabled while holding the feather. I mentioned that I had noticed a difference in members' expressions. The group agreed with this observation, saying that they felt their words and feelings were issuing from a deeper place. One person said that the talking circle eliminated her need of having to "jump into the discussion" in order to be heard. She could sit silently and listen to others, knowing that she would get to speak "in her own time."

The use and conceptualization of time in a group is important. Time is pivotal to social work with groups, as it greatly influences the form and course of the group. It is time that serves as an organizing principle for the delineation of goals, developmental stages, phasic movements, and interventions. Moyse-Steinberg (1996) recommends that practitioners view time "pluralistically rather than distributionally or linearly" (p. 5). Pluralistic time is time that is multiply engaged; that is, all members are involved irrespective of who is speaking. By approaching time from a pluralistic framework, workers can maximize meaningful time for all group members. Time is not an asset to be possessed or monopolized by individual members, but rather a "dimension, inescapably and invariably used by all things at once" (p. 9).

First Nations conceive of time as cyclical, symbolized by the circle, "a form of continual recurrence of natural patterns" (Regnier, 1994, p. 132). The belief that time belongs to everyone is inherent to talking circles, where the structure represents the circularity of time, the order of the cosmos, and each person's innate right to experience time, not only while speaking but also while listening. Although Moyse-Steinberg suggests that group time becomes "filled time" and mutual aid opportunities arise for all members through "self-referential" listening, talking circles ask that one gives one's attention to the speaker both in prayer and in thought. Because we are all interrelated, and the design and method of talking circles reflects this fact, to listen with one's entirety to the speaker in the circle is to learn also about oneself, for the other is but an extension of the self, as the self is but an extension of the other. For this reason, intentional self-referential listening is extraneous in talking circles. The "true community does not arise through people having feelings for one another . . . but through, first, . . . taking their stand in living mutual relation with a living Centre, and, second, . . . being in living mutual relation with one another" (Buber, 1958, p. 45). Because the experience of I-Thou reciprocity is heightened in talking circles, the opportunities for mutual aid are many.

Of the existing social work group models, talking circles are most similar to mutual aid groups. First Nations have always believed that "healing and transformation should take place in the presence of the group because we are all related to one another in very basic ways and we can always use the support and insight of each other" (Walkingstick Garrett and Osborne, 1995, p. 35). Although some might assume that the round-robin method used in talking circles would extinguish the power of mutual aid by undermining groupness and inviting the classic problem of individual work in a group format, the sense of groupness possessed by First Nations people is not fostered by an interactive discursive style as it is for non-Aboriginal people. It is the circle, the smudging, the prayers, the heartfelt listening, and the philosophical tenet of fundamental interconnectedness that allows for a group-as-a-whole experience. The round-robin method *is* interactive, perhaps not to a Western eye but it is to the First Nations person, because it is active and involves others; and First Nations understanding is such that the adjective *active* cannot possibly exist in the context of a group without the prefix *inter.*

Gitterman (1989) underscores acceptance as instrumental to the building of mutual support in groups. Acceptance "is demonstrated by such actions as conveying to another their worth, demonstrating care and interest, and offering suggestions without value judgments" (p. 6). The talking circle, which "traditionally serves as a forum for the expression of thoughts and feelings in a context of complete acceptance by group members," is designed for mutual support (Walkingstick Garrett and Osborne, 1995, p. 37). Each person "is given the opportunity to speak without interruption" and "others listen closely in order to contribute to solutions" (Morrissette, McKenzie, and Morrissette, 1993, p. 103). Although suggestions are offered in talking circles, they are shared only obliquely; and this indirectness is not to be confused with a limitation of design. First Nations people generally do not offer advice or direct suggestions either inside or outside of talking circles, because to do so would be to interfere with another's self-determining capacity (Muller, 1975). The talking circle reflects all that is sacrosanct to First Nations culture, and is thereby enabling, not inhibiting, to First Nations people. Although Knight (1990) purports that "the leader capitalizes on the underlying bond that members share" (p. 203) in a support group, in talking circles it is the group-as-a-whole (including the elder) that makes use of the unmistakable bond of commonality, a bond that is assumed a priori, experienced existentially within the group, and reinforced culturally and structurally via the model.

Although the elder occupies a leadership role in the talking circle, the group is not allonomous—for allonomous describes a group that is "controlled by stimuli acting on an organism from outside" (Lang, 1972, p. 78), and the elder is certainly not outside the circle. The elder is a significant constituent—as are all the other group members—in that she performs essential functions, for example, the opening and closing prayers. Here it must be cautioned that the role and presence of the elder should not relegate the talking circle to transitional group status: circles closely resemble autonomous groups, "a more mature social form, which is capable of an entitative life of its own" (Lang, 1972, p. 83). However, First Nations people would have difficulty with the term autonomous—even if used only as a terminological expedient—for they view all of life as being embedded, inextricably interpenetrated.

Most of the literature about mutual aid groups suggests that a good worker in such a group should endeavour from the start to "work herself out of her job" (Middleman and Goldberg, 1988, p. 239; Berman-Rossi, 1992). The elder in a talking circle is in a different position.

She is not a working professional but a recognized community member who fills a time honoured, culturally sanctioned role. For the elder to contemplate eliminating her function in the talking circle, would be to contemplate collapsing the ceremony itself. The elder is as important to the talking circle as is the prayer, the medicine, the smudging, the eagle feather, the circular seating arrangement, and the round-robin format. Middleman's (1987) first practice principle, "think group" is a guiding injunction for the successful group worker, and groupness is similarly elemental in the mind of an elder. Group orientation was an overarching practice principle and social reality in precapitalist First Nations communities prior to European contact. The "development of Aboriginal culture involved the exercise of responsibility on the part of all members for the benefit of the group" (Morrissette, McKenzie, and Morrissette, 1993, p. 93). Although countless atrocities have been perpetrated by the dominant society in an effort to dismantle First Nations cultures, the primacy of the group has remained an unassailable cornerstone of traditional practice and policy (Frideres, 1988; Miller, 1989).

First Nations communities emphasize the collective, but they are not without role differentiation for individuals. The talking circle is egalitarian insofar as no member is better, more worthy, or more privileged than another; but the elder still fills a unique role. Gitterman (1989) identifies the need to establish a clear purpose as the first task for a mutual-support group. Usually the Native community would target a population (e.g., angry First Nations men prone to violence), and the elder in this circle would decide during each session what should be discussed. Stage setting, attending, and managing interactions are all within the purview of the elder whose purpose in the group is to provide guidance and ensure proper functioning of the ceremony. Kurland and Malekoff (1996), who point to the need for the group worker to exercise "judicious use of experience, expertise, and professional wisdom" (p. 2), wonder how the worker can express his or her view without imposition. The elder is not burdened with this same dilemma, for the "term 'elder' is used to describe someone who has knowledge and understanding of the traditional ways of his or her people, both the physical culture of the people and their spiritual tradition" (Malloch, 1989, p. 107). The sharing of views by an elder is an integral and anticipated part of the experience of the talking circle. Berman-Rossi's (1992) suggestion that the group worker be "taken out of the role as sage" so that egalitarian relationships can prevail would, if applied to an elder, hamstring the talking circle (p. 247). It is the elder's knowledge and wisdom that are frequently sought by members in a circle (Malloch, 1989).

Because the elder is a recognized and respected member of the community, and her role in the circle is dictated by a community consensus to honour tradition, her status is considerably different from that of a worker. The elder is not an authority and, therefore, does not incite antiauthority sentiments. Middleman and Goldberg Wood (1990) advise the group worker to be "a power sharer who gives away her power" (p. 92), but the elder has no power, just responsibility. People participating in a talking circle can leave if they are dissatisfied with the elder, provided they exit the circle as traditionally prescribed; for the circle as an institution is more highly respected than the elder. The elder has no power to give away, and relinquishing responsibility is no way to empower the group. The group is empowered in a talking circle through a fulfilling experience, and the experience can only be of a rewarding kind if the elder amply performs her role. Lee's (1997) enumeration of factors diminishing empowerment—"including compromised personal and interpersonal strengths and resources; economic insecurity; physical and emotional stress; and learned helplessness" (p. 19)—pertain to a disproportionate number of First Nations people due to a history of colonization, and the racist and oppressive political practices of the dominant culture. Although Lee maintains "the empowerment process resides in the person, not the helper" (p. 19), the analogous statement for group work is that the empowerment process resides in the group. Because the elder is part of the group, the empowerment process resides in her also; but this is not to say that the elder has power. The empowerment process, similar to time, belongs to everyone. It is Western society with its staunch individualism that is so preoccupied with issues of power. First Nations communities, having a collectivity orientation, are less concerned with a member's individual power, for they see it as adding to the strength of the group.

In *The Skills of Helping: Individuals, Families, and Groups,* Shulman (1992) describes a number of "common patterns of individual-group relationships . . . (e.g., scapegoats, deviant members, defensive members and quiet members)" that require the worker's attention (p. 439). The talking circle, with its unique group structure, has built-in safeguards that prevent the emergence of several problematic behaviours. Scapegoats and defensive members generally do not arise as a type in talking circles because of the sequential ordering of speakers and the imperative of respectful listening. Although quiet members certainly can exist in circles, it is usually not long before they feel comfortable speaking. Elders do not worry that a member's quietness might mean noninvolvement, for silence is a respected and valid option in the circle. An elder would not "feel a responsibility to check with a quiet member and see how [the] engagement [with the group] was going" (p. 482).

The internal leader, someone whose qualities in the group are "often similar to those of the workers" and whose input "assist[s] in helping the group resolve its struggle toward growth" (Shulman, 1992, p. 463), is a categorical type who does manifest in talking circles. I have participated in a circle where a nondesignated internal leader was present. This person shared striking insights, and the whole group, including the elder, felt fortunate for his contribution.

Gatekeepers do not exist in talking circles. These are people whose behaviour "guards the gates through which the group must pass for the work to deepen," when "the group gets close to a difficult subject, the gatekeeper continues to divert the discussion" (Shulman, 1992, p. 467). Because of the round-robin approach, the role of the gatekeeper is virtually eliminated in talking circles. However, there is room for the monopolizer: someone who gets hold of the eagle feather and talks at length, holding the others in audience, depriving group members of their opportunity to speak. In such cases, a member in the circle would usually approach the elder, whispering a request in her ear that the monopolizer be asked to finish speaking. The elder most often agrees, and the member will whisper in the monopolizer's ear that he should think about finishing and passing the feather along. Because of the sophisticated structure and the culturally sanctioned norms, talking circles, for the most part, are not "subject to the vagaries of needy individuals, to spirited controversies with politeness thrown to the wind" (Middleman and Goldberg Wood, 1990, p. 105).

The contours of social work with groups have changed in recent years. In a climate of scientific and philosophical uncertainty, in the wake of a dramatic epistemological shift from positivism, causality, and fragmentation to deconstructionism, probabilities, and holism, social work literature has begun to address the "nature of knowledge, ways of thinking about knowing and how the mind works" (Papell, 1997, p. 14). Social workers have started investigating the assumptions that underlie professional practice and theory, and the relationship between mind and reality—how each affects the other (Hartman, 1990; Papell, 1997). First Nations have always understood mind and reality to be reciprocally related; for all of life's constituents are parts of a whole, where "the parts are forced to interact with each other and take the other into consideration" (Frideres, 1988, p. 218). Because mind, body, and spirit are interconnected, First Nations people would not think of having a healing ceremony or therapeutic gathering without the inclusion of spiritual dimensions. The prayer in talking circles "indicates acknowledgement of higher powers that play a role in our physical and mental well-being" (Dufrene and Coleman, 1992, p. 233).

There is a diametrical movement occurring: whereas non-Aboriginal people are questioning traditional belief systems, social constructs, and political ideologies that form the basis of Western society, First Nations people are embracing their traditional teachings (Ross, 1996; RCAP, 1993, 1995). These teachings have always been intrinsically nonpositivist. Even the languages of First Nations reflect the mutability of life's components and the impossibility of knowing anything with certainty. David Bohm, the renowned physicist, discovered the suitability of Aboriginal languages—which were "richer in words representing the energy, forces and spirit" underpinning seeming reality—for esoteric discussions about quantum mechanics (Ross, 1996, p. 119). First Nations culture focuses "less on the *characteristics of* things than on the *relationships between* things" (p. 116). Although Marsiglia, Cross, and Mitchell-Enos (1998) suggest that First Nations people are distinctive, not so much along racial lines but due to a unique history with the dominant society, I would argue strenuously that First Nations are culturally distinct. And, it is the divergent worldviews possessed by the two cultures that render non-Aboriginal treatment approaches largely ineffectual with First Nations people. But history does play a significant role.

The history of Indian-white relations—a history of racist colonial practices, subjugation, deceit, segregation, deliberate decimation, aggressive assimilative strategies, damaging educational approaches, and abysmal juridical and political policies—has done much to eradicate First Nations' trust in non-Aboriginals. As McKenna (1981) states, "the Holocaust does not begin to approximate the atrocities done to the continent's aboriginal population during the past 400 years" (in Angell, Kurz, and Gottfried, 1997, p. 10). According to McKenna, over fourteen million North American Indians have been killed for the sake of civilization and progress. Sadly, there exists a redundancy between history and current affairs vis-à-vis Indian/ white relations: that is, the marginalization, the oppression, the discrimination, and the systemic racism that have historically characterized the dominant culture's treatment of and relations with First Nations peoples are extant today. Given this history, and the persistence of colonial attitudes, it is not surprising that First Nations people want Aboriginal treatments by Aboriginal service providers (RCAP, 1993). The success of traditional models, the talking circle in particular, is striking (Ross, 1996; Ashby, Gilchrist, and Miramontez, 1987; Edwards and Edwards, 1984; McEvoy and Daniluk, 1995; Morse, Young, and Swartz, 1991; McCormick, 1996; Weibel-Orlando, 1989; Ross and Ross, 1992). Circles used in northern Ontario with sexual offenders were so effective that only two of the forty-eight participating perpetrators reoffended (Ross, 1996). A recidivism rate this low is a forceful testimony of the potency of talking circles. However, there is a need for further research into the effectiveness of this traditional group work methodology.

A chapter examining talking circles as a form of group process in a social work context would be incomplete, a mere academic exercise, without consideration of practice implications for use with all people, Aboriginal and non-Aboriginal alike. What can social workers take from a method so elegant, so paradoxically imbued with complexity and simplicity, to apply in social work with groups? One answer surfaces repeatedly: the sacredness. If workers can approach all groups with the same sanctity that pervades talking circles, then much can be achieved. The understanding of other as self, and self as other, is what brings such reverence to the circle.

> Your spirit
> My spirit
> May they unite to make
> One spirit in healing.

> Basil Johnston
> *Ojibway Heritage*

REFERENCES

Angell, G.B., B.J. Kurz, and G.M. Gottfried (1997). Suicide and North American Indians: A Social Constructivist Perspective. *Journal of Multicultural Social Work*, 6(3/4), 1-26.

Ashby, Marianne R., Lewayne D. Gilchrist, and Alicia Miramontez (1987). Group Treatment for Sexually Abused American Indian Adolescents. *Social Work with Groups*, 10(4), 21-32.

Berman-Rossi, Toby (1992). Empowering Groups Through Understanding Stages of Group Development. *Social Work with Groups*, 15(2/3), 239-255.

Brady, Maggie (1995). Culture in Treatment, Culture As Treatment. A Critical Appraisal of Developments in Addictions Programs for Indigenous North Americans and Australians. *Social Science and Medicine*, 41(11), 1487-1498.

Buber, Martin (1958). *I and Thou*. New York: Scribner.

Duffy, T. (1994). The Check-In and Other Go-Rounds: Guidelines for Use. *Social Work with Groups*, 17(1/2), 163-175.

Dufrene, Phoebe M. and Victoria D. Coleman (1992). Counseling Native Americans: Guidelines for Group Process. *The Journal for Specialists in Group Work*, 17(4), 229-234.

Edwards, E. Daniel and Margie E. Edwards (1984). Group Work Practice with American Indians. *Social Work with Groups*, 7(3), 7-21.

Frideres, James S. (1988). *Native Peoples in Canada: Contemporary Conflicts*. Scarborough, Ontario: Prentice-Hall.

Gall Eagle, Chokeberry (1997). *Beyond the Lodge of the Sun*. Rockport, MA: Element.

Garland, James A., Hubert E. Jones, and Ralph L. Kolodny (1973). A Model for Stages of Development in Social Work Groups. *Explorations in Group Work: Essays in Theory and Practice*. Ed. Saul Bernstein. Boston: Milford House, 1973, 17-71.

Gitterman, Alex (1989). Building Mutual Support in Groups. *Social Work with Groups*, 12(2), 5-21.

Hartman, Ann (1990). Many Ways of Knowing. *Social Work*, 35(1), 3-4.

Johnston, Basil (1976). *Ojibway Heritage*. Toronto: McClelland and Stewart.

Knight, Carolyn (1990). Use of Support Groups with Adult Female Survivors of Child Sexual Abuse. *Social Work*, 35(3), 202-206.

Kurland, Roselle and Andrew Malekoff (1996). From the Editors. *Social Work with Groups*, 19(3/4), 1-3.

Lang, Norma (1972). A Broad-Range Model of Practice in the Social Work Group. *The Social Service Review*, 46(1), 76-89.

Lang, Norma (1979). A Comparative Examination of Therapeutic Uses of Groups in Social Work and in the Adjacent Human Service Professions: Part II, The Literature from 1969-1978. *Social Work with Groups*, 2, 197-220.

Lee, Judith A.B. (1997). The Empowerment Group: The Heart of the Empowerment Approach and an Antidote to Injustice. *From Prevention to Wellness*

Through Group Work. Ed. Joan K. Parry. Binghamton, NY: The Haworth Press, 15-32.

Malloch, Lesley (1989). Indian Medicine, Indian Health: Study Between Red and White Medicine. *Canadian Women's Studies*, (2/3), 105-112.

Marsiglia, Flavio F., Suzanne Cross, and Violet Mitchell-Enos (1998). Culturally Grounded Group Work with Adolescent American Indian Students. *Social Work with Groups*, (2/1), 89-102.

McCormick, Rod (1996). Culturally Appropriate Means and Ends of Counselling As Described by the First Nations People of British Columbia. *International Journal for the Advancement of Counselling*, 18(3), 163-172.

McEvoy, Maureen and Judith Daniluk (1995). Wounds to the Soul: The Experiences of Aboriginal Women Survivors of Sexual Abuse. *Canadian Psychology*, 36(3), 221-235.

Middleman, Ruth (1987). Seeing the Group in Group Work: Skills for Dealing with Groupness of Groups. *Social Work with Groups*, 15(2/3), 1-10.

Middleman, Ruth and Gale Goldberg (1988). Toward the Quality of Social Group Work Practice. *Roots and New Frontiers in Social Group Work*. Eds. M. Leiderman, M. L. Birnbaum, and B. Dazzo. Binghamton, NY: The Haworth Press, 233-246.

Middleman, Ruth and Gale Goldberg Wood (1990). *Skills for Direct Practice in Social Work*. New York: Columbia University Press.

Miller, J.R. (1989). *Skyscrapers Hide the Heavens: A History of Indian-White Relations in Canada*. Toronto: University of Toronto Press.

Morrissette, Vern, Brad McKenzie, and Larry Morrissette (1993). Towards an Aboriginal Model of Social Work Practice: Cultural Knowledge and Traditional Practices. *Canadian Social Work Review*, 10(1), 91-108.

Morse, Janice M., David E. Young, and Lise Swartz (1991). Cree Indian Healing Practices and Western Health Care: A Comparative Analysis. *Social Science and Medicine*, 32(12), 1361-1366.

Moyse-Steinberg, Dominique (1996). She's Doing All the Talking, So What's in It for Me? *Social Work with Groups*, 19(2), 5-16.

Muller, Hugo (1975). *Why Don't You? A Look at Attitudes Towards Indians*. Schumacher, Ontario: J.A. Watton.

Papell, Catherine P. (1997). Thinking About Thinking About Group Work: Thirty Years Later. *Social Work with Groups*, 20(4), 5-17.

Regnier, Robert (1994). The Sacred Circle: A Process Pedagogy of Healing. *Interchange*, 25(2), 129-144.

Ross, Jane and Jack Ross (1992). Keep the Circle Strong: Native Health Promotion. *Journal of Speech-Language Pathology and Audiology*, 16(4), 291-302.

Ross, Rupert (1996). *Returning to the Teachings*. Toronto: Penguin Books.

Royal Commission on Aboriginal Peoples (1993). *The Path to Healing: Report of the National Round Table on Aboriginal Health and Social Issues*. Ottawa: Minister of Supply and Services.

Royal Commission on Aboriginal Peoples (1995). *Choosing Life: Special Report on Suicide Among Aboriginal People*. Ottawa: Minister of Supply and Services.

Royal Commission on Aboriginal Peoples (1996). Volume 3: *Gathering Strength*. Ottawa: Minister of Supply and Services.

Shulman, Lawrence (1992). *The Skills of Helping: Individuals, Families and Groups* (Third edition). Itasca, IL: F. E. Peacock Publishers.

Walkingstick Garrett, Michael and W. Larry Osborne (1995). The Native American Sweat Lodge As Metaphor for Group Work. *The Journal for Specialists in Group Work*, 20(1), 33-39.

Walsh, Joseph, Heather E. Hewitt, and Adrienne Londeree (1996). The Role of the Facilitator in Support Group Development. *Social Work with Groups*, 19(3/4), 83-91.

Weibel-Orlando, Joan (1989). Hooked on Healing: Anthropologists, Alcohol and Intervention. *Human Organization*, 48(2), 148-155.

Chapter 11

New Perspectives in Group Work for Working with Sexually Abused African-American Children

Claudia Lawrence-Webb

Sex between parents and children has always been taboo in virtually every society. *Incest,* the term used to describe this activity, means "soiled" or "impure" (Rathus, Nevid, and Fichner-Rathus, 1998). Child sexual abuse is an abuse of power inappropriately expressed sexually between an adult and a child. Between 1986 and 1993, it increased more than twofold, with girls three times more likely to be abused than boys (U.S. Department of Health and Human Services [U.S. DHHS], 1999). Those from the "lowest income families were 18 times more likely to be sexually abused" (U.S. DHHS, 1999, p. 3). This difference has remained stable.

Group work is one of the most promising and effective methods of dealing with child sexual abuse. This chapter focuses specifically on group work with latency-age and preadolescent African-American girls who have been sexually abused. Other works discuss group work with this particular age population (Shaffer and Brown, 1998; Schact, Kerlinsky, and Carlson, 1990; Kitchur and Bell, 1989; Carozza and Heirsteiner, 1983), but none give a specific approach for working with African-American girls, except for Pierce and Pierce (1984).

CHILD SEXUAL ABUSE:
RACE, CULTURE, AND ETHNICITY

Although children of color are disproportionately represented in the child welfare system in the United States (Leashore, Chipungu, and Everett, 1991; Lawrence-Webb, 1994), they experience forms of sexual abuse similar to other populations, but differ in areas regarding the age of onset, familial/significant other response to the disclosure, the likelihood of pregnancy, source of disclosure, familial and community perception of the sexual abuse, and the psychological impact of the abuse on the child survivor (Kenney, Reinholtz, and Angelini, 1997; Rao, DiClemente, and Ponton, 1992; Fontes, 1993; Roosa, Reinholtz, and Angelini, 1999; Mennen, 1994; Lira, Koss, and Russo, 1999; Sanders-Phillips et al., 1995; Lindholm and Willey, 1986; Gordon, 1989). African-American children, as with other child survivors, usually disclose their abuse to their mothers, in comparison to other children of color (Asians, Hispanics, and Native Americans), some of whom are less likely to disclose the abuse to their mothers (Asians) and some of whom are more likely to disclose the abuse to their mothers (Hispanics, Native Americans) (Fontes, 1993; Rao, DiClemente, and Ponton, 1992). Also, African-American children are less likely to live with the perpetrator in a biological two-parent situation in comparison to their other counterparts (other children of color and Anglos). Studies vary in terms of their findings regarding this variable (Mennen, 1994; Rao, DiClemente, and Ponton, 1992).

According to Derezotes and Snowden, Wyatt, and Russell, Schurman, and Trocki, as quoted in Sanders-Phillips et al. (1995), the higher percent of single-parent family, female-headed households among blacks may increase the risk of sexual abuse by an unrelated assailant. Sanders-Phillips et al. (1995) believe that the nonbiological relationship that sexual perpetrators have with the children may contribute to the mother's ability to believe the child's allegations and to provide support. This does not excuse the behavior or decrease the responsibility of ownership for the child's victimization by the perpetrator. Sudarkasa's (1981) conceptualization of African-American families regarding consanguineal (blood/biological ties) versus conjugal (family by marriage) has broad implications concerning their behaviors, attitudes, and perceptions of child sexual abuse.

AN AFRICENTRIC GROUP WORK MODEL
FOR WORKING WITH AFRICAN-AMERICAN GIRLS

Group Characteristics and Components

Group Purpose

The purpose of the group was to help African-American girls work through their sexual abuse issues utilizing an Africentric therapeutic group model of intervention. The Africentric model utilizes African philosophy as its focal point, employs spiritual values, and is culturally sensitive to the African-American experience in its service delivery.

Group Size, Structure, and Format

Groups with these populations should be no larger than ten participants. Ownership of the group by its members is encouraged by the group facilitators to allow the participants to have some control over their destiny (Olgilvie and Daniluk, 1995; Haley-Banez, 1999; Gemmill, 1986). Group rules are generated, recorded, and posted by the group members with consequences and a group decision-making process to handle group infractions. They should be structured, time-limited groups that last approximately one-and-a-half to two hours and meet on a weekly basis for fourteen to sixteen weeks. Time-limited, well-structured groups were chosen for these populations for specific reasons:

- Developmentally, children these ages respond better to structured activities because it gives them a sense of control in their lives when there is little control (Wilson, 1980; Kunjufu, 1984).
- It has a beginning and end to the successful completion of a process that fosters a sense of accomplishment among children who are seen as failures (Haley-Banez, 1999; Hazzard, King, and Webb, 1986).
- Provides a sense of ethnic and racial identity with support that there are "others like me," while decreasing a sense of isolation (Olgilvie and Daniluk, 1995; Schacht, Kerlinsky, and Carlson, 1990).

- Initiates the process of examining relationships with parents and/or significant others as a means of reestablishing their trust in adults as a source of protection, with emphasis on extended familial support systems, such as a grandmother, since a sizable number of these children are placed in kinship care (Zuravin and DePanfilis, 1997; Scannapeico and Jackson, 1996).
- Serves as an educational and preventive measure for addressing "crises" as a result of the sexual abuse as well as the emotional and psychological reframing of internalized responsibility for the perpetrator's behavior (Gil, 1996; Boyd-Franklin, 1989).
- Developmentally, children are dealing with issues of interpersonal relationships with peers (Wilson, 1980; Kunjufu, 1984; Gil, 1996; McKay and Gonzales, 1999).
- Facilitates children's use of individual therapy as a tool for addressing more in-depth issues that are unable to be addressed in a group atmosphere (Boyd-Franklin, 1989; Gil, 1996; Hazzard, King, and Webb, 1986; James, 1990; Ratican, 1992).
- The children's perception of the group during the process should be nonthreatening, fun, and sensitive to the individual and group needs (Hazzard, King, and Webb, 1986; Gil, 1996).

The groups should be held in an atmosphere conducive to the members, whether they are latency or preadolescent, with access to numerous art supplies, games, and other materials that capture the attention of the participants. For preadolescents, one can use short videos with preadolescent themes such as physiological development, self-esteem, etc. Materials cannot be too advanced or too childish or the group will lose interest. For example, one of the movies that we showed that was serious and humorous was *Am I Normal*. We chose it because of its use of humor regarding puberty. Its sound information and length as a video provided adequate time to view and hold a group discussion on puberty. This integrated evaluative process provides an avenue for identifying, discussing, and promptly addressing behavioral and environmental changes appropriately, and in the best interest of each child (Shaffer and Brown, 1998).

Role of Group Facilitators

Two group facilitators should be employed who complement and support each other. In preparation for working together, the two facilitators should explore their own personal feelings on issues of abuse and sexuality, limit-setting techniques, understanding the conceptual framework of the Africentric perspective, ethnic and racial perceptions, awareness of the cultural and historical experiences of the population group to whom group services are being provided, therapeutic styles, comfort level with handling and resolving conflict, along with assessment and documentation skills.

Group facilitators should discuss in depth the implementation of fair treatment, respect, and appropriate consequences for the group infractions via group discussion. This process involves several skill development areas such as decision making, problem solving, defining appropriate expectations, setting limits and defining boundaries, self-assertion and advocacy, fair treatment, respect for differences and for one another, and communication. Practicing and internalizing these skills empowers the children and increases their self-confidence and inner strength to address adequately issues within their environments.

Group facilitators must be able to read group process and develop therapeutic intervention strategies throughout the group's process without the group feeling a total loss of control. Group limit-setting, by the group, should be consistent and equitable for all participants (Smokowski and Rose, 1999; Haley-Banez, 1999). A clear balance between flexibility and structure must be maintained with this population, because the children's needs are constantly changing throughout the therapeutic process. Sensitivity to these changes is enhanced when facilitators review every group session upon completion, and document the group process (Burnard, 1990; Randall and Wodarski, 1989; Gemmill, 1986), addressing the elements of group process shown in Table 11.1.

It is not advisable to mix populations of different ages and developmental stages. Doing so forces the group facilitators to make issues too broad and complex for younger members and too simplistic and elementary for older participants. The issues for prepubescent eleven- to thirteen-year-old girls are different from latency-aged girls aged eight to ten. Prepubescent participants see themselves as being older and more mature than latency-aged children. Many verbalize their offense at being in a group with "little kids." In addition, their concerns are more about body changes, dating boys, contraception, pregnancy, sexual abuse in relation to sexual relations, and the physiological de-

TABLE 11.1. Group Process Documentation Format

Group Participation	Information Processed	Group Climate	Utilization of Group Facilitators	Individual Roles Within Group
Group alliances, conflicts, and boundaries	Group's reaction to information processing	Behavioral indicators of difficulty with topics of discussion, activities, individually raised issues, group issues	Group and individual responses to limit setting	Need for additional services or immediate intensive, individual intervention

velopment of boys. Eight- to ten-year-olds are entrenched in separation of the sexes, are ambivalent about relationships with the other gender, enjoy playing games, and are still psychologically immature despite their display of pseudomaturity.

Linking with Parents/Support Units

Establishing a group for latency-aged and preadolescent African-American children requires close and open communication with the parents or caregivers of the children. Many African-American parents are distrusting of the child welfare system because of its negative perceptions of them (Lawrence-Webb, 1994; Scannapeico and Jackson, 1996). Parents must be encouraged to play an active part in the child's group experience in order to manage behaviors and address issues that may evolve as a result of the child's group experience.

For example, one of the girls in the group shared that the abuse was more extensive than she had shared with her parental caregiver. In addition, since attending group she was having problems sleeping at night because she was remembering more of the abuse. Contacting the caregiver regarding what the group member was experiencing was much easier because the facilitators had already started building an alliance with the caregiver and had prepared her for some of the things that might happen with the group member as she went through the process. We were able to be a support to the group member and to her caregiver, by referring the caregiver for additional supports to further assist the group member in working through the concerns expressed. Caregivers had an opportunity to establish rapport with the group facilitators before the group started, through several phone calls that discussed group purpose, the caregiver's perceptions of the group, collecting basic information from the caregiver regarding the child, and notifying the caregiver that the child had been selected to participate in the group; arranging for transportation for the child to attend the group meeting, explaining what could happen with group participants, and encouraging caregivers to contact us if they had any concerns about the individual group members.

The group facilitators have a responsibility to explain the general format, purpose, and expectations of the group as they personally contact each parent or caregiver to request permission for his or her child's participation. In addition, parents or caregivers may themselves be involved in a separate group. Group facilitators should be sure that the parent or caregiver support unit is one that believes that the abuse occurred and the child is not at fault for the situation. The purpose of maintaining contact with the children's parent(s) or caregivers and individual therapists is to aid group facilitators for evaluative purposes by providing a holistic view of each child in the home and within his or her external environments to the home. A lack of communication with systems impacting upon the children while going through the therapeutic group process can lead to dysfunction in the children's environment, self-perception, and significant relationships that may be expressed within the therapeutic group context (Olgilvie and Daniluk, 1995; Randall and Wodarski, 1989; Carozza and Heirsteiner, 1983).

Transportation

Transportation for group members is a must for providing greater participation. Relying on parents and caregivers to bring the children results in low group attendance because of other pressing issues that may require the caregivers' or parents' attention in meeting the basic needs of the child (e.g., employment, court, lack of parental or caregiver transportation, lack of a reliable transportation system to get the child to the group). Agency-provided transportation also provides group members with an opportunity to begin forming social relationships before and after group sessions as well as ensuring that the child is returned home safely. It also lends itself as an opportunity for group members to be supportive of one another. Anecdotal evidence from numerous group services supports these perceptions.

The Group Process

All group participants should be required to participate concurrently in individual treatment to assist in handling issues that may need further examination and intervention than is possible in the group process. Individual treatment is critical to crisis resolution when a group issue activates a personal crisis for a group member. These forms of treatment, individual and group therapy, should be complementary and supportive of each other during the child's therapeutic group process. Individual therapists should be abreast of the therapeutic group experience. Group facilitators and individual therapists should communicate frequently during the group process for updates and feedback on issues pertinent to each individual member. The evaluative process during the child's group experience is necessary for the group facilitators and individual therapists to meet the specific and individual needs of each group member (Smokowski and Rose, 1999; Burnand, 1990).

Once parental support and cooperation have been obtained, group facilitators should contact each referred child personally to determine her willingness and readiness to participate. In conjunction with this activity, the facilitators should develop a structured outline of topics that allow freedom of expression in the group process through such mediums as free play, open discussions, decision making, and flexibility. For example, group facilitators may opt to use the game of SASA (a therapeutic treatment game used with sexually abused children) in the preadolescent group, as opposed to using Candy Land (a regular children's board game played by latency-aged children). Candy Land guides children through a fantasyland of obstacles and challenges until the first person reaches the candy at the end of the trail. The game teaches important skills such as taking turns, sharing, and color matching. SASA is a board game used to allow children to express their feelings and thoughts about the sexual abuse. The children earn chips for following the instructions on the card as they proceed around the board. The greatest accumulator of chips is the game winner. Activities must be able to coincide with the group theme or topic for each particular group session. If one is discussing self-esteem, perhaps the exercise should be one that addresses self-esteem in a way that engages adolescents through the use of a variety of popular magazines that are consumed by African-American preadolescents such as *Essence, Ebony, Right On, Jet,* or *People.*

Throughout the therapeutic process of the group, the children are reframing and redefining the impact of the abuse and their role in the abuse. These reflective techniques are critical to helping them cognitively evaluate the sex abuse process itself as well as its impact on their self-perception and their perception of how they think others perceive them within their environment. The internal strengths and coping mechanisms used by the children to survive the abuse are emphasized and highlighted within the group process. Their management of environmental pressures and negative perceptions of the experience are part of the empowerment and strengths perspective. This process captures Barbara Bryant-Solomon's (1967) definition of empowerment, which defines empowerment, as "a process whereby people belonging to a stigmatized social group can be assisted to utilize or increase abilities or skills to influence their lives" (p. 28).

Case Examples

Other examples of the daily need to draw on internal strengths are promoted in terms of the African-American experience. The following are two examples, one dealing with the issue of self-identity and perception in terms of physical beauty, the other dealing with the issue of protection in society from those who seek to harm others, an issue that emanated from a discussion about the Ku Klux Klan.

One member had a preoccupation with the hair and complexion of one of the group facilitators and another group member who was biracial. She frequently referred to them as beautiful and wished she was "lighter" with "good hair," because then she would be pretty. She believed that her sexual abuse was punishment for being ugly and dark. Group members and facilitators talked about images of beauty as defined in American culture and its symbolism. Other forms of beauty were discussed and the children were asked to compare the different forms of beauty and their "realness." African forms of beauty were discussed and emphasized with examples of these forms of beauty utilized in Western and American culture. Another group member discussed her concerns regarding her perception of why she was abused by stating that how she looked was not the reason for her abuse. The biracial group member then confronted the individual group member and the rest of the group when they asked her to explain how people she thought were "prettier" also experienced sexual abuse. This process helped the identified member to begin redefining her self-image and to define her abuse experience differently. This was later reemphasized and reinforced through two group activities involving self-image and self-perception. The first activity had members look in a full-length mirror and give a description of how they saw themselves, and the second activity required members to trace their body outlines on paper and draw in their facial/body features and clothing. Empowering the group member through knowledge, discussing the strengths and stigma of being African American, identifying coping skills for such negative perceptions, plus cognitively redefining and reflecting on these perceptions helped her to grow.

Group members were selecting pictures for a collage to illustrate situations of protection and safety. In the process of engaging in this exercise, one of the group members found a picture of a rally of Klansmen in traditional garb, with white hoods that shielded their faces. In this instance, the children were unable to identify this group of marchers as being a source of danger to African Americans. The group facilitators shared some very basic knowledge about the Klan organization, their perceptions of African Americans, and other select groups, which initiated a brief discussion. What evolved from the discussion was whether group members knew how to identify whom or what kinds of things may be a source of danger. The facilitators emphasized with group members that people do not have the right to harm others. This led to identifying situations where members thought it was safe, but the behavior of the people or person around them made them feel uncomfortable or unsafe in their presence. Questions were raised about why some adults engage in behaviors to hurt others. Ideas about how to protect oneself from sexual abuse and other types of situations were brainstormed by the group and listed on a flip chart. This discussion was re-emphasized in later group sessions on self-protection and identifying supportive adult individuals to whom the children could turn for help. Issues regarding women and violence were also discussed within the context of the evolving discussion.

CONCLUSION

The major goals of groups with African-American preadolescent females are to help them begin an examination of the role of victimization, prevent future abuse, develop new coping skills, achieve a holistic self-examination along with disclosure, attribute responsibility to the perpetrator, and reestablish trust within themselves and others through the utilization of an Africentric perspective of intervening with sexual abuse. The benefit of using this model with preadolescent African-American girls is its cultural sensitivity laced with feminist theory and cognitive-behavioral techniques that help to empower them. A year after the completion of the group process, only one child was reported as being reabused.

REFERENCES

Boyd-Franklin, N. (1989). *Black families in therapy.* New York: Guilford Press.

Bryant-Solomon, B. (1967). *Black empowerment: Social work in oppressed communities.* New York: Columbia University Press.

Burnand, G. (1990). Group development phases as working through six fundamental human problems. *Small Group Research,* 21, 255-273.

Carozza, P.M. and Heirsteiner, C.L. (1983). Young female incest victims in treatment: Stages of growth seen with a group art therapy model. *Clinical Social Work Journal,* 10, 165-175.

Fontes, L.A. (1993). Disclosures of sexual abuse by Puerto Rican children: Oppression and cultural barriers. *Journal of Child Sexual Abuse,* 2, 21-35.

Gemmill, G. (1986). The mythology of the leader role in small groups. *Small Group Behavior,* 17, 41-50.

Gil, E. (1996). *Treating abused adolescents.* New York: Guilford Press.

Gordon, M. (1989). The family environment of sexual abuse: A comparison of natal and stepfather abuse. *Child Abuse and Neglect,* 13, 121-130.

Haley-Banez, L. (1999). Diversity in group work: Using optimal theory to understand group process and dynamics. *Journal for Specialists in Group Work,* 24, 405-423.

Hazzard, A., King, H.E., Webb, C. (1986). Group therapy with sexually abused adolescent girls. *American Journal of Psychotherapy,* 60, 213-243.

James, B. (1990). *Treating traumatized children.* New York: Lexington Books.

Kenney, J. W., Reinholtz, M.S., and Angelini, P. J. (1997). Ethnic differences in childhood and adolescent sexual abuse and teenage pregnancy. *Journal of Adolescent Health,* 21, 3-10.

Kitchur, M. and Bell, R. (1989). Group psychotherapy with pre-adolescent sexual abuse victims: Literature review and description of an inner city group. *International Journal of Group Psychotherapy,* 39, 285-311.

Kunjufu, J. (1984). *Developing positive self-image and discipline in black children.* Chicago, IL: African American Images.

Lawrence-Webb, C. (1994). African American children in the modern child welfare system: A legacy of the Flemming Rule. *Child Welfare,* 76, 9-30.

Leashore, B., Chipungu, S.S., and Everett, J. (1991). *Child welfare: An africentric perspective.* NJ: Rutgers University Press.

Lindholm, K.J. and Willey, R. (1986). Ethnic differences in child abuse and sexual abuse. *Hispanic Journal of Behavioral Sciences,* 8, 111-125.

Lira, L.R., Koss, M.P., Russo Felipe, N. (1999). Mexican American women's definitions of rape and sexual abuse. *Hispanic Journal of Behavioral Sciences,* 21, 236-265.

McKay, M.M. and Gonzales, J. (1999). Multiple family groups: An alternative for reducing disruptive behavioral difficulties of urban children. *Research on Social Work Practice,* 9, 593-608.

Mennen, F.E. (1994). Sexual abuse in Latina girls: Their functioning and a comparison with white and African American girls. *Hispanic Journal of Behavioral Sciences,* 16, 475-486.

Olgilvie, B. and Daniluk, J. (1995). Common themes in the experiences of mother-daughter incest survivors: Implications for counseling. *Journal of Counseling and Development,* 73, 598-603.

Pierce, R.L. and Pierce, L.H. (1987). Child sexual abuse: A black perspective. In Hampton, R.L. (Ed.), *Violence in the black family: Correlates and consequences,* (pp. 67-85). Lexington, MA: Lexington Books, D. C. Heath and Co.

Randall, E. and Wodarski, J.S. (1989). Theoretical issues in clinical social group work. *Small Group Behavior,* 20, 475-499.

Rao, K., DiClemente, R.J., and Ponton, L.E. (1992). Child sexual abuse of Asians compared with other populations. *Journal of the American Academy of Child and Adolescent Psychiatry,* 31, 880-886.

Rathus, S.A., Nevid, J.S., and Fichner-Rathus, L. (1998). *Essentials of human sexuality.* Boston: Allyn & Bacon.

Ratican, K.L. (1992). Sexual abuse survivors: Identifying symptoms and special treatment considerations. *Journal of Counseling and Development,* 71, 33-39.

Roosa, M.W., Reinholtz, C., and Angelini, P.J. (1999). The relation of child sexual abuse and depression in young women: Comparisons across four ethnic groups. *Journal of Abnormal Child Psychology,* 27, 65-76.

Sanders-Phillips, K., Moison, P.A., Wadlington, S., Morgan, S., and English, K. (1995). Ethnic differences in psychological functioning among black and Latino sexually abused girls. *Child Abuse and Neglect,* 19, 691-706.

Scannapeico, M. and Jackson, S.M. (1996). Kinship care: The African American response to family preservation. *Social Work,* 41, 190-197.

Schacht, A.J., Kerlinsky, D., and Carlson, C. (1990). Group therapy with sexually abused boys: Leadership, projective identification, and countertransference issues. *International Journal of Group Psychotherapy,* 40, 401-417.

Shaffer, J. and Brown, L. (1998). Survivors of child abuse and dissociative coping: Relearning in a group context. *Journal of Specialists in Group Work,* 23, 75-96.

Smokowski, P.R. and Rose, S. (1999). Postgroup-casualty status, group events, and leader behavior: An early look into the dynamics of damaging group experiences. *Research on Social Work Practice,* 9, 555-575.

Sudarkasa, N. (1981). Interpreting the African heritage in Afro-American family organization. In H.P. McAdoo (Ed.), *The black family* (pp. 37-53). Beverly Hills, CA: Sage Publications.

U.S. Department of Health and Human Services (1999). *Executive Summary of the Third National Incidence Study of Child Abuse and Neglect.* Washington, DC: U.S. Government Printing Office.

Wilson, A.N. (1980). *The developmental psychology of the black child.* New York: Africana Research Publications.

Zuravin, S.J. and DePanfilis, D. (1997). Factors affecting foster care placement of children. *Social Work Research,* 21, 34-43.

Chapter 12

Worker Self-Disclosure in Group Work

Estelle Hopmeyer

INTRODUCTION

This chapter focuses on the practice of self-disclosure by the social group worker. It examines the impact of self-disclosure on pregroup planning, on group participants, and on the group processes and outcomes.

The definition of therapeutic relationship includes agreement that one person, the client, will openly discuss his or her personal life, and the therapist will function in a manner that will further the client's psychotherapeutic gains. Implicit to the goal of a psychotherapeutic relationship, however, is a one-way intimacy in which the client is the primary self-discloser. Discussion of the therapist's personal life is not necessarily part of the process; however, a therapist's personal revelations *are* frequently a component of psychotherapy. Therefore, questions arise regarding what is disclosed, when, and why (Simon, 1988).

The author, along with a mother whose adult daughter killed herself, founded the Family Survivors of Suicide Self-Help Group. The mother facilitated the group while the author initially attended meetings as a social work consultant. Several years later, the author received a phone call from another social worker in Québec City who requested a meeting because she was planning to develop and facilitate a group for survivors of suicide in her city. The Québec City social worker explained that she was planning to run a support group in which she would assume a "facilitator" role. As she was leaving the meeting, the woman asked the "doorknob" question, "Should she tell the group that she, too, was a survivor of suicide?" The author had the good sense to ask her what the underlying issues were for sharing this information with the group. She responded that she would be concerned that she would then have both professional and experiential power. Good group work practice requires that the worker/facilitator transfer power to the members so that they can become the helpers for one another. Riessman (1976) describes the "helper therapy principle," where members help themselves by helping others through the use of their own expert knowledge.

Although the bulk of the available literature on the subject of self-disclosure focuses on the client doing the self-disclosing, there are only a few articles pertaining specifically to the self-disclosure of the therapist. This insufficient coverage of social group work facilitation as it relates specifically to the social group worker's self-disclosure was the major impetus for examining this issue. The need was identified to develop a useful set of guidelines to assist social group workers when they are confronted by the decision of whether to use self-disclosure within their social group work practice.

Anderson and Mandell (1989) found that the most highly endorsed reasons to disclose were to promote feelings of universality, to give the client encouragement and hope, to model coping strategies, to build rapport, and to increase awareness of alternative viewpoints. These findings suggest that self-disclosure may be used at every stage of counseling. This chapter presents several practice examples that will highlight the complexity of using the skill of self-disclosure within the group work context. Although the practice examples presented herein are rather specific to our experiences and professional activities, we believe that the guidelines developed from them are easily transferable to other areas of practice and can be applicable in a wider range of practice situations.

DEFINING SELF-DISCLOSURE

Worker self-disclosure is a conscious, intentional technique in which clinicians share information about aspects of their lives outside the counseling relationship. Self-disclosure, as was defined by Danish, D'Augelli, and Brock (1976), was further subdivided into: past self-disclosure, in which the counselor disclosed about a problem previously experienced that resembled the clients' concern; and present self-disclosure, in which the counselor disclosed about a problem currently held that mirrors the concerns of his or her clients.

Counselor self-reference is the sharing of information about oneself with clients (Danish, D'Augelli, and Hauer, 1980). The two major types are (1) self-disclosure, or statements of factual information about oneself, and (2) self-involving responses, statements of emotional reactions to one's clients. These two types of self-reference have been further differentiated according to their positive and/or negative connotations (McCarthy, 1982). Positive self-disclosure conveys information that is similar to the client's experience (e.g., "I also remember questioning my goals when I was in college"); negative disclosure conveys dissimilar information (e.g., "It's different for me, I didn't struggle that much growing up"). Positive self-involving statements convey the counselor's positive feelings elicited by the client (e.g., "I'm happy that you're making so much progress"); negative self-involving statements convey negative feelings (e.g., "I'm uncomfortable with the way you keep denying that anything is wrong").

Guideline No. 1

Professional self-disclosures should be positive (e.g., "I've been there/am there and truly know, but I am different from you and your journey may be different"), not negative (e.g., "I'm doing better than you are!").

Clinicians report that their major reasons for self-disclosure are fostering the therapeutic alliance, facilitating client disclosure through modeling, helping the client not to feel so alone, improving contact with reality, decreasing client anxiety, helping the client consider different viewpoints, and increasing counselor authenticity (Anderson and Mandell, 1989; Simon, 1988). Primary reasons for not using self-disclosure include concern over moving the focus from the client, interfering with transference, taking too much counseling time and thus reducing client disclosure, and role confusion (Anderson and Mandell, 1989).

Theories of self-disclosure in interpersonal relationships (Steele, 1975) posit that people avoid disclosing personal information when they believe their disclosures may communicate undesired images or adversely affect relationships with others. Adverse outcomes of disclosure may include rejection by others, inability to form meaningful relationships, and loss of self-esteem and the esteem of others. Similarly, Rosenfeld (1979) observed that individuals avoided disclosing information about themselves that they believed would adversely affect their subsequent relationships. It appears, then, that anticipated consequences of self-disclosure during formative meetings of therapeutic groups strongly influence the frequency and quality of those messages. Social group workers who are aware of the nature of members' concerns about self-disclosure may develop interventions to help members identify and process their concerns during early group-developmental stages (Robison, Stockton, and Morran, 1990). Rosenfeld also identified certain differences between men and women in reasons for avoiding self-disclosure in relationships. Generally, men tended to avoid disclosures in order to maintain control in relationships; women avoided disclosing in order to prevent relationships from being harmed and to avoid being hurt in relationships.

Guideline No. 2
Worker self-disclosures need to be guided by an assessment of the way in which the self-disclosure will affect the life of the group (i.e., too much personal information may detract from the group's purpose, by focusing too much on the worker).

For Weiner (1983), this does not indicate or imply that the therapist deserts his or her professional role. Rather, it acknowledges that therapy is an ongoing process and one in which the therapist is considered to be another human being in relationship to his or her clients, a situation in which the therapist gives more to clients than mere professional expertise. According to Weiner, being oneself recognizes that not only the client but also the therapist has both a past and a per-

---

Guideline No. 3
Roles and/or boundaries have to be clearly thought out and identified and negotiated with the group.

---

sonality—variables that for Weiner constitute a significant element in the therapeutic process (Mathews, 1988).

Self-disclosure is used, to a greater or lesser degree, by the majority of practitioners, irrespective of theoretical orientation. It is considered valuable and ethical by most counselors (Mathews, 1988; Berg-Cross, 1984; Robitschek and McCarthy, 1991; Simon, 1988).

Guideline No. 4

Workers should feel free to share what could be useful for the group, within the boundaries of privacy and personal comfort—this models appropriate and acceptable behaviour for the group members.

SOCIAL GROUP WORK

The social group work literature devotes limited attention to this controversial subject. The exchange of appropriate personal information generally is accepted as a necessary and desirable component of successful therapeutic groups.

Shulman (1999) addresses the issue of when "the affect is directly related to the content of the work" (as when the worker has had a life experience that is similar to, or the same as, that of the client) and suggests that "self-disclosure of people's experiences and feelings, when handled in pursuit of purpose and when integrated with the professional function, can promote client growth" (p. 165). Shulman goes on to elaborate on how workers can synthesize both the personal and the professional, to deepen the work being accomplished within the group context.

At the 22nd AASWG International Symposium on Social Work with Groups, Toronto, Canada, October 2000, there was a presentation that dealt, both directly and indirectly, with worker self-disclosure (Maram and Ruhala, 2000). The presenters addressed the issue of workers who experienced a medical condition similar to that of the group members. One of the presenters had begun the group after diagnosis, and the other received the diagnosis during the life of the group. Both chose to adopt the facilitator/member role. The presentation dealt with several relevant topics that can be summarized as follows:

1. How are boundaries or roles negotiated and maintained when workers are in the process of coping with and resolving their own issues that are similar to those of the group members? (Guideline No. 3)
2. How can the expert authority of the worker be handled as only one truth of many? (Guideline No. 1)
3. How can the worker deal with his or her personal issues that make him or her feel vulnerable—without feeling like a "professional failure"? For example, is it acceptable to spend time on his or her own personal issues and concerns, as opposed to having and maintaining the focus on the needs, recurrences of illness symptoms, etc., of the group members? (Guideline Nos. 2, 4, and 5)
4. Can workers take time off from the group to give themselves permission to focus on their own needs, concerns, issues, etc.? (Guideline No. 6)

Guideline No. 5
If there is no cofacilitator to provide checks and balances, the lone facilitator should seek ongoing consultation or supervision to provide this support, as well as to assist him or her in dealing with his or her own issues and needs within the group context.

Guideline No. 6
Time away from the group may be important for both the worker and the group members, thus ensuring that the primary focus remains on the group members' needs and issues. Workers can use "self" as an example in certain instances (empathy), but it should not become the primary focus of the group.

In the McGill Centre for Loss and Bereavement, several groups have been initiated by professionals, specifically relating to losses that they themselves have personally experienced. Examples of these groups include: perinatal death, loss of a child, nonbereavement loss groups (for example, coping after a difficult birth experience), adult children of mentally ill parents, and HIV/AIDS-related bereavement groups.

In the perinatal death group, the facilitator identifies herself at the moment of first contact with potential group members as having experienced a perinatal death. She does this to assure group members that she truly understands their experience since perinatal loss is often considered to be a disenfranchised grief (Doka, 1989). This is contrary to what Glassman and Kates (1990) recommend. They suggest that self-disclosure is most often used in the group's middle phase, where the worker is viewed as "unique and differentiated." They caution that before this phase, as members struggle with their own power and control in relation to the practitioner, self-disclosure by the practitioner may lead the members to negative comparisons of their own abilities and successes (Glassman and Kates, 1990, p. 181). They further suggest that early worker self-disclosure "puts the practitioner into the position of being a hallmark of special ability, often leaving the members feeling incapable by comparison" (p. 181). Kurland and Salmon (1998) discuss the uncertainty and discomfort that workers may have about sharing personal information with the group, either at the beginning or during the life of the group.

Guideline No. 7
If planning to self-disclose, it would be preferable to disclose early in the pregroup planning stages or during the initial group introduction session.

It has been our experience that group workers do need to heed this caution by assuring the group that although they, the group facilitators, have lived (and are still living) the experience, their journey through grief was and/or is unique to them. Most of the group members are then reassured and feel hopeful that they, too, will survive.

Guideline No. 8
Group members may see the facilitator as a model, but the worker must consistently and continually remind the group that there are individual and unique ways of handling and coping.

Several years ago, the author supervised a master's student who was working with a group of HIV-positive gay men. He was gay himself but was HIV negative. He agonized over the fact that once the members learned that he was HIV negative, he would lose credibility with the group. However, the unexpected happened. When the group members asked and learned of his status, they expressed their gratitude to him for "caring enough" to work with them.

Guideline No. 9

Group facilitators need to be "in charge" at all times, of when and what to share of their own personal life. This should not be done under pressure from group members.

Further, they rejected his designed model for the group, which had them assuming primary control over the group (in the self-help model), and asked him to "care for them" by assuming the central position of doing the program planning and group facilitation. We decided that it was more empowering for the group if the worker acceded to these requests than to insist that they assume more responsibility for the life of the group.

The student has had extensive experience in facilitating HIV/AIDS-related bereavement groups over the past ten years. Although having had many friends and/or acquaintances die of HIV/AIDS, for the first five years the student did not share with the group members exact experiences of being directly involved in the care and loss of a close relationship due to HIV/AIDS-related death. The role of the student in those earlier groups was one of facilitator. It was clear that the group members also required a great deal of support and encouragement throughout the course of the group. The student's role within the group was perceived by the group members as being the source of "expert" knowledge in grief and bereavement. After several years of facilitating these groups, the student became the primary caregiver for a brother at the end stages of the HIV/AIDS disease process. A lengthy period of illness and eventual death occurred, followed by a two-year hiatus from facilitating any type of bereavement-related groups.

Guideline No. 10
Workers should recognize and act upon the need for self-care, which may or may not include taking a time-out from professional group work or substituting a member role instead of the professional role within the group.

When returning to facilitating HIV/AIDS-related bereavement groups, the student faced many unforeseen obstacles to developing and facilitating groups for which there was now a direct link between the experiences of the facilitator and the content and purpose of the group—that being the loss of a significant relationship due to HIV/AIDS. After working through most of these obstacles, the student was again confronted with the decision of whether to disclose that fact, or to continue facilitating these groups without the group members becoming aware of the exact nature of the facilitator's experiences. It was decided that disclosing this information to all potential group members, during the initial screening interview, would be the most appropriate plan of action.

Since this decision was made, there is clear evidence that divulging this personal information has, indeed, had a positive effect on the development of, and therapeutic benefits achieved in, all subsequent HIV/AIDS-related bereavement groups. Specific indications of these benefits can be seen in a much easier recruitment of potential group participants, more long-lasting commitment by the members (i.e., significantly reduced dropout rates), a much higher level of member interaction and participation within group discussions—which includes specific self-disclosure by the individual group members—and the development and maintenance of friendships after the group process had been concluded.

CONCLUSIONS

Guideline No. 11
When contemplating whether to self-disclose within the group context, group facilitators must consider their decision as it relates to:

- *the theoretical orientation from which they work*
- *their own privacy and comfort levels*
- *the intended purpose of the group itself*
- *what purpose the self-disclosure is intended to serve*

We, as professional group facilitators, must examine the effects our self-disclosure may have, not only on group participants and group intervention practice in general but also on other people—including their own families and/or their personal social networks. It might be important to examine the significance of our choice to self-disclose certain information within our professional practice and how it would impact on the significant others in our personal and private lives. It may be necessary to check with significant others before disclosing certain information that would also implicate them. For example, a mother facilitating a Family Survivors of Suicide (FSOS) group needed to check with her living children before taking an active role in the group and breaking the silence of suicide in the media and television. In a sense, she gained their permission to continue despite the risk of any impact her self-disclosure would have on them (i.e., those previously unaware of the family's experience being made aware of it in a very public way). It is imperative that we keep in mind that once we self-disclose, the information becomes public knowledge and the indiscriminate self-disclosure cannot be easily retracted and therefore, once out in the open, the information cannot be contained.

Guideline No. 12
Professional group facilitators are, in fact, part of a family system. Their personal self-disclosure can have an impact on others. There may be a definite need to gain their permission and/or support before disclosing.

In this discussion of group facilitators' self-disclosure, we must also consider that some groups require that the facilitator be someone who has experienced the exact experience for which the group was designed (i.e., many Widows-to-Widows groups are facilitated by a widow who herself has gone through that group process). This point raises the issue of the peer versus the professional facilitation role.

This could then raise ethical considerations relating to someone experiencing the particular problem (be it a similar or the same experience, illness, or loss), and then developing the group for self-healing purposes (i.e., helping his or her their own situation and serving his or her own needs).

This chapter attempted to raise the issues, present some critical questions, and develop a set of guidelines that would be useful for professional group facilitators confronted by the issue of self-disclosure within their professional group work practice. Further investigation and research might look at testing the guidelines presented here in other types of group contexts. Can they successfully be generalized to all groups or might they work better for some types of groups than for others?

REFERENCES

Anderson, S. and Mandell, D. (1989). The use of self-disclosure by professional social workers: Social casework. *The Journal of Contemporary Social Work,* 16, 259-267.

Berg-Cross, L. (1984). Therapist self-disclosure to clients in psychotherapy. *Psychotherapy in Private Practice,* 2, 57-64.

Danish, S., D'Augelli, A., and Brock, G. (1976). An evaluation of helping skills training: Effects on helpers' verbal responses. *Journal of Counseling Psychology,* 23, 259-266.

Danish, S., D'Augelli, A., and Hauer, A. (1980). *Helping Skills: A Basic Training Program,* Second Edition. New York: Human Sciences Press, Inc.

Doka, K. (1989). *Disenfranchised Grief: Recognizing Hidden Sorrow.* Lexington, MA: Lexington Book Publishers.

Glassman, U. and Kates, L. (1990). *Group Work: A Humanistic Approach.* Newbury Park, CA: Sage Publications, Inc.

Kurland, R. and Salmon, R. (1998). *Teaching a Methods Course in Social Work with Groups.* Alexandria, VA: Council on Social Work Education, Publishers.

Maram, M. and Ruhala, T. (2000). When facilitators and support group members share the same medical diagnosis: Implications for practice. Paper presented at the 22nd Annual International Symposium of the Association of Social Work with Groups, Inc. Toronto, Ontario, Canada, October 19-22.

Mathews, B. (1988). The role of therapist self-disclosure in psychotherapy: A survey of therapists. *American Journal of Psychotherapy,* 42(4), 521-531.

McCarthy, P. (1982). Differential effects of self-referent responses and counsellor status. *Journal of Counseling Psychology,* 29, 125-131.

Riessman, F. (1976). How does self-help work? *Social Policy,* 7(2), 41-45.

Robison, F., Stockton, R., and Morran, K. (1990). Anticipated consequences of self-disclosure during early therapeutic group development. *Journal of Group Psychotherapy, Psychodrama, and Sociometry,* Spring, 3-18.

Robitschek, C. and McCarthy, P. (1991). Prevalence of counsellor self-reference in the therapeutic dyad. *Journal of Counseling and Development,* 69(January/February), 218-221.

Rosenfeld, L. (1979). Self-disclosure avoidance: Why I am afraid to tell you who I am? *Communication Monographs,* 46(March), 63-74.

Shulman, L. (1999). *The Skills of Helping Individuals, Families, Groups, and Communities.* Itasca, IL: F. E. Peacock Publishers, Inc.

Simon, J. (1988). Criteria for therapist self-disclosure. *American Journal of Psychotherapy,* 42(3), 404-415.

Steele, F. (1975). *The Open Organization: The Impact of Secrecy and Disclosure on People and Organizations.* Reading, MA: Addison-Wesley Publishers.

Weiner, M. (1983). *Therapist Disclosure: The Use of Self in Psychotherapy,* Second Edition. Baltimore, MD: University Park Press.

Chapter 13

Meals Made Easy:
A Group Program at a Food Bank
for Parents of Young Children

Zelda Moldofsky
Sue Devor

INTRODUCTION

The prevalence of single-parent families, mostly single mothers, has been steadily increasing in Canada. Their work limitations, restricted incomes, and limited social resources are factors that have contributed to the increasing number of children living in poverty. In 1997, 56 percent of single parents were poor. They accounted for 28.4 percent of all Canadians living in poverty, rising from 22.5 percent in the early 1980s (Canadian Council on Social Development, 2000). Compared to children from middle- and upper-income families, poor children are less likely to receive adequate nutrition, and are at greater risk for mental and physical health problems (Human Resources Development of Canada, 1997).

Poor families struggle to stretch inadequate incomes just to cover basic needs. They are often faced with substandard housing, frequently move in attempts to save rent, cannot always obtain nutritional foods, and supplement their food budget with trips to food banks (Canadian Council on Social Development, 1996). Moreover, studies have demonstrated that negative academic and psychosocial

The authors would like to thank the special assistance of Nick Saul, Rhonda Teitel-Payne, and the staff and the clients of Stop 103 for their support and assistance in this program.

outcomes are associated with families where there is insufficient food (Alaimo, Olson, and Frongillo, 2001).

Although there are immeasurable numbers of cooking classes and community kitchens associated with programs for low-income families, published research in social work and psychology regarding the psychosocial issues confronting clients of food banks has been virtually nonexistent (Tranter, 1997). A study in Namur, Belgium, looked at how the poor suffer from isolation and a lack of respect from society. They found that soup kitchens that reached out to the poor and hungry were not always appealing, and questioned how waiting in line for a bowl of soup out of a van contributed to self-esteem. They analyzed the experience of a soup kitchen where customers came as much for socialization as for food (Mulquin, Siaens, and Wodon, 2000).

Meals Made Easy, an interactive group cooking program at a local Toronto food bank, used cognitive behavior strategies to help food bank users increase self-sufficiency by learning to prepare nutritious and economical meals (Moldofsky, 2000). The study showed that there were both practical and psychosocial benefits to the participants.

Since 25 percent of food bank users were single parents and 28 percent were children under the age of twelve (Stop 103 Statistical Data, 1998-1999), the participants in the Meals Made Easy program did not suitably reflect this population. Therefore, this study was designed specifically for parents with young children. We hypothesized that the Meals Made Easy program would benefit low-income parents by addressing their concerns about providing nutritious and appealing meals for themselves and their children.

The practical, nutritional, and social objectives of the program for the parents were the following:

1. To learn efficient and economical ways to prepare nutritious meals that would appeal to participants and their young children.
2. To improve self-esteem and confidence not only in their cooking skills, but also socially through their group interactions with other participating parents.

SETTING AND METHODOLOGY

This study took place at Stop 103, a food bank and antipoverty agency located in west Toronto. The area has a relatively young population with many immigrant families (Davenport West: A Neighborhood Profile, 1999).

The primary objectives of Stop 103 are as follows:

1. To meet the needs of low-income people by providing access to healthy and nutritious food
2. To implement services and programs that support the ability of individuals and groups
3. To address the problems of food access
4. To participate in initiatives that seek to address the causes of and solutions to hunger (Mission Statement, Stop 103, 1998-1999)

In 1999, the staff of four included a full-time paid social worker. One of her responsibilities was to facilitate Meals Made Easy as a regular weekly program. The program had proven to be highly successful and maintained a weekly participation of approximately fifteen people.

Recruitment of Members

One afternoon a week, as the food bank clients waited their turn to receive their food allotment, the facilitators invited parents and their children to an ongoing cooking class in the adjoining program room. Initially, these parents were reluctant to attend. Negative attitudes prevailed about their interest in cooking or baking. It was common to hear mothers say that their children were fussy eaters and would not like vegetarian meals. Nevertheless, with much encouragement, they did come to observe the class, and had the opportunity to participate in making the ongoing recipes. They also had the opportunity to taste what they made and to take extras home with them.

Outreach also took place at a community-dining program and at a Healthy Beginnings program for expectant parents, both cosponsored by Stop 103. Fliers were posted at a nearby community center. Again the common opposition to attendance was based on negative assumptions that their children would not like healthy foods.

The only attending members at the first two classes beginning November 1999 were those drawn from the food bank. Two mothers returned for the third class and up to seven attended the fourth and fifth. Before the sixth scheduled class, renovations of the kitchen facilities unexpectedly took place in the program room at the food bank, and there was no choice but to cancel the class. Since there was no opportunity to prepare the participants for this interruption, and since it was prolonged for a number of weeks, it was not possible to reconnect this group. Members moved, phones were disconnected, some suffered poor health, and there was a loss of interest.

In May 2000, after the completion of the renovations to the kitchen, the initial recruitment strategies were repeated. In the three-month interval, there was time to discuss the program with individual parents at the food bank, community center, and Healthy Beginnings, and to address negative assumptions about a cooking program. Consequently, ten mothers came to the first class of the second scheduled series titled Meals Made Easy for Parents. Attendance was consistent and grew to twelve participants.

The Cooking Class

The classes were open to parents of children under the age of sixteen. Three fathers came to the first interrupted series, but none came to the second scheduled series. Two social work volunteers facilitated the program.

Classes were held once a week from 1 to 3 p.m. This time was selected to accommodate parents with school-age children. Classes took place in a large program room with a kitchen adjacent to the food bank. Classes were free for the participants. Stop 103 subsidized the classes and provided a budget for child care costs, transit fare for those who lived too far to walk, and twenty-five dollars per week for the recipe's ingredients. Children were placed in day care at a nearby site, but could stay in the class if the parent wished. (A few older children stayed with their mothers and participated enthusiastically in the class.) Each member registered upon entering the class and received a name tag and the day's printed recipe. At the end of the sixth class of the series, each person was provided with a folder containing all of the series recipes.

Participants sat around a U-shaped table with cutting boards and required utensils. The ingredients for the recipe were read aloud and each person volunteered for a task to prepare the meal. At the end of the class the mothers tasted what they made and took home a container of the cooked product. Initially, even the younger children were brought from the child care site to taste the food as well, but it was unanimously decided that this caused too much commotion. Since each mother had a container with the food, the children could sample it at home. They did, however, report at the next class how their families enjoyed the recipe.

Structure

The group collectively agreed that they wished to adhere to the list of responsibilities that had been adopted by the Meals Made Easy program. These responsibilities included restriction of private conversations to designated social times, participation in the cooking process, and respectful assistance to participants with limited English.

Description of Cognitive-Behavioral Principles

The same cognitive-behavioral strategies that were employed in the Meals Made Easy program (Moldofsky, 2000) were used in this program as well. These methods were derived from the theoretical principles and procedures derived by Beck et al. (1979). These strategies were used to challenge the negative beliefs of the participants regarding some of their cooking skills and habits, and particularly their negative attitudes regarding what they believed their children would eat. Parents were encouraged to talk about their frustrations in providing nutritious food to children they perceived as finicky eaters. They were encouraged to introduce new food to their families and to examine their own negative attitudes regarding the responses they expected from their children. Other participants also encouraged reluctant individuals, especially new Canadians, to try new ingredients. The caring environment permitted those fluent in English to assist new immigrants when they required translations. The supportive atmosphere enabled the members to laugh at their mistakes and also to reveal that they were unsuccessful in making the most basic foods. One stressed mother admitted continuous failure in boiling potatoes. When the class recipe included potatoes, she was given the opportunity to work with other class members to learn fail-proof methods without shame or embarrassment.

Educational Program

While the meal was cooking, there was an educational program relating to such things as the preparation and significance of legumes, stocking a cupboard, use of herbs, etc. At this time also, participants had the opportunity to describe individually the class recipes they made at home, including innovative variations. Particular emphasis was placed upon the reaction of their children to the foods that they prepared, and to examine any preconceived ideas that could be fostering negative responses from their children about the foods. It was common to hear the mothers say that they knew that their children would not like a particular ingredient, such as raisins or carrots, but they were encouraged not only to try, but also to be aware of their own reaction in influencing the child's response. Members with little English were assisted by those with bilingual skills to participate in this process. Applause, praise, and encouragement followed these individual presentations to foster self-confidence and self-esteem.

Methods of Evaluation

At the beginning of the first and second series, each participant completed an information sheet outlining personal demographics. Since the first series was interrupted there was no final evaluation. However, at the end of the sixth class of the second series, each participant completed a self-assessment in the presence of an external examiner. An interpreter was provided to those with little English skills. Neither facilitator was present during the evaluation.

RESULTS

Demographics of Participants

The first interrupted series, begun in November 1999, had a total of five classes. The second series began on May 1, 2000, and continued uninterrupted for six consecutive weeks. Although a total of thirty-eight people attended the first series, demographic information was obtained only from thirteen. The rest were one-time attendees who were recruited from the food bank while waiting for their food allowances.

In the second series, fourteen members registered, and of the twelve who completed the final self-evaluation at the end of the sixth class, all attended at least four classes (three attended four classes, eight attended five classes, and one attended all six classes).

The demographics of both series of classes were similar and reflected the large immigrant population in the area. There were few differences in the backgrounds of the members from each series. Although the criteria specified parents with children under the age of sixteen, two grandmothers were permitted to participate in the second series. One attended only one class and the other remained until the end of the series. Her daughter was also a regular participant.

The study of the Meals Made Easy program included few members who could not speak English. However, 22 percent of Meals Made Easy for Parents participants spoke very little English, 30 percent were born in Canada, and the rest came primarily from Chinese- (19 percent) and Spanish- (22 percent) speaking countries. The remaining 29 percent had various first languages, including Portuguese, Italian, Punjabi, and Amheric.

Results of Self-Evaluation

All of the participants reported that they wanted the classes to continue. Eighty-three percent said they tried at least one recipe at home, and that their children enjoyed the foods that they were able to taste from the classes. The participants stated that they changed the way they prepared food, and that their children enjoyed their new meals.

Seventy-five percent said they felt that the structure of the class and the name tags were essential and 25 percent noted that it was important. All participants reported that the social aspects of the class were as important as learning cooking skills. One participant wrote in a special request to have an expansion of the social aspect of the program so that participants could get to know one another better and to share child care concerns.

DISCUSSION

Similarities and Differences in the Two Programs

There were similarities in both the Meals Made Easy program and the Meals Made Easy for Parents program regarding attitudes toward cooking vegetarian foods. Both groups responded positively to strategies that challenged negative beliefs, and valued opportunities to create delicious, inexpensive meals that they enjoyed. The members of the present study, however, were more frustrated with their responsibility to provide healthy inexpensive meals to their children, whom they perceived to be very fussy eaters. This resistance was addressed through cognitive-behavioral strategies that challenged these preconceived negative notions (Beck et al., 1979). The mothers were encouraged to examine how their own perceptions of their children's food dislikes influenced the children, and how their attitudes promoted certain reactions. As mothers became aware of their negative impact, changes occurred. Participants were surprised and delighted to see their children enjoy the foods made in the class.

There were also similarities in both programs in altering negative thinking about the participants' baking skills. In both groups many reported that they had been afraid to attempt to make muffins or other baked goods, and were very pleased with their newly discovered skills.

The Meals Made Easy for Parents program provided the opportunity to note the response of the non-English-speaking members of the group. They readily participated and were very effective with non-verbal communication. They benefited from the class encouragement to repeat new English words, especially relating to the foods they were preparing and eating. The atmosphere provided a supportive climate in which members readily helped one another and were willing to share food, containers to carry home food, and care for one another's children when they did attend the class.

Promotion of Self-Efficacy

Cognitive strategies that were used to address the self-defeating notions and beliefs regarding their ability to cook simple foods such as potatoes or to feed their families with nutritious meals were effective. These mothers were able to develop greater variety in cooking. The success they had in making appealing foods increased their self-confidence and self-esteem with other members of their family. It also decreased their stress regarding uncertainties and insecurities around meal preparation.

Social Interactions and Mutual Aid

Both Meals Made Easy and Meals Made Easy for Parents participants reported that the social interactions in the program were as important as the focus on cooking. In the current study there was greater emphasis on the significance of sharing child care concerns. The mutual aid provided by mothers of comparable economic and social circumstances was apparent.

Meals Made Easy: A Modular Concept

This study confirms that the Meals Made Easy programs readily adapt to a variety of groups with special needs. Not only was the program effective in helping low-income mothers of young children gain more self-confidence in meal preparations for their families, but it was also effective in providing social, cooking, and language benefits to new immigrants with little or no English skills.

SUMMARY AND CONCLUSIONS

Meals Made Easy for Parents was derived from a previous Meals Made Easy program. It is an interactive group cooking class that was designed to help low-income people prepare nutritious and delicious meals easily (Moldofsky, 2000). There were similarities in both programs in helping participants develop self-esteem through more positive attitudes toward cooking, and self-efficacy by altering self-defeating notions about their capabilities. Although mutual aid was a significant outcome in the Meals Made Easy program, all of the young mothers in the current study reported that they benefited from their interactions with other mothers, and there was a request that this part of the program be expanded.

REFERENCES

Alaimo, K, Olson, CM, and Frongillo, EA (2001). Food Insufficiency and American School-Aged Children's Cognitive, Academic, and Psychosocial Development. *Pediatrics,* 108(1): 44-53.

Beck, AT, Rush, AJ, Shaw, BF, and Emery, G (1979). *Cognitive Therapy of Depression*. New York: The Guilford Press.

Canadian Council on Social Development (1996). *Canadian Fact Book on Poverty*.

Canadian Council on Social Development (2000). *Canadian Fact Book on Poverty*.

Davenport West: A Neighborhood Profile (1999). Draft of Demographics.

Human Resources Development of Canada (1997). Strategic Policy Communications Canada, The National Child Benefit: Addressing Child Poverty.

Moldofsky, Z (2000). Meals Made Easy: A Group Program at a Food Bank. *Social Work with Groups*, 23(1): 83-96.

Mulquin, ME, Siaens, C, and Wodon, QT (2000). Hungry for Food or Hungry for Love? Learning from a Belgian Soup Kitchen. *American Journal of Economics and Sociology*, 59(2): 253-265.

Tranter, B (1997). Encouraging Words: Content Analysis of the Social Worker, 1987-1996. *The Social Worker*, 65(3): 155-156.

Chapter 14

A Social Group Worker As a Resident in an Independent Living Facility

Betty L. Welsh

INTRODUCTION

This chapter is the story of how I, as a resident volunteer, brought about some changes in a senior residential community through the use of various types of groups—interest, support, task, discussion, and service—under two different management styles. My point of view, therefore, is of a recipient of services as well as that of a social work professional. The following tale is of a five-year journey creating prevention programs and activities to promote and strengthen the physical, psychosocial, and mental health of residents as they age.

* * *

I view this community through my social work eyes. Using my ecological approach, I envision the mental health of residents inexorably linked to the complex interdependent systems of their family members, staff, and the health care system. This perspective requires the ability to move with comfort and skill throughout this ecological environment, to work at every system level, and to adopt multiple roles. As an insider there is the potential to touch lives not accessible to professional staff members. On the other hand, there are areas best left to the professionals serving us.

Four days after moving to the independent living section of this three-level care facility with my husband, he suddenly became ill and subsequently passed away six weeks later. We moved here so we could travel more, but suddenly I found myself alone in a spacious two-bedroom apartment in a handsome, three-story brick building.

The facility has 240 apartments with all the comforts of home minus responsibilities for maintenance, main-meal preparation, and house-keeping. The three buildings, one for each level of care, sit on twenty-nine acres of land. A small river borders the property on the west side and a thriving wetland borders the east side, giving the feeling that you are in the country even though you are in the midst of a metropolis.

This senior residence is a not-for-profit enterprise—a subsidiary of a local hospital health care system. When it was first built, the independent living component was viewed as a facility for active adults over the age of sixty-five, where they could age gracefully in place and move to other levels of care when needed.

The demographics of the community reveal an aging population with the mean at eighty-three years; 75 percent are women, 25 percent men, and 13 percent couples. Although racial and ethnic diversity is the goal, the population consists of white, Christian, middle- and upper-middle-class residents. This is a well-educated and well-traveled population. Aging has taken its toll with many—including vision and hearing loss. All have experienced losses of friends and family and now that of their familiar home and neighborhood.

Elders come to terms with change in their life situations in different ways. There are those whose glass is half-full, and those whose glass is half-empty. There are those who immediately explore the activities that meet their interests and those who isolate themselves either because it feels good and is right for them or because they are depressed or uncomfortable socializing.

Another dynamic important to recognize is the fact that each age group—residents in their seventies, eighties, and nineties—is marked with a variation of values. An example is a major discussion we had regarding proper dress in the formal dining room. Those in their nineties insisted on banning blue jeans and shorts as attire for residents or guests, and the younger elders did not see that as an issue, and desired a more relaxed dress code.

When I arrived five years ago the staff was led by a director, a retired military officer whose management style reflected his former training. Although this administrator did not object to my leadership in developing the early groups, he referred to them as "just activities." The need for services for residents who showed signs of depression was dismissed as unnecessary in an "independent living community."

Two years later the director resigned under the burden of additional responsibilities due to hospital reorganization to cut costs. The maintenance and housekeeping departments were outsourced, resulting in a complete turnover of staff. This was a difficult period for residents. They liked the staff, and felt the tremendous loss. The uncertainty of what the future would hold became a great concern for many of the residents. The steady state had been seriously disturbed and it would take time to stabilize. At that time, I had just become president of the resident association. I worked with my board to ensure residents full opportunity to say their good-byes as each staff member left. My request to the corporate vice president to involve residents in the selection process of new administrators was granted. The result was the hiring of Mrs. A., the corporate administrator for geriatric services, and Mrs. B., her assistant responsible for our independent living unit.

To accomplish what I have contributed to this community, or what any social worker accomplishes, requires support and sanction of the administration. Being president of the resident association gave me the opportunity to work more closely with both administrations, with whom a degree of respect and acceptance developed. The second administration, however, had a greater appreciation of a collaborative relationship between staff and residents.

Looking back over my early months here, I remember feeling as though I were on a cruise ship. There was entertainment, bingo and cards, an exercise program, "shore" trips and crafts, games of Trivial Pursuit, and discussions of current events. Being on a cruise can be wonderfully relaxing but over time not using available skills and talents is diminishing. There was a gap that kept us from contributing the knowledge and skills that keep minds active by participating in decision-making processes that affect us. Whenever possible I vowed to involve residents in the planning process and to encourage them to take leadership roles in developing programs of interest to them.

As the "new kid on the block," I listened to and observed my fellow residents from diverse backgrounds and began to participate in some of the activities. Upon assessment of the environment, the characteristics of the population, services, and programs offered, I set my goals. These included the development of programs and groups that would aid residents to age successfully (Rowe and Kahn, 1997, p. 143), ones that would ease the transition from living in the outside community to living in congregate housing, and programs that respect and encourage individual potential and support for an individual's aspirations. Essential is the development of communication links, creating a sense of community, and, by all means possible, programs that provide mental stimulation and encourage creativity.

The following is a brief description of the five types of groups that evolved over this five-year period, to meet the previously discussed goals.

INTEREST GROUPS

The interest groups evolved either from my interest or those expressed by residents. They were open-ended and existed as long as the interest lasted. My role was more that of a facilitator—guiding, organizing, and encouraging.

1. The *Bird Walk Group* focused on learning about and enjoying the outdoor environment that surrounds this particular community. For the five to ten walkers who joined me once a week, the activity proved relaxing and rewarding. For some, a deep spiritual connection was felt. The program is now part of the Wildlife Committee.
2. The *Play Reading Group* grew out of a request from the Fireside Chat discussion group to stimulate the creative minds of those who enjoy drama. The group, which averaged five to seven members, encouraged each member's potential. Groups, however, end as well as form. When this group had served its purpose and recognized it was time to end, it did.
3. The *Creative Writing Group* was originally a class. When a teacher was no longer available we decided to continue on our own. As facilitator, I helped members explore what they wanted from the group. Members were not interested in learning how to write but rather wanted to write their stories and share them with the group. We were in a time of life for reflection, and members who participated experienced some therapeutic benefit (Ray, 2000). As we have shared who we are, a closer relationship has developed.

SUPPORT GROUPS

Support groups aid their members in improving their life situations. They encourage problem solving and promote a degree of openness to share difficulties being faced. The leadership role in such groups takes on a therapeutic quality.

Low-Vision Support Group

This group meets monthly. It was designed to help residents who were experiencing a loss of sight, mainly due to age-related macular degeneration, to develop ways of coping with the loss. Guests from vision agencies and individuals who have made the necessary adjustments to living with this disease provide information and resources for the group. This group of ten to twenty residents evolved from the volunteer reading service discussed later under the heading Service to the Community.

This group has been instrumental in providing a reading machine in the library and the installation of "National Radio Information Service," which is heard on one of our in-house television stations. Low-vision residents participate with sighted residents in a newly formed book club through the use of books on tape. Last year nine members volunteered to work with three students from the Institute of Gerontology, in which the residents expanded the students' knowledge of the aging process and congregate living. The residents in turn received copies of their life history as recorded by the students. As one resident said, "I felt useful. I was able to help the students to have a better understanding of what the life of a senior is all about."

DISCUSSION GROUPS

The intent of a discussion group is to provide participants with opportunities to share and discuss topics of interest to them by developing a strong sense of member ownership in direction and content.

Fireside Chat

Fireside Chat is a discussion group named after Franklin Roosevelt's famous radio program. It originally met around the fireplace in the library. Twelve female residents attended the first meeting. The group began to expand and more chairs were brought into the library. It was getting crowded and yet the acoustics, the comfortable chairs, and the fireplace were all part of the reason for its success.

During the time of the first administration, the assistant administrator announced without previous discussion or warning that the group would meet the "next week" in the Rotunda Room, a large multipurpose room where the acoustics were poor, the chairs were hard, and the ambience was absent. I immediately protested. It was true that a change was necessary, but how to handle the size of the group was up to the group. It must be the group's decision, not the administration's. Otherwise, our right to make a decision about our future was being stripped, rendering the group powerless.

In the ensuing two weeks, the big staff turnover occurred, and Mrs. A. replaced this administrator. We invited Mrs. A. to meet with us so we could work together on the necessary change. In a briefing with her before the meeting, I stressed the importance of the group being a participant in the decision to relocate, otherwise it would destroy the group and all that had been built to date. At the next Fireside Chat, after some discussion, we came to a solution with Mrs. A.

The crisis we faced together served to solidify the group. We now number thirty to forty residents a session and the sharing and participation makes the hour pass quickly. There is laughter and good humor that influences the whole community as members share some of our discussions with others and at the dinner table. Fireside Chat has played a significant role in creating a feeling of community.

TASK GROUPS

A task group is formed to accomplish a task. It usually ends when the task is finished. The group leader is responsible for guiding the members toward accomplishing the designated task. When a committee is developed, members are empowered to plan, resolve challenges, and utilize resources.

The Wildlife Committee evolved from the Bird Walk Group when we asked the Grounds Committee permission to install bird feeders during the winter months. Bird feeders were then bought and installed outside a solarium window for all to enjoy. This activity, combined with a wildlife column I write for the monthly newsletter, influenced the Grounds Committee to recommend to the resident association that a separate committee be formed—thus the creation of the Wildlife Committee.

Tasks undertaken by committee members include tending a small wildlife library of books and magazines, maintaining the bird feeders, and planning wildlife activities for the community.

Over time, we partnered with the environmental studies department of a nearby university. Six interpretive signs, installed along the nature path, were designed by two students as a class assignment. A committee member made the frames and posts in our woodshop. In addition to our interpretive sign project, naturalists provided several lectures to our total community on beekeeping, maple syrup processing, and several slide film presentations on birds.

Four Show Committees were developed over a three-year period. The task for each was to showcase residents as active, involved elders who have accomplished much in their lives and continue to learn and grow. For each show, a committee of five to seven members whose personalities and talents complemented one another was formed. The short-term nature of the committee appealed to some residents who were hesitant to get involved in any long-term commitment. An evaluation at the end of each show led to the creation of the next show.

1. The Art and Hobby Show was the first show, and was repeated two years later by request. Its goal was to showcase resident talents and market some creative ongoing community activities. Associates (staff) were given time to visit the show, thus providing the dining-room staff and housekeepers with the opportunity to learn the creative side of the residents.
2. The Antique Show exhibited a collection of the resident's antiques. A sample of the 3,000-piece glass collection of one resident, plus lamps, samplers, furniture, dishes, diaries, and other memorabilia delighted the many visitors.
3. The International Festival was designed to present the ethnicity of residents and to share travel experiences. Over forty countries were represented through the displays. Residents worked in small groups representing countries in Great Britain, Scandinavia, Western Europe, Africa, and Asia to develop their displays. An international lunch buffet preceded the event. Desserts from different countries were served in the exhibit hall.

4. The Golden Elephant Sale, which is now an annual event, had a different purpose—to dispose of unwanted goods in the apartments. The committee decided that funds collected would go to providing scholarships for associates. Since it is against policy to tip any service worker, this seemed to be one way of showing appreciation.

Three publications were written, published, and distributed by task groups: *Wildlife in Our Own Backyard, Celebrating the Century* and *Welcome to Hudson's*. The latter two provided residents with the opportunity to write stories that will be cherished by their families.

1. Alice, a new committee member, initiated writing *Wildlife in Our Own Backyard*. She asked me to work with her daughter, an avid birder, to produce a booklet about wildlife on our grounds. Harry, a resident who is a master with computer graphics, agreed to design the cover. Alice contributed money to cover the cost of publication of a copy for each resident. Alice, at ninety-one, passed away two weeks after the booklet was published. Her legacy lives on.

2. *Celebrating the Century* was developed by the Creative Writing Group to encourage other residents to write about life events to celebrate the century. Ruth, age ninety, who loved to write, said that it was worth a try. Each week we read some of our own work, and then we collected stories from others, reading and critiquing them. There were several residents who had stories to be told but were unable to write due to loss of vision or arthritis. A committee member took notes and put the story together. As we worked as a team, the excitement grew with each new story submitted. The ninety-eight-page book with forty-eight writers that resulted, is organized by decades and includes poetry, snippets, and stories. It was illustrated and formatted by our computer whiz, Harry. Ruth passed away at age ninety-two, several months after the book was published, and in tribute to her we renamed the group—The Ruth Cramer Creative Writing Group.

3. *Welcome to Hudson's* is in honor of a famous department store that was closed and scheduled to be imploded. The store held many meaningful memories for residents. Following a discus-

sion about experiences with the store, I asked if members might like to record their memories of the grand old store and the result was the publication of *Welcome to Hudson's*. It contains twenty-eight memories of the old Hudson department store. Once again Harry volunteered to create the cover and illustrations. He also took the initiative to add some history as an introduction. The task committee, which I chaired, was formed from members of Fireside Chat. Seven hundred copies were printed and distributed by residents to friends across the country. Several hundred copies were purchased by the City Historical Museum, which was running an exhibit on the Hudson's store. An executive of a documentary filmmaker company bought a copy and chose five of our writers to be interviewed for the film he was making—two of those interviews are included in the documentary, which aired on public television.

SERVICE TO THE COMMUNITY

Communication among residents and between programs and committees aids in creating a community. As president of the resident association, I had the opportunity not only to develop communication among the seven committees and among residents but also to link some of our work with the larger health care system for recognition and support.

1. The *In-House Messenger Service* was developed when our mail carrier complained to me that residents were illegally leaving notes for other residents by slipping them through the cracks of the mailboxes. With the help of the exercise instructor, who continually encouraged residents to walk the halls to obtain additional exercise, we recruited fourteen residents to daily deliver in-house mail. One of them agreed to be the organizer and monitor the process. It has become an essential communication link to our community.
2. A *Low-Vision Reading Group* was formed prior to the formation of the Low-Vision Support Group. The service was developed to read newspapers and magazine articles three times a week. The large-print schedule of meeting times and readers is distrib-

uted to the twenty-five members every three weeks. Periodic meetings are held with the twelve readers to share experiences and evaluate the service offered. Evaluation by the recipients of the service is also conducted.

3. An in-house *Video Club* produced by residents presents a half-hour program each week shown weekdays at 3:00 p.m. Three years ago, with Joe, my fifteen year-old grandson who owns a video camera and a desire to pursue a filmmaking career, and Ron, an eighty-five-year-old resident with thespian experience who was a member of the Play Reading Group, we started the video program. Programs include segments of community news; interviews with new residents, staff members, and visiting guests; and clips of major events and programs. We now have a crew of ten. Ron, Charley, Elmer, and the new activity director have completed videographer training at the local cable station. Joe was present every Saturday morning for filming and editing of each program. Upon requesting and receiving funds from the hospital foundation, we were able to purchase our own camera equipment. Joe is now in college and we are now self-supporting.

OUTCOMES

Changes have taken place since I began my crusade. There is a greater feeling of community; more residents are involved in creating and designing programs thus making their lives more meaningful. This is especially important at a time when society and mainstream America has decided that life after retirement has less purpose. The programs and activities have successfully encouraged and promoted the strengthening of the physical, psychosocial, and mental health of many of the residents.

The Wildlife program, Messenger Service, Low Vision Support system, the Ruth Cramer Creative Writing group, Golden Elephant Sale, and the Video programs are now part of the fabric of the organization. With the increase of participatory programs, the number of volunteers has increased threefold. There is now a yearly recognition of our eighty volunteers both within our community and as a part of the Corporate Healthcare System. Both administration and residents have benefited.

It is rewarding to see the relationship of one program to another. For example, poems and stories from the Writing Group are published in the *Acorn,* our monthly newsletter, and filmed by the Video Club. The relationship between the Low-Vision Support Group and the new Book Club, and the development of programs as an outcome of Fireside Chat, provide other examples that no group is an entity unto itself, thus creating a degree of synergy.

In 2000, the Michigan Association of Services and Homes for the Aged recognized The Ruth Cramer Creative Writing Group with the award for Best Innovative Program in honor of our publication, *Celebrating the Century.*

My role here is changing with several groups and programs being built into the structure. I, however, continue to lead some groups because of the pleasure it gives me. With the new administration and activity director, I have found an openness to discuss ideas for programs, which they then carry out with residents. The total experience not only demonstrates the impact of groups on the welfare of a senior residence, but highlights remarkable accomplishment that can be achieved when several system levels collaborate.

REFERENCES

Ray, R. E. (2000). *Beyond Nostalgia, Aging and Life-Story Writing.* University Press of Virginia, p. 19.

Rowe, J. W. and Kahn, R. L. (1997). Successful Aging. *The Gerontologist,* 37(4), p. 433.

Chapter 15

From Fragile to Wild:
Group Work As the Transforming
Element in Redressing Social Inequities
for Older Women

Merike Mannik

THE CONTEXT

From fragile to wild—what does this actually mean for older women? Fragility operates on multiple levels—physical fragility (with the onset of chronic conditions and disability); emotional fragility (with the loss of valued roles, diminishment of support networks, or the questioning of self-worth and abilities); and imposed fragility (being unfairly labeled with a societal tag that says "past use-by date")—culminating in the fragility of social justice. Transforming from fragile to wild involves breaking barriers to participation to enable older women to "access education and training programs . . . and pursue opportunities for the full development of their potential" (UN, 1991), so that they can take up full citizenship.

Barriers to participation in education for older women are both attitudinal (ageism, sexism, and stereotypes) and structural (practical barriers). These include physical and mental frailty, social isolation, family and community attitudes, financial circumstances, societal stereotyping of older women, and internalized negative beliefs and attitudes (Sachse et al., 1999; Bennink and Blackwell, 1995). The widespread stereotyping of older women results in undermining their

The author would like to acknowledge the support provided by Dr. Carol Irizarry from the Flinders University of South Australia in the development of this chapter.

self-esteem—a factor contributing to low participation rates in education (Sachse et al., 1999)—and diminished opportunities for community involvement.

The model outlined in this chapter is based on Helping Hand Aged Care's Successful Ageing program—the social work arm of an innovative rehabilitation and therapy service called Healthy Lifestyles, which provides counseling and educational programs for people over sixty years of age in Adelaide, Australia. Successful Ageing aims at providing the opportunity for older women to increase their participation in society and to expand their options through increased knowledge, skills, and appropriate levels of support. In this service, group work serves as the medium for transforming perceptions of powerlessness (fragility) to mutual empowerment (wildness) for older women.

Barrier-Breaking Aspects of the Program

At its most fundamental level, the program breaks barriers to participation in learning by ensuring immediate relevance of program content, providing more time to assimilate new information, creating a supportive rather than a competitive learning environment, adopting experiential methodologies, and offering programs at nominal or no cost. The program recognizes potential physical barriers to participation, and accommodates for diminished hearing, sight, and reduced mobility. In acknowledging the need to be responsive and flexible to the needs of older women to overcome the barriers to participation, the group work takes place in a variety of settings, ranging from the home, to library meetingrooms, to community halls, to educational institutions.

Theoretical Underpinnings

The model draws on theoretical approaches outlined in literature on empowerment (Lee, 1994); mutual aid (Shulman, 1992); feminism (Dominelli and McLeod, 1989); and community development (Cox, 1987; Kramer and Specht, 1975), utilizing an ecosystemic perspective that recognizes the unity of persons and environments and of working with both entities (Germain and Gitterman, 1980, 1987).

Socioeducational groups, formed for purposes of education, socialization, and support, are a key part of the model. These groups are underpinned by social learning theory, whereby the group experience is essentially viewed as an educational experience. Within this context, group transactions promote consciousness raising, redefinition of self and/or aspects of one's personal and social world, and a better integration of knowledge, values, feelings, and action—all of which serve to promote successful problem solving and adaptation (Goldstein, 1988).

Trajectory of Barrier-Breaking Groups

The trajectory of barrier-breaking groups has five interrelated components—consciousness building, competency building, social capital building, community building, and citizenship building (see Figure 15.1). As people move through the trajectory they reduce their fragility and increase their "wildness." Movement can occur in any direction, as the trajectory experience is highly individual and participants define their own pathway. In empowerment terms, the trajectory enables shifts to occur "from egocentricity to group, community and social centricity" (Lee, 1994, p. 24). Each component of the trajectory is outlined in turn.

CONSCIOUSNESS-BUILDING GROUPS

These groups are aimed at addressing both the attitudinal and structural barriers faced by older women through a consciousness-building process that involves breaking through self-imposed boundaries formed by the internalization of negative societal attitudes and beliefs (Freire, 1972, 1975). The groups examine internalized values and external conditions that result in feelings of powerlessness, addressing common themes of self-blame, ageism, and sexism. Each group serves as a forum for developing the connection between private troubles and public issues (Schwartz, 1974), linking personal issues with the wider societal oppression of older women, thereby rejecting victim blaming and deficit approaches (Freire, 1972). Bonds of sisterhood are built, based on common situation, with mutual aid playing a pivotal role in effecting shifts toward self-empowerment among group members.

⇧ 5. FULL CITIZENSHIP-BUILDING GROUPS

Features:	Linkage to:	Worker Roles:
• Taking social action to change oppressive systems • Facilitating access to community-based learning programs and educational institutions • Full participation building	• University of the Third Age • Senior Colleges • Neighborhood Houses • Workers Education Association • Universities	• Mediator • Community educator • Negotiator • Advocate

⇧ 4. COMMUNITY-BUILDING GROUPS

Features:	Programs:	Worker Roles:
• Locality based • Community development focus, involving other service providers and community organizations • Conducting groups in partnership to raise profile of group, reduce invisibility, and promote inclusiveness • Collaboration and pooling of expertise • Community leadership and involvement building	• Home Alone • Community in Action • Help Yourself to Health • Regaining Your Control • Kickstart Your Life	• Cofacilitator • Coordinator • Networker • Community developer

⇧ 3. SOCIAL CAPITAL-BUILDING GROUPS

Features:	Programs:	Worker Roles:

• Volunteer facilitated
• Provision of valued roles for older community members as group leaders, peer tutors, teachers, facilitators, and/or project contributors
• Contribution building
• Social membership building
	• Oral History
	• Computer Demystification
	• Who's Pulling the Strings?
	• Home-Based Groups
	  –Reinvent Yourself
	  –Music Appreciation
	  –Creative Writing
	• Study Circles (kit centered)
	  –Aboriginal Reconciliation
		• Coordinator
		• Networker
		• Resource mobilizer
		• Peripheral resource
		• Community developer

⇧ 2. COMPETENCY-BUILDING GROUPS

Features:	Programs:	Worker Roles:
• Strengthening of individual capabilities, potentialities, and problem-solving skills • Increasing adaptation and coping abilities • Rehearsing new skills using role-plays • Focus on role transitions and life events • Interpersonal relationship building	• Stress Management • Communication Skills • Conflict Resolution • Confidence and Self-Esteem • Coping with Change • Successful Grandparenting • Retirement As Regeneration • Intimacy and Sexuality • Improve Your Memory	• Facilitator • Active resource • Educator • Learner • Enabler • Partner • Challenger • Modeler

⬆ 1. CONSCIOUSNESS-BUILDING GROUPS		
Features:	Programs:	Worker Roles:
• Consciousness-raising focus • Challenging of stereotypic roles and notions • Unlocking the secret desires of the heart • Personal and collective vision development • Action plan development and implementation • Sisterhood building	• Exploration of Learning Pathways (ELP) • Wild Women's Weekends • Return of the Wild Woman • Unity in Diversity	• Facilitator • Active resource • Educator • Learner • Enabler • Partner • Challenger • Modeler
THEORETICAL UNDERPINNINGS:		
• Empowerment, Social Learning, Adult Learning, Feminism, Life Model, Mutual Aid, Community Development		

FIGURE 15.1. Trajectory of Barrier-Breaking Groups

Wild Women's Weekends

Wild Women's Weekends are an example of a consciousness-raising group that uses activity as the catalyst for opening up rich dialogue and an increased depth of discussion. A two-day intensive program devised as a fresh alternative to bus tours and bingo for older women who want to get more out of life, the weekends were created in conjunction with older women needing to get out of a rut and develop fresh life direction.

Wild Women's Weekends combine creative process with mutual support in empowering older women to increase the choices in their lives. Activities include self-reflective exercises focusing on values clarification and achieving life balance, discovering the Goddess within, massage, deep-listening circles, meditation, and designing a fresh map of life. Spur-of-the-moment program inclusions, initiated by some of the women, have included skinny-dipping in a hot tub at midnight with glasses of chilled white muscat and topless bushwalking through the vineyards at sunset.

Many older women who attend the Weekend have low levels of self-esteem, having taken on board the negative valuations of themselves imposed by others and having experienced age- and sex-based discrimination. Many are also at a crossroads in life, having experienced recent widowhood, retirement, changed health status, or relocation. Personal change and an increased awareness of women's oppression is promoted in the group through the use of structured exercises, the sharing of personal experiences, and consciousness-raising techniques.

For example, story sharing through a deep-listening circle is pivotal in deepening connectedness and a sense of belonging and in re-affirming the participants as both women in their own right and as part of a collective of women. The women draw inspiration from one another's stories of survival and success, with the shared experience enabling the reinterpretation of individual stories to occur in light of the broader, common themes that emerge. Story sharing serves as a mechanism for discovering commonalities in situations, generating discussion around barriers to achieving self-actualization, and involving individuals in a power analysis of their circumstances (Cox, 1991; Home, 1991).

Collaging is used as an ending activity in the group as a creative means of personal goal-setting—designing a fresh map of life. Through the collages many of the women unearth alternative reflections of themselves (as goddesses, as warriors, as doers, as adventurers, as sexual beings), which counter negative, stereotypic self-images that hinder action-taking.

Spirituality As Part of Empowerment

An important aspect of the work in consciousness-building groups is to recognise the spiritual dimension of each woman. Spirituality describes what lies at the core of each individual's being and forms an essential dimension that brings meaning to life. It is an area often ig-nored or overlooked in defining components of empowerment, how-ever its inclusion is merited as part of a holistic approach (Harald, 1994), particularly for older women.

Incorporating spirituality into an empowerment approach involves identifying what spirituality means to each individual. It necessitates looking at what is deeply meaningful to women in terms of their be-lief systems, discovering what lies at the core of each woman's being and exploring what would bring greater meaning to each woman's life. It encompasses honouring the individual uniqueness of being and discovering ways to express it, through the personal and collec-tive, as part of everyday living. What is it that makes each older woman's spirit sing? What are the secret fires that burn within and how can they be ignited? It is important to recognise that "thought, feeling, and action become integrated into expressions of a sense of self-worth only when they are in harmony with one's primary values, spiritual commitments, and ethical covenants" (Goldstein, 1988, p. 29).

Consciousness-building groups, forming the kernel or starting point of barrier breaking, lead on to the next component of the trajectory—competency-building groups—which enable older women to develop the knowledge and skills needed to effect personal change and move beyond oppression.

COMPETENCY-BUILDING GROUPS

These are socioeducational groups that "seek to increase practical knowledge and skills as well as develop interpersonal connection and communication skills through group participation" (Cox, 1988, p. 119). Competency-building groups seek to strengthen individual capabilities, potentialities, and problem-solving skills, thereby increasing adaptation and coping abilities.

The groups perform an important role-attainment function, assisting older women to learn roles that they aspire to fulfill (Garvin et al., 1985). They serve as an important next step toward self-actualization for women who have designed a fresh map of life through Wild Women's Weekends. They can also serve as a main point of entry to the trajectory, although more marginalised older women usually need consciousness building to occur first. Competency-building groups teach skills for living, such as assertiveness, conflict resolution, and stress management. New skills and ways of relating can be rehearsed and reviewed in the group through role-plays.

Many of the groups look at life-stage issues of loss and adjustment (e.g., grandparenthood, retirement, widowhood, memory loss, onset of chronic illness, sexuality) and the myths associated with aging. Groups increase participant awareness of these issues, assisting with the resolution of developmental conflicts, encouraging behaviour change and assisting older women to cope with the consequences of these changes. Competency-building groups enable older women to build and reassess interpersonal relationships and to redefine sexuality, work, and achievement in nonsexist and nonageist ways.

Negative valuation through discrimination may manifest itself in lack of interpersonal and technical skills, resulting in reduced effectiveness in performing valued social roles (Solomon, 1976). An example of creative programming to combat this barrier to participation is the conducting of courses in interpersonal communication skills, emphasising androgogical skills acquisition, listening skills, and group dynamics. These serve as confidence and skill builders for some older women, while acting as "refreshers" for others with some teaching experience.

The skills learned or enhanced are then used by some participants to teach or facilitate groups in their local communities and/or applied in other volunteering roles such as one-to-one peer support. An empowering component of the teaching or facilitation roles for older women relates to "helper therapy" (Gartner and Reisman, 1984), whereby helping another to learn often results in an increased level of personal competence and reinforced learning for the helper. This leads into the next component of the trajectory—social capital-building groups—which serves as a practice ground for skills learned in competency building and signals a further move away from learned helplessness/dependency and seeing the professional as the "expert."

SOCIAL CAPITAL-BUILDING GROUPS

These groups focus on contribution building by providing valued roles for group participants and older community members as group leader, peer tutor, facilitator, and/or project contributor. As well as creating an avenue for older women to be valued and utilised in the community for their knowledge, experience, and wisdom, social capital-building groups are social membership-building.

Ongoing, peer-facilitated, home-based learning groups (such as creative writing groups, poetry reading circles, computer interest groups, music appreciation, current affairs, conversational English, and reinventing yourself) and community facility-based groups (such as computer demystification and oral history) assist to develop informal support networks in the community in lieu of longer-term professional support. Most of the group facilitators are older women who have moved through the consciousness-building and/or competency-building components of the trajectory.

For example, Allison, eighty-four, attended a Wild Women's Weekend to self-renew, reevaluate her life, and develop fresh direction. From this, she identified the need to build her assertiveness, confidence, and self-esteem, so she enrolled in conflict-resolution skills and a confidence and self-esteem course. A former teacher, she then enrolled in the interpersonal communication skills course as a refresher, after which she became the facilitator of an ongoing home-based reinvent yourself group for older women. The community development component of social capital-building groups gathers further impetus in the next component of the trajectory.

COMMUNITY-BUILDING GROUPS

These groups, through community development, seek to promote active citizenship and change in partnership with communities. The strong focus on a community development approach helps to combat social exclusion and to promote wider participation. The development of partnerships with communities serves to reverse the trend of socially excluding elderly citizens. Conducting information provision groups in partnership with other service providers, community organisations, and older women reduces the invisibility of older women and promotes inclusiveness.

Community-building groups have been developed, in partnership with older women and community organisations, in response to learning needs identified by older women in the community. For example, the Home Alone course—a partnership venture with the police department, a bank, and a local council, which looks at addressing issues relating to home and personal security, electronic banking, home maintenance, and social isolation—was set up in response to concerns raised in relation to these matters by many older women attending the consciousness- and competency-building groups.

The groups have a primary function of information provision, providing older women with the knowledge and tools for self-help. With high community visibility, community-building groups highlight the needs and concerns of older women to the broader community. They also provide a valuable forum for testing out ideas with others, creating an action plan with peers, and developing a community response to some of the issues raised. The groups build community leadership and involvement, as they may result in the development of social action groups, with community leaders emerging from the groups to take responsibility for further action. This leads into the final component of the trajectory.

FULL CITIZENSHIP-BUILDING GROUPS

These groups involve full participation building by breaking institutional barriers to participation in learning, enabling older women to access community-based adult education as well as formal education. The worker role involves advocating for the building of bridges between informal and formal education, increasing the awareness of education service providers of the barriers faced by older women to education, and to facilitate effective linkage to the education system for group participants from the other parts of the trajectory. There is an important role for the worker in promoting an understanding of how older people learn to ensure that methodologies used consider older people's preference for experiential learning, courses are of immediate relevance, and materials used take into account diminished physical ability.

For group participants who have moved through the trajectory, full citizenship building may involve taking social action to change oppressive systems. The worker's role is to take action with, not for, group members. As a result of social action, the environment is made more responsive to people on a larger scale, above and beyond the group.

For example, a group of older women—who had moved through the trajectory by attending a home-based computer demystification session followed by a six-week peer-conducted computer course—effectively lobbied for changes to enrollment procedures and financial policies at a local college to enable them to attend a word processing course held there. As a result of their lobbying, the college introduced a concession policy for seniors, less intrusive enrollment procedures, relocated the course to a more accessible room, and effected changes to teaching methodologies—making their courses more accessible to all older people. For the group of older women, their social action enhanced their problem-solving capacity and increased their sense of self-esteem, hope, and empowerment, effecting both personal and social change.

WORKER ROLES

Over the course of the trajectory of barrier-breaking groups, the primary focus of the worker shifts in line with the changing goals and contexts of the groups. More direct social work intervention occurs at the beginning of the trajectory, where vulnerabilities, personal pain, barriers to participation, and sense of powerlessness are usually the greatest. At the consciousness- and competency-building stage, the role of the worker includes that of educator and active resource transmitting their knowledge and skills to group participants, modeler, facilitator, learner, enabler, partner, and challenger (Freire, 1972; Cox, 1988; Lee, 1994).

At the social capital-building and community-building stage, the worker takes on the primary role of community developer by promoting change, challenging social exclusion, and advancing full citizenship; fostering the empowerment of individuals and groups by increased involvement in decision making; performing an educative function in relation to the community and the organisations within it; and by drawing together and developing new forms of association and organisation (Drysdale and Purcell, 1999).

At the full citizenship-building stage, the worker acts "as a connector to the various aspects of working with groups such as making approaches, forming alliances, looking at alternatives, facilitating access, encouraging action and appraising the outcome" (Muir, 2000, p. 77). In line with the concept of community-based learning, part of the role of the worker across the trajectory is to work on the boundaries between systems, seeking to create and develop learning communities.

CONCLUSION

In summary, the trajectory of barrier-breaking groups helps to overcome social obsolescence and its symptoms of exclusion and reclusiveness by enabling older women to mobilise and build on their knowledge, skills, and creative potential, liberating their capacities to move toward self-actualisation and full citizenship. The trajectory of group work experiences serves to increase opportunities, motivation, confidence, self-esteem, participation, social membership, visibility, competencies, contribution, valued roles, and community inclusion—all of which improve quality of life and enhance the capacity of older women to live independently as active, valued, and contributing community members. "Through collectivity people draw the strength they need to empower themselves and attain actualised, unique personhood (and) social responsibility" (Lee, 1994, p. 24), enabling the fragile to become the wild.

REFERENCES

Bennink R and Blackwell P (1995). *Access for All in Adult Community Education: Overcoming Barriers to Participation Report.* Adult Community Education Unit, Dept. for Employment, Training and Further Education, Adelaide, South Australia.

Cox EO (1988). Empowerment of the Low Income Elderly Through Group Work. *Social Work with Groups,* 11(4), pp. 111-125.

Cox EO (1991). The Critical Role of Social Action in Empowerment Oriented Groups. *Social Work with Groups,* 14(3/4), pp. 77-90.

Cox, FM (Ed.) (1987). *Strategies of Community Organisation: Macro Practice,* Fourth edition. Itasca, IL: Peacock.

Dominelli L and McLeod (1989). *Feminist Social Work.* London: Macmillan Education.

Drysdale J and Purcell R (1999). Breaking the Culture of Silence: Groupwork and Community Development. *Groupwork,* 11(3), pp. 70-87.

Freire P (1972). *Pedagogy of the Oppressed.* Harmondsworth, England: Penguin.

Freire P (1975). *Education for Critical Consciousness.* New York: Seaburn.

Gartner A and Reisman FE (1984). *The Self-Help Revolution.* New York: Human Sciences.

Garvin CD, Glassner P, Carter R, English R, and Wolfson C (1985). Group Work Intervention in the Social Environment. In Sundel M, Glassner P, Saari R, and Vinter R (Eds.), *Individual Change Through Small Groups,* Second edition (pp. 277-293). New York: The Free Press.

Germain CB and Gitterman A (1980). *The Life Model of Social Work Practice.* New York: Columbia University Press.

Germain CB and Gitterman A (1987). Ecological Perspective. *Encyclopaedia of Social Work,* Eighteenth edition, Volume 1. Silver Spring, MD: NASW, pp. 488-499.

Goldstein H (1988). A Cognitive-Humanistic/Social Learning Perspective on Social Group Work Practice. *Social Work with Groups,* 11, pp. 9-31.

Harald J (1994). Death, Life and Empowerment in West Indian Women's Groups. *Women and Environments,* 14(1), pp. 16-17.

Home AM (1991). Mobilizing Women's Strengths for Social Change: The Group Connection. *Social Work with Groups,* 14(3/4), pp. 153-171.

Kramer R and Specht H (1975). *Readings in Community Organisation Literature,* Second edition. Englewood Cliffs, NJ: Prentice-Hall.

Lee JAB (1994). *The Empowerment Approach to Social Work Practice.* New York: Columbia University Press.

Muir L (2000). Evolving the Curriculum: Groupwork and Community Based Learning. *Groupwork: An Interdisciplinary Journal for Working with Groups,* 12(1), pp. 72-82.

Sachse M et al. (1999). *Lifelong Learning and Older People: A Discussion Paper for the Office for the Ageing.* Department of Human Services, South Australia.

Schwartz W (1974). Private Troubles and Public Issues: One Social Work Job or Two? In Klenk R and Ryan R (Eds.), *The Practice of Social Work,* Second edition. Belmont, CA: Wadsworth, pp. 82-101.

Shulman L (1992). *The Skills of Helping Individuals, Families and Groups,* Third edition. Itasca, IL: FE Peacock Publishers, Inc.

Solomon B (1976). *Black Empowerment: Social Work in Oppressed Communities.* New York: Columbia University Press.

United Nations General Assembly (1991). Resolution No. 46/91.

SECTION IV:
SOCIAL JUSTICE IN SOCIAL WORK
EDUCATION AND RESEARCH
FOR SOCIAL WORK WITH GROUPS

Chapter 16

Group Passage to the Profession:
The Field Seminar
in Social Work Education

Michael Phillips
Carol S. Cohen
Linda Hutton

INTRODUCTION

Every September at Fordham University, groups of approximately fifteen students entering foundation-level field placement gather for their first field seminar session. They cross a broad age span, and come from different cultural and ethnic backgrounds, both influencing the type of life experiences they bring to the seminar. Relatively few are male. Each student chooses his or her own place, some taking chairs at the rear of the room, some sitting in isolation, and some seeking refuge in small clusters, sipping coffee, and wondering aloud what the seminar experience might be like. There exists a mixture of feelings: excitement, hesitation, and vulnerability. Although many worry about what is to come, most are also filled with hope and anticipation.

Similar scenes occur at social work programs throughout the United States, and although having some unique qualities depending on their institution, they share many things in common. This chapter will discuss the way these seminars can serve as mutual aid groups to facilitate the transition from social work student to social work professional. As suggested by a student, the authors have chosen to think of this process as a passage. This chapter traces the voyage through participant voices expressed in process recording of group sessions, contemporaneous journal entries, and retrospective reflections in a focus group. The preliminary sections suggest contexts for thinking about the field seminar, including those of field education and social work practice with groups. The chapter concludes with reflections about these mutual aid groups, their applicability to integrating the professional social worker role, and the applicability of such groups in other settings.

FIELD EDUCATION
AND PROFESSIONAL DEVELOPMENT

A principal outcome of education in the social work foundation is the development of a set of generalist skills, applicable to practice with a variety of systems and client populations. Field seminars can bring together classroom and field practicum experiences to support this development. The "conscious, disciplined use of one's self and one's abilities" (Phillips, 1954, p. 43) is fundamental to the social worker role. Through the integration of classroom and field learning, students form an understanding of what it is to be a social worker, and what it means to take responsibility for one's practice. Those who have preprofessional social work experience must "unpack" their experiences and review them from a new perspective. For those without such experience, it involves building an understanding of the structure and processes of professional social work practice. Regardless of previous experience, students share the common task of integrating a variety of inputs into a coherent professional sense of self.

Constructing the professional self is an abiding theme in social work literature. Mary Richmond (1922) suggests that "the good case worker must be born and made," cautioning the profession that "its element of error is the failure to recognize how much is being done in social work to develop a native gift through training and specialized experience" (p. 7). Professional education programs need to create structures, through which these "native gifts" can interact with the input of instructors, clients, and fellow students to form the social work professional. Grossbard (1954) expands this idea, noting that learning in social work involves more than adding new facts. It also requires "giving up the old and familiar for the new and unknown" (p. 381). Conceptualizations of field instruction draw from these ideas and commonly describe the experience as a "planned change process," consisting of "some degree of personality development and change in which knowledge becomes personalized, skill becomes individualistically stylized, and a vocational self and identity become part of one's ego identity" (Siporin, 1982, p. 176).

FIELD SEMINAR AS A GROUP EXPERIENCE

Field seminars are common in social work programs (Lewis, 1988; Mary and Herse, 1992) and take on a variety of forms as they try to help students integrate classroom and field learning. Groups are ideal vehicles for helping participants achieve individual goals, such as developing the professional self through sharing experiences of growth and change. With thoughtful facilitation, they can become reservoirs of power resources, available to members through the giving and receiving of support (Hirayama and Hirayama, 1986). However, just because a number of students and an instructor are assigned to meet together, a field seminar does not necessarily constitute a group in the social work frame of reference. Field seminar instructors need to make a conscious choice to convene the seminar as a group experience in which students engage in a common enterprise of mutual aid in order to achieve professional goals (Birnbaum, 1984; Lynn, 2000). Instructors must balance viewing each student's quest for development and their agency experiences as highly idiosyncratic with exploring the learning challenges they share in common.

In order to incorporate goals of social justice into the seminar, the worker/instructor must provide opportunities for member/student empowerment. Social work groups are highly varied, but all effective groups are directed toward achieving member goals through the purposeful focus on common objectives. Seminars that incorporate key features of mutual aid and social justice meet the criteria for social work groups and for sound learning environments in which to develop professional skills and identity.

Group workers, or as in this case, seminar instructors, must prepare themselves by understanding the institutional context and need that define the purpose of the group (Kurland, 1978). Following the group work model, instructors must explicitly contract with student members, insuring their informed consent in the group process and understanding the seminar's purpose and content. The conditions that are nonnegotiable and imposed by the social work program, such as rules for attendance and scope of authority of the leader, must be openly discussed. Instructors must identify those areas open to input from members, such as developing systems to present practice issues and choices about participation.

Since this is a designated part of students' education, it is important that instructors have a clear sense of what can be accomplished. Having this sense does not mean that instructors take over the group. Rather, they set the boundaries within which the work will be done. The purpose of the seminar is:

> To provide an opportunity to work together and collectively focus on issues in field placement in order to integrate and help fill in gaps between classroom and field experiences, help tackle particular practice issues, and share information needed for education and career planning.

The instructor proposes that such a purpose is consistent with his or her overall goal to successfully enter the social work profession, and invites discussion. Through exploration of purpose, students begin to locate themselves as members of the seminar, and develop a preliminary understanding of what joining the group entails.

Instructors also explain the structure for the seminars in terms of life span (ten sessions over an academic year), session duration (two hours), and place (at school). Content, determined by instructors and students, includes: planned discussion of practice issues, student case presentations, educational-program information, and "checking in" regarding what has transpired in the field experiences between seminar sessions. Although role-plays, readings, process recordings, and other strategies are used in seminars, the predominant form of communication is group discussion. Thus, field seminars become models for practice, as in vivo experiences of collective action and reflection. With these conditions met, field seminars become groups as classically defined by Olmstead (1959):

> A plurality of individuals who are in contact with one another, who take one another into account, and who are aware of some significant commonality—an essential feature of a group is that

its members have something in common and that they believe that what they have in common makes a difference. (p. 21)

It is the nature of this "significant commonality" that helps in balancing the level of heterogeneity (diversity between students and field placements) and level of homogeneity (student status) in the seminar groups. Such groups can tolerate a high level of diversity in membership when what they share in common is experienced intensely (Gitterman, 1989), in this case the experience of being immersed in professional education. The common purpose binding students and instructors in the seminar is powerful; all are devoted to the successful completion of the field education experience and the graduation of students into the social work profession.

The experiences described in this chapter will demonstrate how field seminars link individual struggles with those of other students and facilitate exploration of parallel processes with clients engaged in their own transitional passages. Each of the following sections devoted to a metaphoric point in the field seminar journey begins with the reflections of students. These comments become longer as the voyage continues, paralleling the increased ownership and participation of students in the seminar over the course of a year. In addition, excerpts from instructors' recordings are presented to evoke the seminar process.

FIELD SEMINAR JOURNEY

Preparing for the Voyage

I recall in the first seminar feeling intimidated by others and concerned what the other group members might think of me if I shared my clinical experiences and difficulties.

The field seminar is a required course and certainly not initially thought of by students as a mutual aid group. The first task confronting the field seminar leader is that of creating a group setting and group-oriented expectations. This task is complicated by both student expectations that the instructor will be the primary source of needed information and the amount of information, which must be covered, in that initial session. Typically, in the first session, which takes place prior to the students' entry into the field, the function of the field seminar is defined. The role of the instructor as faculty advisor is also clarified. Specifically, the students are advised that the focus of the field seminar includes the following:

1. The sharing in the group of field-placement issues
2. The "melding" of class material and field experiences
3. Discussing the appropriate application of theory to field situations
4. Tackling specific practice issues
5. Providing a place for mutual support and collaboration
6. Providing a venue for the free flow of information needed for educational planning

Frankly, the initial field seminar session resembles more a traditional class than a mutual aid group. The transformation to mutual aid occurs progressively in the following stages: (1) the description of the seminar, (2) clarification of the common task, (3) the demand for work, and (4) establishing a climate for risk taking. An example of this transitional process from the instructor's notes follows:

> I briefly described the purpose of the seminar and told them I was responsible for deciding if their practice merited a passing grade. In deciding this I would be looking at their ability to interview, make assessments, contract, use resources, and handle case termination. I told them that in judging their work I would also be looking at their ability to take risks in their learning. If, for example, they took an action based on a clear rationale they would get credit for that even if the activity did not achieve the desired outcome. Finally, I said that in our learning together we would be working from specific examples of experiences they had. This served as a bridge to asking for volunteers to role-play a first interview between a client and worker. This early call for work was met with mixed reactions.

The underlying interest in the students' successful completion of their fieldwork experience establishes a common basis that binds together seminar members and instructor. However, even though the purpose is the successful completion of their first-year placement, students' roles in that process have yet to be defined. Instructors must clarify the benefits of collaboration and underscore the need to share in the group. They must further define that they are vested with the responsibility of deciding whether the student passes fieldwork. The instructor may go on to review students' learning needs and how they will be judged.

Signing on to the Voyage

In that first session we became immediately aware of the complex blend of individual personalities and "superordinate" properties of group structure. We were struggling with the same familiar challenges of our personal lives and the new life of social worker that we had come to embrace, moving from well-intentioned citizen to professional, skilled practitioners. . . . We knew when the phrase "the conscious use of self" was used that this would be a different experience.

In order for risk taking to occur, there must be a demand for it coupled with a sense of safety in the group. In the early stage, the instructor provides support for risk taking. As group members take on more responsibility for the group, their sense of safety strengthens. Group members begin to share more freely their field-placement experiences. Instructors often move to a role-play, conveying the message that the group will be looking at specific work. This method also provides an opportunity to model process recording (by writing key phrases on the board), and reinforces the idea of taking risk. Students with no prior social work experience often seize this opportunity to prepare themselves for their first experience with a client. The feelings of safety in the group allow for exploring and applying technique and theory to practical situations (Birnbaum, 1984). The following process note illustrates this point:

> After a brief role-play of a first interview I thanked the student volunteers for their willingness to "stick their necks out and provide a learning opportunity for all of us." I asked the group if they had any thoughts on what they had seen. There were a lot of positive comments about how the worker had tried to help the client. I then turned to the student playing the worker and asked: "Do you think you can help this client?" She said she thought she could. I then asked the "client" whether she thought the "worker" could help her. She said "no," and I asked, "Why not?" She said that the worker seemed to have decided what she, the client, should do and was not really listening to her. I asked the

group what they thought. Some said it was up to the worker to
define what was to be covered, and another said that the worker
was helping the client by telling her what she needed to do. I
asked if that was the function of the social worker. Several said
the worker knew what would help, and others questioned the
right of the worker to decide for the client. They asked me which
was right and I said, "Well, let's look at the work." I turned to
the student who had role-played the "client"; she said her ideas
were not really being sought. I asked her, "Would you mind
showing us exactly what you would do differently?" She agreed
and the two students reversed roles and the role-play began
again.

Sailing Out

In those early integrative seminars we wanted to be open, to leave previous
lives behind to absorb this new life and new way of thinking wholeheartedly. We
constantly looked to the professor for all the answers to our myriad problems. As
a group of first-year social work students, we sought the perfect "right" answer.
We wanted blueprints of practice, diagrams, and definitive solutions. We feared
surprise and so retreated to caution. We desperately wanted to know what was
in store so that we would not be caught off guard by new possibilities. Our passage to newness was filled with the black potholes of chaos in the classrooms, in
the agency field placement, and often in our own personal lives. The newness
was fearsome for us and we guarded against it.

The previous extract from a postseminar focus group reflects an
initial uniform desire for direct advice and safety. This need is rarely
raised directly; rather, students express concerns about the neighborhoods in which they will need to work. The instructor can help students share their fears and ways of coping in new and occasionally
dangerous neighborhoods. The issue of being safe expands to issues
of being safe in the seminar, and is intimately connected to issues of
confidentiality. These issues are explored in the following extract
from a second session where the instructor was trying to help the students see that they have an active part in defining both what would be
done in the seminar and in creating a climate of safety:

After discussing child abuse reporting and confidentiality, L.
raised questions about the supervision she was receiving. She
said she had an excellent supervisor. However, the supervisor
did not provide her with enough support and she did not feel

safe. Another student in the same setting agreed. I said that it is difficult to learn if we do not feel safe and wondered whether the discussion was not also a way of talking about us in the group. Could it be about confidentiality here and feeling safe here? I wondered how they felt. After a long wait, one student said that he felt nervous because, after all, I was judging them and would be grading them. Another was then able to say that she had concerns about feeling that sometimes it seemed as though they were under attack. Other students said they did not feel that way. They emphasized that we were here to learn. After further discussion I asked what I could do to make them "feel more supported, feel more safe." They said the discussion had helped.

I said it was strange no one mentioned confidentiality and maybe we had to agree among ourselves about this. They struggled with this and agreed that they needed to be sensitive to each other's need for confidentiality. They were okay with the idea that people might want to discuss with others some of the issues raised in the group. They said that identifying who was involved should be avoided. I agreed that I could also live with that.

Coping in a Sea of Turbulence

The field seminar group was similar to one of those weird spring days when all of a sudden the sun comes out among the clouds. Over time we became our own explorers and discoverers. We began to inquire together to find answers, and we turned to one another as our best hope for inventing and discovering the world of social work. In the process, we came to know that being open also entailed acknowledging and incorporating our own experienced lives. We learned to honor one another in our different roles, recognizing that everything depends on context and on the unique relationships available in the moment. From one another we learned what was possible, and were often inspired by another's success to continue our own search. We were experiencing that we were "all in this together." Those of us who were beginning our own group work in agencies tried to recreate the unfolding model of group work in the seminar. The seminar became a safer place and we moved toward a deeper experience of group work. I remember being surprised that someone else could understand how I was feeling as I struggled with clients who had enormous difficulties in their lives. When we shared, we experienced a sense of validation and of being understood that had almost nothing to do with spoken words. Temptation for a "quick fix" still beckoned enticingly, yet we found no quick fixes in the integrative seminar. The journey was beginning to be difficult, demanding, exhausting. Finding safe inlets and familiar shores was more challenging. Adapting to this new life and changing ourselves was hard for all of us. Over time we felt more engaged and connected with one another and several emotional risk-taking self-disclosures followed. As each of us risked sharing our thoughts and feelings, we began to feel more and more trusted with information; we felt we knew how to listen and speak to one another and collaboration seemed truly honored. It seemed that we had come together as a group and sometimes it also seemed that we were inventing new ways of doing things. The demand for work intensified both outside and inside the group seminar.

The voyage is not all smooth sailing. Students resist taking responsibility for the work and the instructor must reach beyond the obstacles and make a demand for work. In the beginning phase safety and confidentiality are at the core of the work. As is reflected in the following excerpts, in the middle phase students struggle with the role of the instructor and reach out to each other in discussing common concerns regarding client engagement, how their value system impacts their practice, and issues of diversity. In the process they confront and challenge one another as well as offering advice and support. As they come to own the group they move away from seeking the instructor's advice and develop their own understanding of what to do.

> G. talked about her group of drug abusers and how "they try to impress me with their lives. They saw me as this white, middle-aged, middle-class woman and I said to them 'Don't be so sure I don't have my dark side too.'" I asked the group what they thought about G.'s response. G. interrupted, saying: "With my clients, I need to connect with them in some way." She went on to describe how she had connected with a particular client by discussing recipes and food. This she felt shifted the dynamics because they had something in common. N. told of finding commonality with a client through poetry. L. said that one could do the same thing through emphasizing the differences between client and worker. I wondered what she meant, and she said this could provide an opportunity for the clients to educate you. For example, she might have asked a client to tell her about cooking. "It gives them the chance and you a chance to demonstrate that you are listening to them and that you care."

> L. said it was hard sometimes to feel for one's client. She said she had a client who is always talking about her pain and how that annoys her. She went on: "What I wanted was for her to admit that things weren't so bad. Finally, I realized that it was my bias. She is only forty-five and she is crippled with arthritis. I had thought this could only happen to old people. What we need

to do is educate ourselves about differences. Seek information so you can understand their experiences."

N. said, "I have been dealing with a Hispanic victim of domestic violence and it seems to me that the woman is wondering if she should go back with her husband. What troubles me about this case is that the mother is sleeping in the same bed with her eleven-year-old daughter. That's not healthy." I asked her when this began. The student said it started when the battering father moved out. N. continued: "I've been trying to make her see that this is not a good thing." I said that knowing what to do was dependent upon being aware of what the dynamics of the case were. I asked if anyone wanted to speculate about that. One student said that this was a regression on the part of the child, that the child was anxious and wanted to be close to her mother. Several others agreed. A Hispanic student challenged that interpretation, saying that it was not uncommon for children to sleep in the same bed with their mothers. N. reiterated that she believed such behavior was unhealthy. The Hispanic student responded, "Since this girl is eleven, what's unhealthy?" The student passionately replied that this is the time of separation from the parent and this would block the child's psychological development.

Another area of concern among students is their relationship with their supervisor. In parallel with the process in the field seminar, students at first seek to have the supervisor define what they should do. Should the relationship become conflictual, students have a tendency to not share their work with their supervisor. As may be seen in the following, through the process of group work in the field seminar, students become more self-confident and are more able to use their supervisor effectively.

E. said she has been wondering how much to share with her supervisor. I responded, "And?" She continued, "I think I have a kind of spiritual thing with my clients, and this is hard to share with the supervisor." The student elaborated, saying, "The supervisor is so uptight about what I am doing that I am focusing on how I am fitting her expectations." M. said that her supervisor is always negative even though she knows she is doing a good job. Z. said that her supervisor tells her only that she is doing a great job, so she is not sure she can trust her. L. indicated that after listening to these comments, she felt less alone in her conflict with her supervisor and now felt more ready and capable of demanding the kind of help she should be getting.

In the middle phase there is an increased emphasis on reaching out to other group members for help. As the phase ends students begin to look more critically at their own work with a mixture of fears of failure and a growing belief in their own capacity to help. This reflects the growing professional self. These themes are reflected in the following examples:

Z. began by asking what to do about her group. She briefly described the situation and questioned whether she was doing any good. Was she giving them the information they needed? N. said she should not worry about knowing all the answers or having all the information, and wondered why she felt she had to have all the answers. The student said she felt the members in her group were depending on her. The field seminar group members reassured the student and suggested she might focus on helping the group members help one another.

M. said she had a client who continues doing the same things, making M. feel that she is a bad social worker. I asked if anyone else ever felt that way. Several answered they did. I asked the group what they thought a social worker was there for. Among the answers were, "to help people" or "to talk with them about what needs to be done." I reflected back, "What needs to be done?" One student responded, "It is not really what needs to be done. You need to give your client a chance to make choices." Another said she found she had to be patient. F. said that her agency is demanding that she help the client. She added, "They even want me to take home the client's phone number. Originally, I did it, but I'm realizing I need space to have time for myself." L. indicated she also didn't know what to do. "Both Fordham and the field have so many expectations." E. said that things were better for her since she had changed her expectations, and went on to say that she now judges herself by what she does, not the outcome.

Ending the Voyage

> Mary expressed a sentiment we all agreed on: we had been able to rely more on our relationships with one another in the here and now. We saw meaningful self-disclosures grow from abstract theoretical concepts, into living archetypes of group dynamics. When we risked sharing our thoughts, our sense of isolation decreased, our communication skills improved, and we began to help each other in noncritical, nonjudgmental ways. We had caught hold of new meanings for ourselves, meanings that were reflected in the relationships within the field integrative seminar. A student summed up her experiences this way: "I am thinking of a half circle. I have made the beginning and I'm half way there, but I have a way to go still." As the voyage came to a close and we prepared to disembark, we had found the freedom to become.

The next to last session of the field seminar is devoted to termination and is an effort to prepare students for their own termination experience. Invariably, one or more students have already had an ending experience with a client, so the student experience is used as a backdrop for the field seminar work. In these sessions students' feelings of having failed to "get more done" with the client reemerge. It is a feeling that if only they had used the perfect words, all would have been different. The group leader must avoid saying it is OK and stay with the students' pain.

Group members discuss what they found beneficial in the field seminar and, with encouragement from the instructor, what they would have liked to have done differently. An example of reaching for the negative aspect follows:

> After a discussion of the benefits of the seminar, I said, "Even in the best things there are some problems or issues, and we should talk about what should have been done differently. In that way you can help me do better in the future." After a long pause, E. responded that she would have wanted more role-plays. "More role-plays to be in the moment. To show what we could do so we can learn." Others added similar comments, and I responded, "It sounds to me as though you wanted to try out ideas here before you did them with your clients."

The final session is devoted to the seminar's own ending process. Instructors use a wide variety of methodologies for dealing with terminations. Some ask students to suggest metaphors that represent the work in the field seminar. This technique has often been both illuminating and reflective. In this last session the theme of loss is pervasive and many students speak movingly about losses in their own lives and in their professional lives. Students also ponder how much they still need to learn to be a professional social worker.

My image is of thunderstorms hitting and then it all goes away. All of the things that were going on with me this year. But being here has helped me get what I need. I still feel incomplete, but I can move on.

CONCLUDING COMMENTS

Over the years there has been a parallelism in the issues raised for discussion in the seminars. Field seminars initially deal with the fears students have as they enter unfamiliar communities to do unfamiliar tasks. Even for students with social work experience, there is a new and different way of relating to colleagues. Many discuss their struggle to change from a role defined by paperwork to that of a professional ready to take personal responsibility for the work. A familiar struggle for both beginners and those with previous experience is letting the client be responsible for the work. This struggle is parallel to students' movement in the seminar from looking to the instructor for advice to drawing on their own insights and experiences in practice with clients.

Essential to mutual aid is that the work connects to students' concept of reality. Mutual aid groups are ideal for this since they work on the intersection between the personal, the group, and the larger environment (Schwartz, 1971). For a mutual aid group to exist, it is not enough to just be in a room together. A skilled leader is needed to help the group develop a clear sense of common purpose, in this case the students' desire to become professional social workers. As group members feel their common struggles are being addressed, they can share their deepest concerns and reach out for and provide support and advice to others.

A second common area of concern is that of safety, in the development of a safe climate. This is essential to students' readiness to explore the more complex issues such as diversity. Students are able to acknowledge how their own values impact upon their work; they challenge each other to look with a critical eye at their own work. As with all groups, movement is not always linear, but these seminars do reach a middle phase in which storms can precede a stage of maturity and solid work. It is easy to allow such field-integration seminar groups to deteriorate into gripe sessions. The instructor must put out a demand for work. When one demands movement toward confronting unsaid issues and exploring solutions, the real work of the group begins. This sometimes painful process both models practice and stimulates the work of the group.

Over time students learn not to accept the actions of the instructor uncritically, rather they incorporate those behaviors they can use in their work. In this process they come to see that there are many ways of achieving a given end. They recognize the need to develop their own personal professional style for which they will be responsible. This process is better done in a group where a range of viewpoints is reflected. Toward the end, students undertake an appraisal of what they know and what they have yet to learn. This dual realization is essential to the development of the professional social worker. Endings are characterized by movement away from the group, since termination generally signals a graduation into a higher level of practice.

The groups described here are not dependent upon a particular organizational structure, rather they are dependent on an instructor's willingness to guide rather than control the classroom process and a willingness to look at students from a strength perspective, recognizing their capacity to provide a learning environment for one another. Armed with this faith in the students' capacity for self-organization, one can focus upon, in Schwartz's words: "helping group members define where they need to dig, providing them with tools with which to dig, but calling upon them to do the digging" (Schwartz, 1978, personal communication). Although group members will initially respond with resistance, expecting the professor to provide specific advice, the desire to take control of their own destiny will lead them to use one another rather than the professor as the sounding board for learning. In that process, the field seminar experience brings together abstract and reality. The experiences described demonstrate how the field seminar conducted as a mutual aid group can link the struggle of individual students to the collective purpose of becoming a social work professional.

REFERENCES

Birnbaum, M. (1984). The integration of didactic and experiential learning in the teaching of group work. *Journal of Education for Social Work, 20*(1), 50-58.

Gitterman, A. (1989). Building mutual support in groups. *Social Work with Groups, 12*(2), 5-2.

Grossbard, H. (1954). Methodology for developing self-awareness. *Social Casework, 35*(9), 380-386.

Hirayama, H. and Hirayama, K. (1986). Empowerment through group participation: Process and goal. In M. Parnes (Ed.), *Innovations in social group work: Feedback from practice to theory; Proceedings of the annual group work symposium* (pp. 119-132). New York, London: The Haworth Press.

Kurland, R. (1978). Planning: The neglected component of group development. *Social Work with Groups, 1*(2), 173-178.

Lewis, P.J. (1988). Utilization of andragological principles in a bachelor of social work program. Doctoral dissertation, Hunter College of the City University of New York.

Lynn, M. (2000). Student perceptions of faculty advisement through the integrative seminar. Doctoral dissertation, New York University.

Mary, N.L. and Herse, M.H. (1992). What do field seminars accomplish? Student and instructor perspectives. *Journal of Teaching in Social Work, 6*(2), 59-73.

Olmstead, M.S. (1959). *The small group.* New York: Random House.

Phillips, H.U. (1954). *Essentials of social group work skill.* New York: Association Press.

Richmond, M.E. (1922). *What is social case work? An introductory description.* New York: Russell Sage Foundation.

Schwartz, W. (1971). On the use of groups in social work practice. In William Schwartz and Serapio R. Zalba (Eds.), *The practice of group work* (pp. 3-24). New York and London: Columbia University Press.

Schwartz, W. (1978). Personal communication.

Siporin, M. (1982). The process of field instruction. In B.W. Sheafor and L.E. Jenkins (Eds.), *Quality field instruction in social work* (pp. 175-197). New York: Longman Press.

Chapter 17

Justice in Teaching: Teaching As Group Work

Mari Ann Graham

Education in the United States has traditionally been an individual matter. That is, individuals receive individual grades for their individual efforts and achievements. Individuals are admitted to institutions of higher learning because their individual test scores and academic histories justify their acceptance. Individual mastery of content has been the hallmark of a good education.

Paradoxically, education is delivered in a group context: the classroom. With the exception of the occasional group project or use of small groups in the classroom, teachers treat the classroom as a collection of individuals. A lecture is delivered to a group of students with little attention to group process. Even when discussion is permitted or encouraged, the goal is that such discussion facilitate individual learning. Group dynamics and process from this perspective are peripheral to what is taught and learned.

The constructivist paradigm of teaching and learning offers the possibility of resolving this incongruence. It makes group process central rather than peripheral. The teacher is a facilitator of a constructivist process rather than an expert who disseminates information to individuals. In this context, the classroom is a dynamic group and teaching is a form of group work.

Many social work educators, although interested or committed to group work, do not know how to teach from this orientation. "Grounded discussion" is a teaching tool developed in response to this need. This teaching method is described in the latter half of this chapter. But first, a discussion of the constructivist paradigm of teaching and learning and a rationale for why this paradigm of teaching is particularly relevant to social work education is offered.

CONSTRUCTIVIST PARADIGM
OF TEACHING AND LEARNING

As Fosnot (1996) observes, constructivism is not a theory of teaching. It is a nonpositivist theory of knowledge and learning. It attempts to describe what knowing is and how one comes to know. Based on work in psychology, philosophy, and anthropology, constructivists describe knowledge as temporary, developmental in nature, nonobjective, internally constructed, and socially and culturally mediated. Even though constructivism is not a theory of teaching per se, it does suggest radically different teaching methods or interventions.

First, knowledge or "facts" cannot be passed on or transmitted to students. According to this paradigm, objective reality does not exist. There are no objective "facts" that must be "covered" by the teacher and transmitted to students. Moreover, facts cannot be specified in advance or known by the teacher in advance. Even if objective facts did exist, they could not be transferred to learners because according to this paradigm, students cannot incorporate the teacher's knowledge as their own. Instead, what exists (for both teachers and learners) are multiple, subjective constructions of reality that are socially and experientially based. Teachers, therefore, are not expert disseminators of information; they are catalysts in a constructivist process. Learners construct their view of reality and their choices in relation to it, and examine their value judgments and the political implications of their choices in relation to it, *as do teachers*. Both teachers and learners are engaged in a process of mutual discovery.

The aim of this sort of education is to help students more consciously and deliberately construct their realities around particular topics or issues. The role of the teacher is simply to facilitate this constructivist process (Graham, 1997). Dialogue or discussion in this paradigm is a means of creating a constructivist process. Student-centered discussions along with interactive media, music, drama, and literature are all used to assist students in the creations and re-creations of their own realities. Constructivism hinges on attention to perceptual differences and differences in frames of reference. Both students and teachers construct their own meanings within their own contexts. They cannot do otherwise, by definition.

RATIONALE FOR CONSTRUCTIVIST TEACHING
METHODS IN SOCIAL WORK EDUCATION

There are a number of critiques suggesting that *how* we teach *what* we teach in social work education is often incongruent (Brigham, 1977; Dore, 1993; Weick, 1993, 1997; Graham, 1997). Specifically, there are incongruences related to the profession's emphasis on:

- The strengths perspective
- Responsiveness to the needs of diverse and at-risk populations
- Authenticity
- The centrality of values and ethics

These incongruences represent issues of social and economic justice in the classroom for which the constructivist paradigm of teaching and learning potentially offers liberation.

The strengths perspective applied to teaching would suggest that teaching needs to build on client (student) strengths rather than unduly emphasize student deficits. Just as practitioners who emphasize their expert status and authority relative to clients are in danger of reinforcing "problem-saturated perceptions" (or other feelings of inadequacy), teachers who strictly adhere to an expert model of teaching run the risk of undermining student empowerment by subtly reinforcing student perceptions of inadequacy. Even when students complete a course and get satisfactory grades, feelings of incompetence may persist due to the subtle impact that this paradigm has on the student's sense of self. A constructivist teaching approach, on the other hand, makes every student a cocreator of knowledge since all knowledge is held to be temporary, developmental in nature, nonobjective, internally constructed, and socially and culturally mediated. The aim of this sort of education is to help students more consciously and deliberately construct their realities around particular topics, issues, or methods of practice. The constructivist teacher understands that students are also experts and assists students in discovering what they already know.

In an edited collection of works on this topic, Saleeby (1992) concludes that human service professions have generally developed a language that "sickens and does not heal," and that this affects not only clients but practitioners as well. He notes that practitioners can hardly be about the business of empowering their clients if they themselves feel weak or alienated from their work via the dominant paradigm in the workplace. The same may be said of social work education and the learning environment. If educational strategies are organized around assumptions that presume deficits in students (chiefly their ignorance and its many forms), how can educators escape the subtle, disempowering implications of this paradigm with respect to their teaching?

Although the Council on Social Work Education mandates that accredited programs demonstrate compliance with nondiscriminatory policies and affirmative action guidelines, this standard is not necessarily demonstrated in the ways teachers relate to diverse and at-risk students. Although some efforts are being made to become more inclusive in this regard, traditional pedagogy often fails to recognize or validate experiences, knowledge, skills, and learning styles that are considered marginal by traditional academic standards. These student voices and experiences become institutionally marginalized despite intentions to make the classroom more just. Students, regardless of their background or experience, are expected to receive educational "transfers of information" in whatever form they are presented and demonstrate their understanding according to standards set in advance by the teacher.

The constructivist orientation, with its rejection of "objective facts" and its emphasis on social constructions of reality, offers a lens through which diverse perspectives may be seen and experienced. It does not take away the conflicts that are created; it legitimizes them while offering a perspective that is large enough to hold the various points of view in creative tension. A constructivist perspective can level the playing field among students and between teachers and students. That is, privileged experiences are not automatically valued more than marginal ones. Both have a place and are important in this context. This orientation is especially important at a time when even social work educators who are committed to responding to the needs of diverse and at-risk populations have difficulty knowing how to respond to diverse and at-risk students because academic institutions are still organized around positivist assumptions of teaching and learning.

Vodde and Gallant (1995) point out that traditional pedagogy fosters the suppression of "student-lived experience" in favor of learning the facts. This, they point out, leads to a lack of integration of personal experience, which in turn results in a loss of authenticity. For students who learn this way, the process of necessity becomes technical and mechanical. The emphasis is on saying and doing certain things that are considered professional and appropriate. But students need to be concerned not only with doing; they also need to be concerned with being—being who they are so that they can be fully present with clients. Merely talking about concepts such as these without integrating them into one's lived experience creates even higher levels of anxiety in students who become excessively preoccupied with getting it right (Vodde and Gallant, 1995). This ability to be is difficult to quantify or measure. The constructivist paradigm offers a complementary way of seeing that has the potential for elucidating nonquantifiable concepts such as personal authenticity.

Allen (1993) draws attention to the irony that although the social work profession is value-based and value-driven, social work educators continue to teach students in ways that obscure the centrality of values relative to actual practice. She notes that from the traditional perspective, the only ethical stance for a clinician is that of a "value-free, objective expert." Constructivism, on the other hand, rejects the notion of objectivity and suggests instead that the ethical stance is one of "responsible participation." She goes on to note that clinical social workers have an ethical mandate to "acknowledge their active participation in creating images of their clients, their problems and their possibilities for change" (p. 32). Yet in traditional classrooms this kind of process is seldom reflected to allow students to have the opportunity to experience it for themselves.

Social work educators talk "about" the importance of values and ethics, and the teaching methods themselves obscure the primacy of values with respect to actual practice. Values are treated "objectively"—here they are; know them; memorize them. Precisely *how* values impact perceptions, assessments, and intervention strategies, and how students might become more conscious of this process, is often left unattended. What appears important is that students learn the values of the profession and somehow demonstrate that knowledge. The constructivist paradigm, on the other hand, assumes no transfer, but rather requires that students examine the biases of all theory presented including their program's biases, biases of the profession, and their own personal biases. Allen (1993) notes that this may be the most demanding challenge of the constructivist paradigm with respect to social work education, and Weick (1997) notes that a constructivist approach to teaching and learning "allows us to think about values in a new way" (personal communication).

The preceding discussion illustrates the need for teaching practices that affirm student strengths, are sensitive to the needs of diverse and at-risk students, underscores the critical importance of authenticity, and demonstrates the primacy of values and ethics. Although the need for constructivist approaches to teaching has been acknowledged with respect to these issues (Laird, 1993), there have been relatively few methods and/or techniques articulated that can be used across the social work curriculum. This is where grounded discussion comes in.

GROUNDED DISCUSSION

Grounded discussion is a process in which teacher and students attempt to construct their realities around a particular topic or content area. The discussion is "grounded" because:

- the facilitator presents a question that is grounded in his or her lived experience with the subject;
- students ground their understanding of the topic in their lived experience with the subject;
- the process makes possible a grounded understanding of the topic that is seen as a requisite to making evaluations or judgments that would otherwise be premature or superficial; and
- grounded understanding is seen as integral to the person in contrast to knowledge that is outside the person.

Grounded discussion is a student-centered discussion that takes on a life of its own. In order for this to occur, both students and facilitators need to be authentically present. Particular attention is given to helping facilitators show up in this way since they are typically trained to be in charge and have answers, both of which often create obstacles to their capacity to be fully present with students and limit student capacity to be present.

There are a number of preparatory steps as well as steps in facilitating the discussion. These are graphically depicted in Figure 17.1.

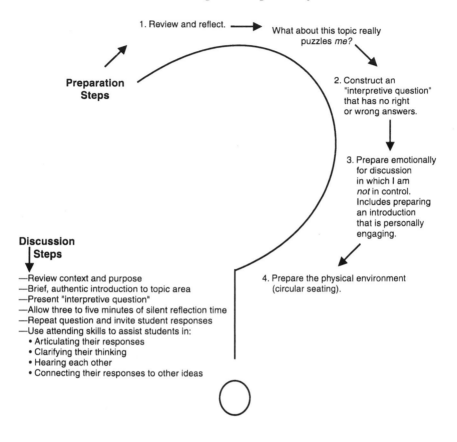

FIGURE 17.1. Implementing Grounded Discussion

Preparing for Grounded Discussions

Grounded discussions require a different kind of teacher preparation. Traditional preparation would involve the teacher identifying important ideas to be covered during the discussion, perhaps identifying strategies for making sure that the key points are brought out and convincingly relayed to students. This is consistent with the expert role, and from this perspective discussion is simply another tool or means of assuming that role. The teacher's task would be to guide the discussion based on his or her or judgment as to what needs to be covered. This type of discussion and preparation might be referred to as a content-driven process based on the expertise of the teacher.

A discussion from a constructivist paradigm, however, needs to be more process driven in order to be congruent with constructivist principles that deny the existence of objective facts and that hold as central the meaning-making processes of students. It is the process of constructing meaning, becoming aware of one's own constructivist processes as well as the processes of others, that is central to grounded discussion. Therefore, a different kind of preparation is required, one that attends to the necessary elements of a constructivist process rather than particular content.

The first step in preparing to facilitate a constructivist discussion is careful review and reflection related to the content to be discussed. This content includes not only required readings, but any other medium of expression that speaks to facilitator's understanding and experience of the content. Things such as film clips (previewed by the instructor in advance), practice scenarios, process recordings, songs, or poetry are all examples of various forms of expression that contain constructions of reality that are relevant to the content under review. The purpose of this reflection is *not* to make judgments about what is most important from the teacher's perspective. Similarly, the purpose is *not* to figure out the correct interpretation of the expression, identify what is true about it, or otherwise evaluate it. The purpose of this review and reflection is to identify areas or issues that provoke questions for which no clear-cut answers are apparent. In short, the facilitator seeks to answer the question, What about this topic really puzzles *me*? These areas of genuine uncertainty with respect to the topic represent a measure of the facilitator's vulnerability with respect to the subject. This vulnerability on the part of the instructor is critical to the process because it makes possible a dialogue with students based on mutuality.[1]

Once the facilitator has identified areas of genuine uncertainty, he or she is ready to proceed to the second step of preparation—construction of an interpretive question. An interpretive question is a question that does not have a right or wrong answer. Posing a question that does not have a right or wrong answer makes it possible for the instructor to authentically inquire about the subject and model a search for truth.[2] Authentic inquiry on the part of the instructor and the accompanying vulnerability prevents the instructor from squelching the discovery process by conscious or unconscious attempts to control the discussion. It also gives students permission to explore their own "lived experience" of the material.

The third step of preparation has to do with the psychological and emotional readiness of the facilitator. This preparation is concerned with preparing the instructor for some loss of control. Since the instructor needs to be willing to let the discussion take on a life of its own, some mental and emotional preparation is necessary. This involves different things for different people and is highly dependent upon the level of instructor self-awareness. For some it might mean writing out the question or issue and the reasons it was selected, reviewing it several times before the discussion, and doing some relaxation prior to meeting with students. Still others might need to meditate, pray, or take a walk as a way of grounding themselves in the issue and preparing themselves for an experience of vulnerability and relinquishing control. The important thing is that the facilitator gives deliberate attention to preparing himself or herself for the process, and then does whatever he or she needs to do to maximize his or her capacity to be fully present during the discussion.

This emotional and psychological preparation also involves preparing an introduction to the topic that is authentic and personally engaging. This introduction is brief, three to five minutes, and is intended to ground the facilitator, i.e., establish his or her connection to the content, as well as provide an opportunity for students to experience the facilitator as a person. This brief, heartfelt introduction models the process of grounding that students will hopefully experience during the discussion. Examples of introductions might include telling a personal story, reading a poem, playing a clip from a video, or whatever expresses the affective as well as cognitive dimension of the topic for the instructor.

The fourth and final step in preparation involves preparing the physical environment. Circular seating should be arranged prior to the discussion. The room should be a comfortable temperature and distractions should be minimized.

Facilitating the Discussion

The first step in facilitating the discussion is reviewing the context surrounding the discussion (e.g., what the assigned reading is for the day, topic(s) for the day, and the purpose of the discussion). The purpose is presented in the facilitator's own words and includes some general reference to the importance of integrating student experience with the topic, i.e., making it "real."

The second step of facilitating the discussion is a brief, authentic introduction to the topic area. This step requires that the facilitator introduce the topic of discussion in a heartfelt way, i.e., a way that exposes some vulnerability with respect to the topic, some sense of why the instructor believes the topic is important. As already noted in the preparatory section, this introduction is intended to be brief, and serves the purpose of grounding the facilitator, revealing the authenticity of the facilitator to the students, modeling the willingness to be vulnerable in the group, and engaging both students and facilitator in the process.

The third step of facilitating the discussion is the presentation of the basic interpretive question. The facilitator says something such as, "I'd like to begin the process by sharing with you something that puzzles me about the reading/topic. I'd really like to get your thoughts on this. I want to give you a few minutes of silent reflection time to jot down any thoughts and ideas you have, as well as organize your thoughts before we begin. Here's the question." It is important that the facilitator communicate that the question does not have a right or wrong answer. The facilitator then presents the basic interpretive question, which may be stated orally, written on a blackboard or a flip chart, and/or transmitted on an overhead projector.

The fourth step of facilitating the discussion is silent reflection time. The facilitator instructs the students that they will have three to five minutes to reflect on the question/issue before the discussion begins. The facilitator encourages students to write their responses on paper (for their own reference only) as a way of organizing their thoughts. The facilitator then allows three to five minutes of silent reflection.

The final step of facilitating the discussion involves a number of facilitative behaviors that are important to the life of the discussion. When students appear ready, the facilitator repeats the interpretive question and invites students to share their responses. As students share their ideas, the facilitator uses basic group-process skills to help students do the following four things:

1. articulate their responses (identify them; draw them out)
2. clarify their thinking (their logic, assumptions, inferences)

3. hear each other (listen carefully to other student responses)
4. connect their responses (make linkages between their responses and the question as well as to the text and other student responses)

The group process skills used to achieve these four purposes cannot be arranged chronologically because they are dependent on the nature of student responses to the question and the facilitator's intuitive sense of what is most important to do at that point in the discussion. As facilitator of this classroom group, he or she does the following things:

1. Conveys interest in student responses via basic attending skills
2. Restates or paraphrases student responses *only* to assist students in clarifying their thoughts or to make certain that students are physically able to hear what each other is saying[3]
3. Connects student responses back to the basic question
4. Connects student responses to other student responses
5. Encourages students to give examples from their own experience of what they are talking about
6. Encourages students to connect their responses to the text and to other student responses
7. Does *not* try to control or direct the discussion; goes with the flow; offers his or her perspective only when asked so as not to dominate the discussion
8. Allows the process to take on a life of its own; stays with one question until there is a sense that students are finished with it before moving on to other questions or issues
9. Identifies themes, recaps or summarizes the discussion

As a coinquirer and collaborator in the process, it is also important that the facilitator authentically respond and spontaneously react to the process. Care must be taken, however, that the facilitator does not dominate or control the discussion with his or her point of view. Facilitators are instructed to consider that they are simultaneously facilitating the discussion, and also modeling member behavior.

RESULTS

Grounded discussion achieves a number of educational outcomes and procedural objectives. Research data (Graham, 1999) suggest that it helps both students and faculty experience the subject as "alive" and "cocreated," fosters fairly high levels of student engagement, moderately high levels of student-to-student interaction, and is perceived by students and faculty as being congruent with social work practice. It helps students experience and appreciate the complexity of a topic, increases awareness of values including the impact that values have on perceptions and judgments, and increases awareness that perceptions of reality are grounded in personal experience. This method helps both students and educators connect course content with their own experience and integrate knowledge as opposed to acquiring it as an external commodity.

Unanticipated benefits include the perception from both faculty and students that retention of content is significantly improved and the ways that students report being personally affirmed and stimulated by the process. Challenges associated with this method include teacher ambivalence in giving up the leadership role, boundary issues between students and teachers, and how often this method can or should be used given current expectations in academic institutions.

Students identified a couple of different types of affirmations or validations that they received from this method of discussion. They noted that grounded discussion "helps you realize how much you know." This sense of having what they already knew "pulled out of them" and becoming more conscious of what they already knew seemed important to them. They reported that what they did not know about the topic was offset or balanced by what they discovered that they did know. Another type of validation articulated by students has to do with the building of ideas. As one student put it,

> When I think of something and then someone else builds on the idea and takes it in a different direction, I don't know what it is that happens, but it's a really powerful experience.

And from another student,

> You feel validated and you feel alive, like all of a sudden, you're part of the creation, not just here for somebody to dump a bunch of stuff in your lap.

Both students and facilitators reiterated their perceptions that these kinds of discussions appear to be more memorable. That is, content is more likely to be retained over a period of time. As one student noted,

> I have to come back to the retention thing. I have a problem with my memory [laughter]. I'm serious. And when I read something I have to read it over and over. If I read it and then something like this took place after the reading versus a lecture where you're just taking notes, I think that would help a lot for the retention of material.

CONCLUSION

Grounded discussion is a particular type of discussion that is grounded in a constructivist theory of knowing. Both instructor and students participate in the cocreation of knowledge and become grounded in a topic area. Grounded discussion makes group process central to learning rather than peripheral to it. The facilitator prepares for the discussion in a different way and facilitates a discussion around an interpretive question using group-process skills. As a form of group work, this teaching method achieves a number of educational outcomes and procedural objectives consistent with social justice principles and social work practice.

NOTES

1. Mutuality is not possible if one person is more vulnerable than the other. A client (or a student) that begins from a position of vulnerability due to a problem (or presumed ignorance) cannot engage in a mutual relationship with a social worker (or teacher) who has the answer. Such a relationship is inherently unequal. Although not necessarily bad, this inequality sets up issues of power and control, which both persons can reinforce in the other, and which often impedes the free-flow of expression from the person of lesser power. If the person of greater power chooses to operate from a position of real (not contrived) vulnerability, mutual relating, although not guaranteed, is at least theoretically possible.

2. Truth here refers to the subjective rather than the objective connotation of the word, i.e., truth that is grounded in his or her lived experience.

3. Overuse of paraphrasing or summarizing runs the risk of putting words in their mouths, appearing to interpret or otherwise evaluate student responses, which is considered an inhibitory influence at this point in this process.

REFERENCES

Allen, J.A. (1993). The constructivist paradigm: Values and ethics. *Journal of Teaching in Social Work, 8*(1/2), 31-55.

Brigham, T. (1977). Liberation in social work education: Applications from Paulo Friere. *Journal of Education for Social Work, 13*(3), 5-11.

Dore, M. (1993). The practice-teaching parallel in educating the micropractitioner. *Social Work, 29*(2), 181-190.

Fosnot, C. (Ed.) (1996). *Constructivism: Theory, perspectives and practice.* New York: Teachers College Press.

Graham, M. (1997). Alternative paradigms for teaching and learning. *Journal of Teaching in Social Work, 15*(1/2), 33-49.

Graham, M. (1999). *Design and development of "grounded discussion."* Published dissertation, Mandel School of Social Sciences, Case Western Reserve University.

Laird, J. (Ed.) (1993). *Revisioning social work education: A social constructionist approach.* Binghamton, NY: The Haworth Press.

Saleeby, D. (Ed.) (1992). *The strengths perspective in social work practice.* New York: Longman.

Vodde, R. and Gallant, J. (1995). Skill training as a facet of self-exploration: A qualitative study of teaching social work methods from a postmodern perspective. *Journal of Teaching in Social Work, 11*(1/2), 119-137.

Weick, A. (1993). Reconstructing social work education. *Journal of Teaching in Social Work, 8*(1/2), 11-30.

Weick, A. (1997). Personal communication with the author, November 26.

Chapter 18

Participant Perceptions of Online Group Work with Fathers of Children with Spina Bifida

David B. Nicholas

INTRODUCTION

This chapter identifies participants' perceptions of an online group specifically for fathers of children with spina bifida. Fathers participated in an electronic mail-based group in which group dialogue was conveyed through e-mail messages posted to the entire group. A sample of participants was subsequently interviewed about their perceptions both of the impact of the group and the technology/online format used by the group. This chapter presents interview findings and implications regarding online groups for fathers (for a brief overview, see Nicholas et al., 2001).

BACKGROUND

Online group work specifically for fathers has received limited research attention. Moreover, evaluation of programs for fathers of children with spina bifida has appeared to remain largely unaddressed. Bergofsky and colleagues (1979) are early contributors to this area of

The author wishes to acknowledge the participation and contribution of the following people to the development of this chapter: Gert Montgomery, Christine Stapleford, Ted McNeill, Michelle McClure, and Roger Smith. Also, the author acknowledges project funding from KidsAction Research and is appreciative of the contribution of research assistants Julie Thompson and David Brownstone.

substantive inquiry by outlining the impact of a therapy group for individuals with spina bifida and their families. Clark (1986) later documents the development of collectivities and networks for families. Reported achievements of these entities are described as "bring(ing) families together in an atmosphere that encourages mutual aid" (Clark, 1986, p. 105). Specific objectives attained in these entities include: "altering the environment; information and feedback; providing emotional support; and enhancing competency" (Clark, 1986, p. 106). Clearly, the support and mutual aid offered were experienced as beneficial to families affected by spina bifida (Clark, 1986).

Palm (1997) discusses fathering issues in parent and family education practice including group support (not specifically related to spina bifida). He asserts the value of father-oriented programs and comments that, "the developmental emphasis in PFE [parent and family education] emphasizes the importance of growing into good fathers and outlines some typical and predictable patterns of change" (Palm, 1993; Palm, 1997, p. 170). Potential differences in education and support programs for mothers and fathers reportedly reflect different aims and needs. Of this Palm (1997) comments,

> Although the content and the goals for PFE [parent and family education] may seem to be the same for mothers and fathers, parents of both genders come to parenting from different backgrounds and may have different needs and goals. (p. 173)

Although group work with fathers is advocated (Stein, 1983), inherent problems of face-to-face groups are identified (see Weinberg et al., 1995). Drawing on Palm's (1997) discussion of father-based education and support, groups may be adapted to better address unique needs of fathers. Such adaptations may include implementing preferred styles of communication and content that is of greater relevance for fathers. As an example, relative to mothers, some fathers may have less comfort with the open expression of experiential feelings or affect (Palm, 1997). Accordingly, opportunity to discuss issues and concrete concerns rather than focusing too quickly on "how it feels" may offer greater resonance and utility for some fathers.

Structural and contextual factors in orchestrating a group may also impose barriers for fathers. For instance, the potential accessibility and utility of face-to-face groups may be impeded by factors, such as extended geographic distances (Clark, 1986; Galinsky, Schopler, and

Abell, 1997; Weinberg et al., 1995); transportation challenges (Galinsky, Schopler, and Abell, 1997; Weinberg et al., 1995); stigma (Galinsky, Schopler, and Abell, 1997); and limits on available time for a scheduled group (Clark, 1986; Galinsky, Schopler, and Abell, 1997; Weinberg et al., 1995).

As an alternative, group work offered via online technology may increase the potential for fathers to participate in and benefit from such interventions. Galinsky, Schopler, and Abell (1997) assert that a primary contribution of technology for group facilitation is increased accessibility and convenience for group members. For instance, electronic-mail postings can be composed and read at the convenience (i.e., time and place) of group members (see also Finn, 1995; Weinberg et al., 1995). Also, greater anonymity is reported, resulting in online group participants potentially being able to more quickly identify sensitive issues that might be perceived as too embarrassing to divulge within face-to-face groups (Finn, 1995; Galinsky, Schopler, and Abell, 1997; Weinberg et al., 1995).

In seeking to accommodate unique needs and issues of fathers, in this case fathers of children with spina bifida, an online group was identified as potentially promising. Such a forum for father-based groupwork was viewed as a nonthreatening and accessible environment that simultaneously permitted, as desired by individual fathers, sharing of concerns, issues, experiences, and potential solutions.

THE GROUP

An online e-mail group for fathers of children with spina bifida was initiated in which a total of twenty-five participants were enrolled. Potential participants were drawn from databases of fathers of persons with spina bifida who receive treatment or follow-up in a central Canadian province. They were introduced to the group by receiving a mailed letter describing the online group and inviting their participation.

Upon informed consent and a group registration process, participants were placed on an e-mail list of group members and each were invited to post and review messages. The group comprised only e-mail-based interaction, hence, a chatroom or real-time discussion did not occur. If needed by potential participants, used computers and appropriate software were provided. The group was led by an MSW social worker who monitored group process and intervened as needed (e.g., moderated in extended moments of group silence, sensitively drew out "quiet" members, encouraged further discussion as needed). The group facilitator also assisted with technology questions, concerns, and problems. The online network for the group was hosted by a nationally acclaimed computer messaging network, Ability Online.

Within the group, participating fathers were invited to identify and address issues related to their child's condition and, in particular, its impact upon them, their child, and their family. Moreover, fathers could discuss whatever was of individual and/or mutual interest.

Group participants consisted of fathers whose home locales were geographically scattered. They each had a child with spina bifida who ranged in age from infancy to eighteen years (with the exception of one participant whose child exceeded eighteen years of age). Most participants' children with spina bifida were of latency age and the mean age of children was nine years.

The extent of fathers' participation in the group varied, based on number of posts to the group (e-mail messages relayed by an individual participant). Fathers discussed issues of mutual concern related to fathering a child with spina bifida and the impact of the condition in the context of family life. They shared stories, engaged in humor, and gave and received advice and support. They conveyed to one another their struggles and challenges as well as blessings that were a part of their lives as fathers of persons with spina bifida.

PARTICIPANT INTERVIEWS

A purposive sample of $N = 10$ group members participated in in-depth interviews that addressed perceptions and experiences of the group. Variation in group involvement (number of posts on the online group) was sought in interviewee selection. The age of interviewed participants' children ranged from toddlers to young adults.

With the exception of one interview in which consent for recording was not given, interviews were audiorecorded and transcribed verbatim. Interviews were conducted by a research assistant who was familiar with "long interview" qualitative research data collection and analysis (McCracken, 1988). Interview duration ranged from thirty minutes to two-and-a-half hours. Verbatim interview transcripts were content analyzed by three reviewers who analyzed the transcripts for codes, categories, and themes. Reviewers met to identify and contrast findings in seeking consensus about emergent themes. Peer debriefing occurred with "expert" personnel and participant-represented member checking was conducted ("trustworthiness" criteria outlined in Lincoln and Guba, 1985).

FINDINGS

Interviewed fathers commented on the experience of participating in the online group. Findings included both *perceived benefits* and *perceived challenges* or *considerations* of the online group (see also Nicholas et al. [2001] for a brief and preliminary overview of these findings). Within the broader classification of benefits and challenges or considerations, more specific themes emerged as outlined:

Perceived benefits

1. Information
2. Support
3. A sense of anonymity/privacy
4. Convenience

Perceived challenges or considerations

5. Varying interest/involvement according to topic areas
6. Difficulty with hardware/software
7. Difficulty keeping track of participants and remembering "who's who"
8. Time constraints

Each of these themes is discussed along with verbatim quotes from participant interviews.

Perceived Benefits

Theme 1: Information

Although several fathers did not perceive the group to have necessarily influenced or altered how they viewed or related to their family, some fathers felt that participation in the group was beneficial in terms of increased *knowledge, awareness,* and/or *insight.* A few fathers felt that the group had positively affected how they viewed their child's situation. Several fathers described, in differing degrees, that participation in the group had informed them of different and/or helpful strategies. Most fathers appreciated the information conveyed, as illustrated below.

> "We could help each other with how (a problem or issue) had been encountered in our own situation. . . . Everybody gave how it worked or didn't work, or the things that they tried and that didn't work with their own child."

> " . . . it gave me some ideas to question (health care professionals) about how they were doing it, and if they were using this technique or this consideration. It helped me to pose a little more knowledgeable questions to the doctors, instead of just standing there and shaking my head, 'yes, yes, okay.' "

> "The other real benefit I guess is the comfort in knowing that I am getting more knowledgeable in the condition—and what might be there and what might be up the road ahead. And I guess also to just spend some time thinking about it instead of only dealing with it at home with the day-to-day duties. You are actually getting more into the abstract and what might be an education. I find that enjoyable and feel a little more useful."

Theme 2: Support

Along with information, a sense of support was often noted in hearing and sharing experiences. Accordingly, group dialogue often comprised not only *information sharing,* but apparently in the process, a sense of *acceptance, understanding,* and *emotional support.* This is illustrated in the following fathers' comments.

"Getting information . . . and there is also the support from sharing problems [support]. I guess it is information, but it is also nice to talk to somebody else who has the same problem you do, and to share some of your personal experiences."

"I find it beneficial to share the experiences and to see how other people cope with them."

"Dad's able to talk about the *realities,* not just the medical issues from a doctor's perspective."

A few participating fathers commented that the group seemed to decrease isolation or loneliness, as illustrated below.

"Sometimes it is pretty tough to read about some of the problems that the other kids went through, [and] their parents. I have, I guess, a little less loneliness in respect to what makes us different from other families."

"What seems to be a common experience is unless you have a kid or close relative with heavy-duty problems, the other people just really don't understand."

"I don't get out much because of the family and work and things like that. . . . So making new friends and socializing, it was actually really helpful."

Although fathers differed in their perceived sense of camaraderie with the other participants, most seemed to appreciate and respect the comments and experiences of other fathers. For some the opportunity to, as one father remarked, "talk to somebody who has gone through the same stuff," seemed important and helpful:

"It is one thing to talk to a social worker and it is another thing just to talk to somebody who has gone through the same stuff. It is a lot easier to talk to them and say this is my experience and what was your experience, and then try to find the common strings in there. That kind of bonded together, you know, made a few friends online."

"And just the amount of information was tremendous. Learning from different people's experiences, and getting to talk to other people and say OK, well this is what can be expected or this is what could have happened. Just sit there and say at least we know that somebody else is going through it, and how they dealt with it and things that they did, and it really helped. It was really good."

" . . . to see what kind of problems other people went through, and see if I went through the same thing. You know, just to see what was going on in other peoples' lives. It was pretty interesting."

Theme 3: A Sense of Anonymity/Privacy

The online network encouraged the expression of fathers' experiences and perceptions. Some felt that computer technology allowed them a place to "independently ponder" and write thoughtful considerations about their experiences. For some fathers, this perhaps more "open expression" was thought to be encouraged in the perceived "privacy" of being "alone" rather than in a face-to-face forum. This perception of anonymity and openness is exemplified in the following.

"You were sort of anonymous, if you will. You were sort of anonymous in the sense that you could reveal as much as you wanted or as little as you wanted. . . . I saw stuff . . . there that I do not think we would talk about face to face."

"I think it has a lot to do with anonymity. . . . And you can just let it all out and they can respond back without any repercussion. Most people have a hard time talking face to face with somebody. . . . I think that helped out quite a bit for a lot of people."

"It was just a little more of a freedom, I guess, to say some stuff you maybe not have said in person."

Theme 4: Convenience

Fathers often commented about the convenience that was offered by the online group. From the perspective of several fathers, participation in a support group would not have been possible without the convenience offered through online capacities. Accordingly, fathers appreciated being able to participate (i.e., "log on") from their home or workplace at times that they chose. The following quotes illustrate this appreciation for the convenience and accessibility of the online group.

"It is a nice comfortable place. . . . There is nothing like sitting in your own home and reading it (online group comments) when you want. It is not like having to go out, or make arrangements for somebody to come and visit, or that type of thing. You can just pick it up and do it when you want, and sign off when you want. Any time of day or night."

"You do not have to wait on anybody or schedule with anyone. Just go ahead and do."

"By being able to do that in the comfort of my own home at whatever hour I chose, that is why it was the medium of choice . . . . It was convenience with a capital C."

Perceived Challenges or Considerations

Theme 5: Varying Interest/Involvement According to Topic Areas

Although fathers expressed finding common experiences with other participants based on their children's condition (e.g., "Nobody knows who you are but they know that you are a person who has had the same experience . . ."), they also presented in online dialogue a variety of issues that were particular to their own unique situation. For instance, their children's ages widely varied, hence there was an array of diverse developmental issues and age-related concerns. Also, some medical issues were more or less relevant for various fathers. Several fathers stated that their interest in a specific discussion over a period of time varied according to the topic/issue. For instance, when the dialogue focused on a medical issue (e.g., a specific treatment/ intervention) or an age/development-specific concern (e.g., school issues) that did not coincide with their child's situation, some fathers described feeling less interested and/or able to comment than when the discussion was more specifically related to their particular situation, as illustrated below.

"Sometimes for a week or two, some of the dads would get onto a topic that did not relate [to me], so I would just read them and see if there was anything that did relate to [my child]. . . . I wouldn't have a comment or anything because it just doesn't fit. . . . But at other times, you get good information."

The diversity of experiences and issues may have limited group dialogue, particularly given the limited number of online posts at certain times during the pilot project timeframe. As an example, one father commented, "I do not think there was as much participation as I would like to have seen. You would go on and there wouldn't be any messages there." Perhaps the wide range of issues and ages of participants' children limited potential commonalities and subsequent dialogue among fathers. On the other hand, several fathers appreciated the information from others (e.g., more experienced fathers) and as such, found it helpful to receive information that did not specifically pertain to their current situation:

> "The other real benefit, I guess, is the comfort in knowing that I am getting more knowledgeable in the condition—and what might be there and what might be up the road ahead."

Theme 6: Difficulties with Hardware/Software

Fathers often commented on technology-related issues. For some, use of the computer was not problematic. However, a few fathers who described "less than desired" or "waning" involvement in the online group seemed to attribute this, at least in part, to (1) unfamiliarity with the technology, (2) technical difficulty with the network, and/or (3) slowness in typing, as illustrated below.

> ". . . Some of the fathers who were not as familiar with the computer as I was faced a certain amount of learning limitations and constraints because of unfamiliarity and needed to grow comfortable with it before they would be participating as fully . . . as those others who just took it as a matter of course."

> "That was another discouraging thing . . . I just don't have an interest in the computer . . . I found that when I wrote, it took me a long time because I don't know the computer."

> "I really had a computer problem. It was quite frustrating. I was more than willing to get into it, but I couldn't."

A few fathers offered potential ideas for easing or reducing necessary steps in accessing the online group. For instance, one father suggested that there would be increased ease in accessing e-mails if "posts" could automatically be deposited into participants' regular e-mail rather than fathers having to access or "log onto" the network directly.

Theme 7: Difficulty Keeping Track of Participants and Remembering "Who's Who"

Of those who more actively participated in the online network, some fathers commented that it was difficult to envision other participants in the network because of their inability to "put a face to the name on the computer." As such, they shared important issues together without having met one another nor having had the opportunity to see or hear those with whom they were sharing. Although some appreciated this anonymity, several fathers also found it challenging because they felt they did not know (or could not remember) who else was in the group. As the group grew in size, a few participants reported losing track of the particulars of each father (e.g., age of father's child).

This lack of identifying information reportedly limited a few fathers in terms of understanding where other fathers were coming from, and consequently inhibited their ability to respond to one another as quickly or as sensitively as they could have. Several means of addressing these challenges were proposed. For instance, online or "mailed out" introductory information or scanned-in photographs were suggested:

> "It would be kind of nice to have a group picture, you know, to have an idea of who it is you are talking to. . . . I found it limited, for me, the personalizing of the people. It was all kind of one big glob of people."

A few fathers commented on the potential benefit of meeting together; however, the practical difficulties of doing so were also recognized (e.g., geographic distances between participants, scheduling challenges), as illustrated below.

> "I was thinking, at one point, that it would have been nice for the group of us to get together. I realize it wasn't feasible, but it would have been nice just to see each other."

Theme 8: Time Constraints

Several fathers stated that a *shortage of time* was a barrier to more extensive involvement in the online group. Fathers tended to be busy individuals, with many responsibilities and pressing priorities. Finding the time for "themselves" and/or time to use the computer was difficult for many given their responsibilities, time constraints, and/or multiple users of the computer in the household, as illustrated below.

> "The only negative part on my side was, again, the time set aside to go through it all. I wish I had spent more time online, but I couldn't."

> ". . . it was just finding the time to do it. But, again, I found the more that I said and the more similarities that I saw . . . prompted me to use it more."

> "We didn't build up enough of a dialogue among ourselves and I know that some of these men were quite busy."

> "There may have been times when I was ready to go, to log on— and the computer was busy."

Despite these challenges in finding time to participate, fathers tended to believe that the online group should nonetheless continue. They conveyed it as offering fathers the unique opportunity for peer-based information and support that would otherwise be difficult to access. Accordingly, fathers offered few alternatives to this forum, and generally suggested that other forms of group work (e.g., a face-to-face group) would impose prohibitive constraints in terms of time demands, geographic distance, inconvenience, and scheduling difficulty.

DISCUSSION

Interview findings and group transcripts suggest that fathers of children with spina bifida experience unique issues and concerns. For some, it appears that these experiences can be productively explored and shared within an online group context. The fathers in this group—many of whom lived substantial distances from one another—were able to come together and meaningfully share elements of their lives. Fathers conveyed to one another challenges and adjustments, as well as blessings associated with their children's condition. In varying degrees, the group was perceived to assist participants by: (1) hearing and sharing some of their challenges, (2) increasing connection with other fathers, and/or (3) providing peer-based insight and information. Consistent with other literature (e.g., Galinsky, Schopler, and Abell, 1997; Weinberg et al., 1995), the convenience, accessibility, and flexibility offered by this online capacity fostered group participation. The text-oriented electronic-mail format was generally reported to effectively facilitate fathers' dialogue.

Participant interviews illustrate perceived benefits of online group work with fathers as well as limiting challenges or considerations, particularly related to the online nature of the group. For instance, based on interviews as well as discussion with some of the fathers throughout the course of the study, it appears that older or less-advanced computer hardware and software and some fathers' unfamiliarity with computer technology limited participation. Generally, fathers who had access to more advanced technology (i.e., hardware/software) and greater comfort or competence in computer utilization, appeared to participate more readily and frequently.

Accordingly, it is advisable that advanced computer technology for participants and accessible (e.g., home-based) technological support/education be integrated within online groups. Availability of advanced hardware/software and technological support serves to foster accessibility to all fathers for whom such a group could be potentially helpful. It stands to reason that persons who continually struggle with the technology will likely give up on the process and subsequently not benefit from the group experience.

On the other hand, if such technology is not yet universally available or viable, participants may be supported in accessing publicly available computers. However, in so doing, the convenience offered through online capacities may be largely thwarted. That is, the opportunity to participate in the group is limited in terms of both when and where participants can access a computer. Notwithstanding this limitation, public venues at which the group could be accessed often include various community outlets (e.g., public libraries). It is expected that over time computers increasingly will be available and accessible to more and more persons.

CONCLUSION

Interview transcript analysis suggests the potential benefits of an online group for fathers of persons with spina bifida. It further illuminates challenges and concerns in conducting online groups for fathers, yet these challenges do not appear to outweigh the potential benefits of this emerging form of group work. Rather, online groups for fathers indeed appear to be a promising endeavor worthy of further study.

REFERENCES

Bergofsky, R.E., Forgast, C.S., and Glassel, A.F. (1979). Establishing therapeutic groups with the families of spina bifida children in hospital setting. *Social Work with Groups, 2,* 45-54.

Clark, E. (1986). The use of single session collectivities with families of spina bifida children. *Social Work with Groups, 9,* 103-111.

Finn, J. (1995). Computer-based self-help groups: A new resource to supplement support groups. *Social Work with Groups, 18,* 109-117.

Galinsky, M.J., Schopler, J.H., and Abell, M.D. (1997). Connecting group members through telephone and computer groups. *Health and Social Work, 22,* 181-188.

Lincoln, Y.S. and Guba, E.G. (1985). *Naturalistic Inquiry.* Newbury Park, CA: Sage.

McCracken, G. (1988). *The Long Interview.* Newbury Park, CA: Sage.

Nicholas, D., Montgomery, G., Stapleford, C., McNeill, T., McClure, and Smith, R. (2001). Technology and practice: Lessons learned in the development of an online group for fathers. *OASW Newsmagazine: The Journal of the Ontario Association of Social Workers, 28,* 10.

Palm, G. (1993). Involved fatherhood: A second chance. *Journal of Men's Studies, 2,* 139-155.

Palm, G.F. (1997). Promoting generative fathering through parent and family education. In A.J. Hawkins and D.C. Dollahite (Eds.), *Generative Fathering: Beyond Deficit Perspectives.* Thousand Oaks, CA: Sage, pp. 167-182.

Stein, T.S. (1983). An overview of men's groups. *Social Work with Groups, 6,* 149-161.

Weinberg, N., Schmale, J.D., Uken, J., and Wessel, K. (1995). Computer-mediated support groups. *Social Work with Groups, 17,* 43-54.

Index

Page numbers followed by the letter "f" indicate figures; those followed by the letter "t" indicate tables.

SPECIAL 25%-OFF DISCOUNT!
Order a copy of this book with this form or online at:
http://www.haworthpressinc.com/store/product.asp?sku=4775

SOCIAL WORK WITH GROUPS
Social Justice Through Personal, Community, and Societal Change

_____in hardbound at $37.46 (regularly $49.95) (ISBN: 0-7890-1815-2)

_____in softbound at $18.71 (regularly $24.95) (ISBN: 0-7890-1816-0)

Or order online and use Code HEC25 in the shopping cart.

COST OF BOOKS_____

OUTSIDE US/CANADA/
MEXICO: ADD 20%_____

POSTAGE & HANDLING_____
*(US: $5.00 for first book & $2.00
for each additional book)*
*Outside US: $6.00 for first book
& $2.00 for each additional book)*

SUBTOTAL_____

IN CANADA: ADD 7% GST_____

STATE TAX_____
*(NY, OH & MN residents, please
add appropriate local sales tax)*

FINAL TOTAL_____
*(If paying in Canadian funds,
convert using the current
exchange rate, UNESCO
coupons welcome)*

☐ **BILL ME LATER:** ($5 service charge will be added)
(Bill-me option is good on US/Canada/Mexico orders only;
not good to jobbers, wholesalers, or subscription agencies.)

☐ Check here if billing address is different from
shipping address and attach purchase order and
billing address information.

Signature_____

☐ **PAYMENT ENCLOSED: $**_____

☐ **PLEASE CHARGE TO MY CREDIT CARD.**

☐ Visa ☐ MasterCard ☐ AmEx ☐ Discover
☐ Diner's Club ☐ Eurocard ☐ JCB

Account # _____

Exp. Date_____

Signature_____

Prices in US dollars and subject to change without notice.

NAME_____

INSTITUTION_____

ADDRESS_____

CITY_____

STATE/ZIP_____

COUNTRY_____ COUNTY (NY residents only)_____

TEL_____ FAX_____

E-MAIL_____

May we use your e-mail address for confirmations and other types of information? ☐ Yes ☐ No
We appreciate receiving your e-mail address and fax number. Haworth would like to e-mail or fax special
discount offers to you, as a preferred customer. **We will never share, rent, or exchange your e-mail address
or fax number.** We regard such actions as an invasion of your privacy.

Order From Your Local Bookstore or Directly From
The Haworth Press, Inc.
10 Alice Street, Binghamton, New York 13904-1580 • USA
TELEPHONE: 1-800-HAWORTH (1-800-429-6784) / Outside US/Canada: (607) 722-5857
FAX: 1-800-895-0582 / Outside US/Canada: (607) 722-6362
E-mailto: getinfo@haworthpressinc.com
PLEASE PHOTOCOPY THIS FORM FOR YOUR PERSONAL USE.
http://www.HaworthPress.com   BOF02